THE CRYSTAL PATH TO AWAKENING

"*Crystal Vision* is one of the most unique and imaginative, yet practical guides to working with crystals that has yet to emerge. Michael Smith and Lin Westhorp have a deep understanding of the earth and how both crystals and humans relate to our planetary home. This perspective clearly emerges throughout their book. I recommend it highly to those interested in crystals, the earth, and ways to bring about healing during the times of earth changes."

— Wabun Wind
author of *Lightseeds* and *Woman of the Dawn*
co-author of *The Medicine Wheel* and *Black Dawn, Bright Day*

"Like a multi-faceted crystal, *Crystal Vision* presents many facets of information to appeal to readers ... for the crystal worker, the book contains numerous diagrams and descriptions on how to construct crystal tools; for others, the book expresses deeply profound and simple truths relating to our connection and relationship with all aspects of creation. By sharing personal experiences, the authors assist us in better comprehending and appreciating the world in which we live and larger world in which we all travel. *Crystal Vision* does indeed lift the reader into higher awareness and increased wisdom."

— Sandra J. Radhoff
author of *The Kyrian Letters:*
Transformative Messages for Higher Vision

"There are few things anyone who works in the field of psionics likes more than new gadgets to build, and *Crystal Vision* is absolutely filled with them. The reader will find that Smith and Westhorp have given an explanation of psionics that is one of the best I have ever encountered. Not only that, but the Psi-Comp device is the first good system for interfacing a home computer and black box that I have seen—easy to build and use. You will like this book."

— Charles Cosimano
author of *Psionic Power* and *Psychic Power*

ABOUT THE AUTHORS

Michael G. Smith was born in Great Bend, Kansas, on March 9, 1947. He has studied ancient knowledge for 30 years and spent time in the 1970s with the Bear Tribe Medicine Society, where he was first introduced to quartz crystals. This inspired Michael to invent the crystal healing rod.

Lin Westhorp was born of American military parents on March 9, 1949, in Frankfurt, Germany. In her teens and twenties, after being thrust into the world of the occult by a series of mystical experiences, she began exploring ESP, astrology, numerology, and reincarnation. She was introduced to channeling and new age philosophy in the late 1970s, and her personal channeling questions resulted in the prediction of her meeting, marriage to, and work with Michael Smith.

TO WRITE TO THE AUTHORS

If you wish to contact the authors or would like more information about this book, please write to the authors in care of Llewellyn Worldwide, and we will forward your request. Both the authors and the publisher appreciate hearing from you and learning of your enjoyment of this book and how it has helped you. Llewellyn Worldwide cannot guarantee that every letter written to the authors can be answered, but all will be forwarded. Please write to:

Michael G. Smith and Lin Westhorp
c/o Llewellyn Worldwide
P.O. Box 64383-728, St. Paul, MN 55164-0383, U.S.A.

Please enclose a self-addressed, stamped envelope or $1.00 to cover costs.
If outside the U.S.A., enclose international postal reply coupon.

FREE CATALOG FROM LLEWELLYN

For more than 90 years Llewellyn has brought its readers knowledge in the fields of metaphysics and human potential. Learn about the newest books in spiritual guidance, natural healing, astrology, occult philosophy and more. Enjoy book reviews, new age articles, a calendar of events, plus current advertised products and services. To get your free copy of *Llewellyn's New Worlds of Mind and Spirit,* send your name and address to:

Llewellyn's New Worlds of Mind and Spirit
P.O. Box 64383-728, St. Paul, MN 55164-0383, U.S.A.

LLEWELLYN'S PSI-TECH SERIES

Crystal Vision

Shamanic Tools for Change & Awakening

Michael G. Smith & Lin Westhorp

(Includes material from *Crystal Spirit*)

1994
Llewellyn Publications
St. Paul, Minnesota 55164-0383, U. S. A.

FIRST EDITION
Second Printing, 1994

Cover Painting: Hrana Janto
Cover Design: Christopher Wells
Illustrations: Lin Westhorp and Linda Norton
Book Design and Layout: Jessica Thoreson

Library of Congress Cataloging-in-Publication Data
    Smith, Michael G. (Michael Gary), 1947-
        Crystal vision: shamanic tools for change & awakening /
        Michael G. Smith & Lin Westhorp.
           p.   cm -- (Llewellyn's psi-tech series)
        Rev. ed. of: Crystal spirit. 1st ed. 1990
      ISBN 0-87542-728-6
        1. Crystal--Psychic aspects. I. Westhorp, Lin, 1949-
        II. Smith, Michael G. (Micahel Gary), 1947- Crystal spirit.
        III. Title. IV. Series.
BF1442.C78S65   1993
133.3'22--dc20   93-41333
                                                  CIP

Llewellyn Publications
A Division of Llewellyn Worldwide, Ltd.
P. O. Box 64383, St. Paul, MN 55164-0383

Printed in the United States of America

Also by the Authors
Crystal Warrior

By Michael G. Smith
Crystal Power

TABLE OF CONTENTS

Introduction

Until the eighties, you may not have heard much about quartz crystals unless you were involved in obscure arcane practices. Then overnight, it seemed, everyone was talking about them. Their sudden popularity reflected an intuitive recognition of the fact that the Earth was on the verge of changes so vast that we needed all the help we could get to gracefully survive a period of relative chaos. Humanity needed to do a lot of growing up in a hurry to reach a higher level than we'd previously achieved.

All of us have come a long way since that time and have seen many changes in our world. In order to cope with changing circumstances, we've had to open our minds to new ideas. One new idea was the discovery that crystals and crystal tools are vibrating at a faster rate than we are, and we can use them to tune ourselves to a higher level. In *Crystal Vision* we offer exercises, techniques, and crystal tools that have helped the authors and others toward growth. We share them with you here to help you on your own exciting journey into the future.

If you've read *Crystal Spirit*, you'll find that the tools in *Crystal Vision* are similar. *Crystal Spirit* was written primarily for people who are adept at building and using crystal devices. Almost as soon as it was published, we realized that we should have broadened our scope. *Crystal Vision* provides that broadened scope, answering difficult questions that may have been troubling you. From the perspective of our own experiences, we share exactly what crystals do and give you information about how they work. We explain how you can use them to improve your life, providing exercises and experiments that you can try for yourself. The crystal tools have been updated to high-tech standards with clearer directions and illustrations. In addition, we suggest simple substitutes that you can use to try out the techniques and exercises offered.

Many readers have asked for more information on the Psi-Comp, an outgrowth of black box technology and radionics. To accommodate them, Michael streamlined the early model and we provided more specific directions on how to build and operate it. For beginners, we added a chapter on radionic principles and directions for building and using your own black box.

As people become more aware of the connection between the physical and spiritual, there is a growing interest in shamanism. The truth is, we're all capable of becoming our own shamans if we accept individual responsibility and acknowledge our power to direct our own lives. Knowledge that was previously held by a few now belongs out in the open. When we decide we're no longer willing to let others determine the course of our lives, we need the facts in order to make informed decisions for ourselves. Toward that end, we included specific directions on how to do your own channeling, past life recall, healing, dowsing, or perform your own Native American pipe ceremonies. With a belief in yourself and an open mind, you can discover the answers to any of your questions by using the techniques provided.

Today, the vision is truly becoming a reality for the new Earth era. Crystals can help you experience your inherent power to create the world of your dreams. If you haven't taken that first step yet, take it now with us, and we'll all discover what wonders we can create together.

PART ONE

Understanding Crystals

Many books have been written about crystals, but few explore their relationship to Universal Energy or tell you exactly how results are achieved with them. The plain fact is, we can't use crystals successfully without first understanding who we are and the way the Universe works. Yes, some people have achieved miracles with crystals, but it was because they knew about and operated within a larger picture. In this section we'll show you that larger picture, and place you firmly within its frame by giving you the information you need to perform your own miracles.

ONE

The Crystal Earth

*Since most people in today's society can't go back to the land,
the land will come back to the people.*

ENERGY FLOW TO A NEW EARTH ERA

A new era for the Earth is evolving. In order to work with crystals, it's important that we take into consideration our place as Earthlings and citizens of the Universe rather than trying to use crystals and crystal tools as if we lived in a vacuum. As we move to a higher vibrational level, so too does the Earth. When we use crystals, not only are we able to amplify our thoughts, but in the process of tuning ourselves to their vibrational level, we are being tuned by the crystals to a higher level where we realize that everything is connected. No successful crystal worker is unaware of this phenomena. It's impossible to get involved with crystals without also becoming aware of the Earth we live on and our place on it.

We, as humans, sometimes forget to think of the Earth as a moving, growing, changing being. Yet this is what she is. It's obvious during peaks of earthquake or volcanic activity, or when we visit areas (like the Grand Canyon) that have been eroded by wind and water. It's especially obvious in the wake of a devastating forest fire, when life regenerates a season later. What's not so noticeable is the Earth's land surface flowing in smooth movements, similar to ocean waves that can vary each day. The Earth has a geomagnetic field, a constantly moving aura of atmospheric weather patterns. She reaches out into space with her upper atmosphere, complete with an ozone layer and radiation belts. This is a very large, alive being we're living on, definitely someone to be taken into consideration.

Many of us are concerned about how we're affecting the Earth's ecology and the way we treat the environment. It may be time for us to go a step further and wonder what the Earth might be doing to or with us. She moves and grows in ways that promote a balance of energies. In order to survive, we must move with her. A new human consciousness is evolving at the same time a new Earth consciousness is growing into being; the two processes are inextricably connected. The result for Earth and humans is the same—growth, an essential condition of all life.

The energy process of balancing stimulates the creation of new forms in the environment, both human-made and Earth-made. Everything on the planet comes from the natural materials that the Earth created, and she provides us with everything we need to live. During cycle changes a lot of the earth moves around, stimulated by over five billion human vehicles who move large portions of the earth, thinking it's their idea. This moving involves simple things like collecting rocks and digging up a garden plot. Human society on a larger scale moves tons of earth, oil, rock, water, and gas in the process of building highways and structures, or when ores are mined and goods manufactured. It's a blow to our egos when we realize that our great civilizations fulfill the same function for the Earth as anthills do. We both move a lot of earth materials from one place to another, changing the physical and energy balance of the planet.

The energy balance on Earth has been changing throughout history from the time we incarnated in physical bodies. In civilizations of the past, a relatively small population moved a lot of rock and earth. The first materials to be mined and moved were copper, silver, gold, gemstones, and crystals. Then larger pieces of earth were moved to various areas.

Giant stone blocks were quarried to build cities and pyramid structures at various sites on the Earth. Who determined where the pyramids were built? Was it humans themselves, or humans responding intuitively and instinctively to the guidance from the Earth Mother?

People are once again delving into the Earth's energy grid patterns and energy vortexes as the wheel of history comes around. Pyramids, which function as generators that channel natural energy, are once again being constructed from plastic, metal, wood, and stone. Sizes range from half-inch quartz crystal jewelry to house-sized wood and stone. All are energy generators that change the balance of energy.

At certain times in Earth cycles of thousands of years, people respond to the Earth's impulse to change and balance the planet's entire field of energy. We like to believe the changes are our own ideas, but the Earth is, in reality, relaying instructions. We respond by constructing forms in the appropriate areas. We are currently responding to a new cycle of the Earth.

If we're responding to the Earth, what is she responding to? The sun and stars are emitting radiations of energy for a cycle change in all the planets. We naturally tend to be Earth-oriented, but the energy is affecting the growth consciousness of all our planets. We often forget to think of planets, solar systems, and galaxies as larger beings that move into new energy growth patterns just as we do. Our Milky Way galaxy is following its path of orbit into a new energy frequency area of the Universe. As it does this, direct energy communication is channeled down the line to suns and their solar systems, from planet to planet, moon to moon, and asteroid to asteroid. All these sources radiate energy to the Earth and the forms that inhabit her: spirit, mineral, animal, and human alike.

This channel of energy communication has stimulated our growth in the areas of awareness and expanded consciousness. We're all getting the same energy at the same time, in ever-increasing amounts. How we, as individuals, handle and adapt to the energy is a personal choice, but we're all exposed to the higher frequencies of energy to an equal degree.

TUNING IN TO EARTH VIBRATIONS

Some of us handle the changing energy more gracefully than others, as we can see from the six o'clock news. But we can all handle it better if we take the time to become aware of it and in tune with it. This flow is of spiritual essence for us, and there are many enjoyable ways of tuning in to it and balancing ourselves.

Hiking or picnicing while rock hunting is one way to get in tune. Fresh air and exercise are a beneficial side effect when finding rocks and crystals to bring home for gardens, yards, planters, and terrariums. We find ourselves agreeably helping the Earth move herself in this manner, while bringing nature, beauty, and good energy into our home environment.

Rock hunting also teaches us to feel the energy of rocks, plants, fish, birds, and animals in their natural home environment. Being close to nature promotes an awareness that we are all connected, and encourages a love of ourselves and other beings.

An understanding of our connection to the living being we call Earth can come to us in simple ways, if we let it. Bringing home rocks for an outdoor rock garden or an indoor terrarium brings us closer to the Earth. It can be as easy as placing a few rocks or crystals in a potted house plant. The contact provides us with energy communications from the plant and mineral kingdoms of the Earth.

The majority of life on the Earth Mother is not going to communicate with us in English or any other human language. If we want to learn about ourselves and nature, we'll have to communicate in the energy/information language of nature. Parts of ourselves, from body cells to higher spirit, don't speak in words of language, but rather communicate in an interchange of energy fields or overlapping dimensions.

That sounds complex and esoteric, but the communication can be as easy as sensing the energy flow in a house plant, a vegetable garden, or flowers in a window box. It can be as enjoyable and relaxing as going for a hike in the country or having a picnic by a river. These activities seem simple and ordinary, but if we pause to immerse ourselves in the ever-changing interactions of earth, air, water, minerals, insects, birds, and animals that surround us, they lead to an understanding of our unbreakable connection to the Earth.

TUNE IN TO THE EARTH AT HOME

If you want to, you can get in tune with nature right at home. Even apartment dwellers have windowsills or balconies where they can study nature by putting out birdseed or growing plants. If you live in a house, your yard can provide you with nature's full spectrum.

For example, the authors' times of tuning and communication often take place while observing the activity in our rock garden, which is filled with rocks and crystals we collected ourselves.

On a large scale, squirrels and birds take turns at the feeders, each taking what they need and then allowing the next his or her turn. Among the squirrels, the nursing mother takes a priority that few are willing to challenge. Although there's a lot of light-hearted bickering during summer's time of plenty, when it gets cold it's not unusual to see three or four squirrels on our two-tiered feeder, while several more wait their turn in an adjacent tree. Our cats, who are always in tune with Earth energy, enjoy the squirrels as much as we do and several times we've caught one of them lying in the feeder next to a munching squirrel. Once we saw our half-grown cat, The Ghost, actually playing a light-hearted game of tag with a young squirrel.

On a small scale, in the summer, long-legged wasps are attracted to the bird bath. Their graceful flight and landings are a joy to behold. As an added benefit, wasps are largely carnivorous and our garden and rock garden are virtually free from caterpillar pests. Other wasps, who are carrion eaters, keep the landscape clean with the help of scavenger ants.

The marigolds, which reseed themselves each year, attract a multitude of honeybees, bumblebees, and butterflies, all busy pollinating the flowers and vegetables. Some of the bumblebees are so large that their weight pulls the flowers over, causing the bees to hang upside down while they feed. We've learned that all our bees and wasps are gentle creatures, intent on fulfilling their function in the ecosystem. Even when we brush them away from a flower or plant, they never attack us.

Occasionally we see the large iridescent ground beetles that live among the rocks scurrying past. They are busy fulfilling their mission, which has thankfully all but eliminated slugs from the area.

Insect and bug activity in our organic rock and vegetable gardens provides us with with a constant source of learning and amazement. One year we were horrified to see the rock garden mint covered with black and orange striped creatures reminiscent of gila monsters. After a few weeks, while we gritted our teeth and left them alone, the ugly creatures attached themselves to the plants while they continued to mature. Imagine our surprise when out of those ugly casings, ladybugs emerged—at first a bright golden color that eventually darkened to red as spots appeared. We'd wondered why our aphid problem disappeared after we started gardening organically. Obviously those creepy monsters, and the pretty ladybugs they became, were eating them.

Beneath all the visible activity taking place in the rock garden lies a more subtle level of vibration exuded by the plants, animals, insects, rocks, and soil interacting together. They emanate an aura of growth, health, and fulfilled purpose that makes the very air vibrate with joyous life. Whenever we're troubled, worried, or hurt, we retreat to the garden, and never fail to regain the knowledge that all is well with us and with the world.

CREATE AN EARTH SANCTUARY

It's possible for anyone to create an Earth sanctuary that heals all ills somewhere in their life. If the weather allows, take your favorite crystal and go where you can observe nature in process. Watching plants, animals, insects, and even people interact can restore a sense of balance and harmony. We're an essential part of the Earth and all her systems, if we'll only take the time to stop and notice.

Even inside our buildings we can achieve a sense of our place in the scheme of things by watching a potted plant or focusing on a dish of crystals and rocks for a few minutes. We all have the time to pull out a favorite crystal at some time during a busy day and gaze into its depths. Take a few minutes to notice the whole of creation inherent in any of these objects, and you'll begin to heal whatever's troubling you. Keep in mind that all matter evolves and changes in the process of crystallization. This includes rocks, plants, animals, and people. Crystallization is the activity of creation, the expression and manifestation of the logical order of creation.

The following quote from Chief Seattle's (Sealth's) speech to the U.S. Government in the 1850s finishes up this chapter in the most fitting way we can think of.

One thing we know: Our God is also your God.
The Earth is precious and to harm the Earth
is to heap contempt on its creator.

In learning to be one with and love the Earth we live on, we also learn to be one with and love ourselves and all creation. Once we learn those lessons, our work with crystals becomes effective.

TWO

The Other Side of the Coin

We like to pretend we never get the blues,
but it just ain't so.

WHEN CRYSTALS DON'T SEEM TO WORK

What do we do when crystals don't seem to be working, or work in what we consider a negative fashion? Few crystal books address this question adequately, but negatives play a large part in any endeavor and need to be dealt with. Crystals are a reflection of ourselves. Crystals and crystal elemental energy respond to our thoughts and emotions. When things don't go right we need to look at ourselves, inside and out, to determine what our thoughts, attitudes, and core beliefs are creating.

Quartz crystal energy beings respond to the finest subtleties and nuances of our mental, emotional, and spiritual consciousness or awareness. They react to our aura of energy, our total bioelectromagnetic energy field, amplifying it to produce quicker manifestations. Quite simply, they enhance our mind programs, whatever they are.

11

To most effectively tune in to and use the energy in crystals, it helps if we think of them as conscious energy beings with a form that's different from our own. It's relatively easy to acknowledge the life force in a member of the plant or animal kingdom, but it is sometimes difficult to accept the same force in a mineral. If you can't relate to the fact that a crystal is a life form, don't worry about it. After all, most of us have been trained from birth to think that way. It can take time to believe what we thought was unbelievable. Even without belief, the crystals are going to enhance what we're programming, whether we're conscious of it or not.

If you haven't been able to detect the life force in crystals, there are several things you can do to tune in to their energy. First, try to keep an open mind about the subject. After all, a lot of people do think crystals work and chances are they aren't all nut cases. At any rate, if you've spent money and time on this book, you might as well consider the ideas in it.

Once you're in a receptive, if still skeptical, frame of mind, get a quartz crystal or a related crystal, such as amethyst, smoky quartz, citrine, etc. You can even use another member of the mineral kingdom in polished or crystal form, if you like. One of our readers said he felt nothing with crystals, but he could feel the energy in a tourmaline. Hold the crystal in your hand until your body heat warms it. The heat speeds up the molecules in the crystal and makes its energy field easier to detect. At that point you should feel at least a faint tingle from its energy field interacting with your own. Sometimes, with a crystal in either hand, the tingle will travel up your arms and across your shoulders, to form a connection. If you don't feel anything at first, keep trying. You're like a blind person learning to feel the presence of a wall or solid object before he or she touches it. You have to develop a sense that you may not have used before. It takes practice.

Another exercise you can do is to warm the crystal, then lie down and place it in the middle of your forehead, in the third eye position. The third eye is a sensitive area, and you may feel the energy coursing down through your body. It's also common to feel a tightness or pain in your forehead, as Lin did at first. Don't worry about the pain. It's probably due to the mind's attempt to tune into an unfamiliar energy and should decrease and disappear eventually. Keep in mind that at least you've proved to yourself that something is actually happening.

For these exercises to be effective, it's necessary to be in a relaxed, receptive state, both physically and mentally. To relax, you can use some of the other exercises in this book, meditate, or just do whatever you do when you're trying to get to sleep. One exercise that we like is to control our breathing until it's deep and regular. We do this by imagining the Universe is filled with particles of love. With each breath, we know that we're filling our body with love—that we *are* love. Without worry or fear to make us tense, our bodies naturally relax. It also helps to choose a time for practice when you're likely to be able to achieve that state. Right after a fight with a friend or in the middle of a stressful day may not be the best times.

On occasion, when we practice with a crystal on the third eye, we go someplace else. By that we mean that for ten minutes or a half-hour we lose track of things. It's not like sleeping, because there's no memory of dreams or thoughts, but rather a blank space in our perception. When we come back we feel relaxed, but not rested, as if we were working hard while we were away. We think that during that time we're probably in direct contact with our higher selves. There's no memory of it because the communication doesn't translate to physical terms. But later, the translation occurs in the subconscious and in our dreams. Whatever it is that actually happens during the blank periods, the effects are beneficial so we don't worry about it.

Once you've proved to yourself that crystals are doing something, you can begin to find out what it is that they're doing and how their energy can benefit you.

WHEN CRYSTAL EFFECTS SEEM TO BE NEGATIVE

Crystals can make some people nervous or edgy at first. The reason for this is that working with crystals, or just having them around the house, car, or office, does two things simultaneously. It not only amplifies our thoughts, which can be uncomfortable if we're in a negative space, but the crystals also tune us to a higher rate of vibration, speeding up our evolution, awareness, and personal growth, along with their own. They amplify and manifest changes and new growth patterns for the evolution of our consciousness. This higher vibratory rate can be physically and mentally uncomfortable while it's going on, but it is a sure sign that growth is taking place.

As most crystal workers are aware, spiritual growth can also mean a change of mates, home, geographical location, or career that stimulates our talents and personal growth. With crystals there's no resting on our laurels. If we don't move toward growth, they and our inner spirit will move us. The process can be interpreted negatively as a loss, or it can be accepted as a gain, depending on our choice and awareness.

Once our growth is started in motion by our choice to work with crystals, it's advisable to accept changes in ourselves and our lives as gracefully and good-naturedly as possible, with the knowledge that our higher consciousness has chosen what's best for us. The Universe is providing what we chose and what we need to realize our choice. In crystal work, energy frequency changes often happen so fast that they can be interpreted as bad. Over the course of time, we can recognize that the changes were a step in the right direction, but at the time they can be pretty traumatic.

CRYSTAL KARMA

Since crystals amplify emotions, you may experience what we call Crystal Karma when you're working with them. Crystal Karma is simply a matter of cause and effect. If we put out negative emotions around crystals, they amplify them and project them back to us. Likewise if our emotions are positive.

Karma can manifest from lifetime to lifetime, year to year, decade to decade—or instantaneously. Karma is the way we teach ourselves lessons that allow us to grow. It's the balancing force of the Universe.

When we're in balance, Karma doesn't exist. When we're not, the Universe moves energy to balance us. We might call it good or bad Karma, but it's just balance. Working with crystals moves energy quickly to bring about this balance. That's what we want because it allows us to stay on the path of growth. It guides us in the same way that a heat-seeking missile finds its target. If we're experiencing events that we perceive as bad, we can look at ourselves and see what thoughts produced them. The same is true of events that we see as good. But we have to be careful when we're trying to judge events because many are neither bad nor good, but are just changes we need in order to grow. If you want to remain just where you are now, you'll probably be disappointed; even without the help of crystals, life tends to move us forward. But if that's really what you want, stay away from crystals.

One of the most common cases of Crystal Karma is the cold or flu that follows an "out of balance" emotional outburst of anger, hostility, or depression. What is happening is that our bodies are manifesting our negativity. A beneficial side effect of the illness is that it's also releasing the negativity so we don't have to carry it around with us any more, as long as we don't continue being negative. In everyday life, it's almost impossible not to build up some negative energy; during times of stress and trauma, our negativity can skyrocket. Illness allows us to release it. When this happens, the best attitude we can take is to accept the fact that we have negativity that needs to be released, and that once it's gone we don't have to be burdened with it any longer.

Lin came to an understanding of the connection between negativity and illness through a series of traumatic events in her life.

When I was a child, before I realized that negativity causes sickness, I was ill a lot. The fact that I was sick made me even more negative, which prolonged the illness and caused more of it. I functioned within this negative cycle until a traumatic situation as a young adult completely changed my outlook.

In 1973, my parents decided to take a trip over the New Year's holiday to their mountain property where they planned to retire. Although I'd never worried about their safety before, I felt a sense of impending doom about the trip. When Mother called me from a hospital on New Year's Day to say that she'd fallen ill, I suddenly realized the reason for my premonition. There was no doubt in my mind that she was going to die soon!

Throughout the next seven months, while the doctors, my family, and my mother herself firmly maintained that she was going to recover, I knew she wouldn't. It was a hard time because Mother had always been the mainstay of our family. Fortunately, her strength during those months helped me to adjust to her gradual decline into illness and to the fact that we'd have to learn to live without her. During that time, I couldn't understand why God would take a person who was needed and loved by everyone she came in contact with, leaving behind someone as worthless as myself. It just didn't make any sense.

My attitude changed dramatically on the day that Mother finally died. When my father told me the news, I accepted it calmly and went to my room to grieve alone. I lay down on the bed and was able to feel only emptiness. Then, out of that emptiness, a vision emerged. I saw my mother as a young child running through an incredibly beautiful field of flowers, where colors were music, and music was joy, the whole bathed in a blinding aura of white light. The little girl, who was my mother, turned back to me briefly, as if to say goodbye, and the joy of the whole of creation was reflected on her face. I suddenly realized that instead of dying, my mother had awakened to a new and wonderful life. From that point on, I began seeing her death in a new light. In order to escape from a body and a life that had fulfilled its purpose, my mother had to die. It was her choice!

I also realized that since she had chosen to die, chances were that my foreknowledge of the event had been picked up telepathically from her. I was grateful that she'd given me the time to prepare for her absence and shown me that she was all right in her new place.

After that I accepted that I'd been causing my own illnesses, but I wasn't sure how I was doing it. It never occurred to me that my negativity was the culprit or that I was capable of giving it up. I used pessimism almost like a talisman to ward off evil. If I was prepared for the worst, then it couldn't hurt me. Of course it didn't work.

An unfortunate side effect of the knowledge that we choose our own deaths was that I decided that if Mother was so much happier being dead, I might be, too. As a result, I deliberately gave myself cancer five years later, during a period when I felt that my life was hopeless.

Fortunately, once I had the disease, I wasn't so sure I'd done the right thing and started working on healing myself. That attitude saw me through a biopsy where the cancer was removed, and the eventual knowledge that I wasn't going to die after all. At that point, I decided that if I couldn't bring myself to die, I'd better start living—to make my life count for something. From then on my life took an upward turn that led me to a discovery of my own power to control my life.

Now I only get sick during times of major transitions or growth. I think of it as cleaning house so I can go on to new adventures. Instead of feeling bad about the sickness, I put myself to bed for a well-deserved rest, read, write, and rearrange my favorite crystals, happy with the thought that I'm ridding myself of the negativity that caused my sickness. It's not usually long before I'm well again and ready to face the future with the knowledge that whatever happens, it's going to be better than what I've lost. And do you know what? So far, it always has been—better, I mean.

CRYSTALS ARE DOORWAYS TO OUR MINDS

Crystals amplify our thoughts and emotions to make things manifest faster. That's why it is so important to know ourselves. Any type of negative emotion such as fear, anger, depression, or jealousy will be amplified, as well as positive emotions like love, peace, kindness, and understanding. That's not necessarily bad. Sometimes it's important for us to become painfully aware of our feelings in order to deal with them so we can move ahead on life's path.

The Universal Energy that flows through crystals and people is impersonal. It doesn't judge how or what is being created, but responds and manifests exactly as the mind of the human creator thinks or visualizes. The use of crystals speeds up the process of cause and effect, sometimes to the point of almost "instant Karma." It helps crystal people speed up their own development and understanding of how the energy works.

As we study crystals, we're seeing reflections of ourselves. The patterns we see in our own actions and reactions show us that we're integrated parts of the whole of creation. We can't turn the energy on or off, but we can guide and channel its expression, direction, and manifestation. Our lives are our individual choice and responsibility. What we think or visualize is what is created and projected. What we are is what we get. In order to get something different, we have to learn to *be* something different. Our beings work energy in whatever way our minds and higher or inner selves determine.

Anyone who works with crystals will have to face themselves, time and time again. Not just those aspects that are pleasing, but also the disturbing ones. This continues until we learn to love, respect, and accept ourselves and others. It's best to avoid harsh judgment and self-criticism as much as possible since they are amplified by the crystals. We need to accept the fact that we're doing our best and that we're getting better all the time.

Keep in mind that when we don't see crystals or crystal rods doing anything at all, they probably are. The energy is subtle and responds to the strength of the mind using it. When our inner beliefs, feelings, and thoughts are in conflict with what our outer thoughts are trying to do, the opposing nature of our thoughts can cancel each other out. Our thoughts and feelings, especially deep-seated ones, affect the crystal beings who produce the amplification of energy or lack of flow.

Crystals augment, amplify, and speed up a process that's already in motion. The process is the programming and creation of our own lives and circumstances by our thoughts. Our thoughts create, and crystals help. Good thoughts and emotions are a must for conscious self-creators to avoid negative feedback and increase the positive.

Crystals also help guide us to the mind of the creator, our higher inner selves ... *all that is.* It is all Mind. Channeling, meeting extraterrestrials, shopping at the grocery store, making love, watching an eagle soar across the sky, or seeing the moon rise full into the night above the Earth are all examples of the One Mind in motion and relationship to itself.

Crystals and crystal books are only guides and helpers on our journey into ourselves. The fact that we create our own conscious experience is the secret revealed by all the great masters and sacred books. As we go towards the twenty-first century, we ourselves are our only true guides in what we create.

THREE

Choosing a Crystal

Our perceptions determine reality.

When we first started working with crystals we, like others, advocated using only those with perfect tips. As our awareness grew, we realized that the imperfections existed only in our own minds and that some of our most flawed specimens projected the best energy. To the best of our knowledge, no other being—spirit, mineral, plant, or animal—perceives something the Earth herself created as flawed or imperfect. Now, although we often use our best specimens for rods or display, we realize that this is for aesthetic reasons, not because their energy is any better.

Our perception of flaws and imperfections is a reflection of our limited awareness as humans. Part of this may be due to our industrial society. We've been conditioned to expect thousands or millions of objects to look exactly the same, stamped out and symmetrical. Nature doesn't work that way. The Universe doesn't create that way, either. There are differences in quartz crystals that are not flaws or imperfections, except to our narrow spectrum of human vision. The characteristics we might consider flaws are part of the energy field transfers that occur throughout nature.

A crack in a quartz crystal that might be considered a flaw can produce the prismatic refraction of light we see as a rainbow. Should we reject that crystal? Of course not. Over the years, we've proved to ourselves the value of cracks, chips, and inclusions in determining a particular crystal's energy patterns and frequencies. The so-called flaw may be the characteristic that causes the energy of a certain crystal to be just right for you or your particular expression. That's why it's sometimes better to choose a crystal by feel, holding it in your hand before you look at it closely. In crystal work, the energy of a crystal is much more important than the appearance.

This also applies to other rock or mineral specimens. Many will be similar in appearance, but you won't find identical specimens of the same type.

We heard a story about a woman who came into a rock shop with a photograph of a friend's rock. She told the shop owner, "I want a rock exactly like this one, with green, red, and yellow spots in the same places." Even though the owner explained that Mother Nature doesn't stamp out identical rocks like a factory, the woman refused to accept the explanation and went away empty-handed without even trying to find a similar rock that would better fit her particular energy.

By adhering to dogma about crystals or minerals, our conscious minds can block our understanding and effectiveness. Keep in mind that Mother Earth sees no imperfections in her mineral kingdom. The rocks and crystals are all doing their energy jobs, growing, changing their vibrations, and behaving according to the Earth's pattern. We can best tune in to their energy by using all of our senses, rather than just our eyes.

Perhaps you don't want to use a particularly flawed crystal in a rod or display for aesthetic reasons, or because it's energy just doesn't feel right for your purpose. That's okay. You can still make use of its energy qualities. We have hundreds of low-quality, chipped, or broken crystals and minerals that we've bought or found in our area on rock-collecting expeditions. Many of them are stuck in the dirt of our house plants and, despite the fact that the plants are over-watered, under-lighted, under-fertilized, and mostly ignored, they flourish with the help of our crystal friends. Similarly, our vegetable, flower, and rock gardens thrive on the good energy our overflow crystals and minerals provide. You can find a place for all your less-than-perfect friends wherever you want to grow things, or anywhere you want an energy boost.

TYPES OF CLEAR QUARTZ CRYSTALS

When crystal people start referring to the many types and qualities of quartz crystals, it can be confusing for the novice. Doorways, phantoms, rainbows, and inclusions can be seen or suggested when you're looking into the interior of a crystal and are pretty self-explanatory. For instance, a phantom can be either the half-formed suggestion of a crystal within the crystal, or a cloudy area in its interior. A rainbow effect comes from fractures in the crystal that form a prism. Inclusions occur when the crystals form around other minerals.

Often you'll hear about crystals with doorways, diamonds, or pyramids appearing on the facets of crystals. Various authors have described specifically how different flaws and anomalies affect the energy of the crystals, but we think that each individual's perception of them is more important. For instance, we've noticed that when we're concerned about money, crystals with diamonds begin to appeal to us. The diamond shape symbolizes money to us, so we're able to tune in to and use the crystal more effectively. For someone else, the same shape might symbolize something entirely different. More often than not, we don't even know why we're attracted to the shape or flaws in a crystal; we only know that on some subliminal level that particular crystal is telling us it's right for the job.

Below, we'll describe some of the more common types of crystals you'll be encountering in this book and in rock shops.

Single termination: Crystals with only one faceted tip.

Double termination: Crystals with a faceted point on each end.

Twins or triplets: Two or three individual crystals that have grown together, side by side.

Crystal clusters: Three or more crystals that have grown out of the same base.

Herkimer diamond: A particularly hard type of quartz crystal found in Herkimer County, New York, and characterized by a rounded diamondlike shape.

Rutilated crystal: Threadlike inclusions, usually of titanium, in the crystal's interior.

Crystal balls or crystal pyramids: Quartz crystals that have been shaped by machinery to achieve these forms.

COLORED CRYSTALS

People often want to know what color quartz crystal they should use when they want a particular result. That's a difficult question to answer. While there are many popular beliefs about the differing properties of colored and clear crystals that make good sense, they don't always hold true for every person all the time. We've found that what works best for us and others is to have a general knowledge of the properties of different crystals, but when the time comes to choose a specific color or type of crystal, we go with the one that says, "choose me." We operate this way because our intuition and the crystals themselves know which crystal we're going to be able to tune in to and work with best at any particular time. As a result, we don't always use the same crystal or crystal tool to get the same result.

Another reason for going with intuition when choosing colored crystals is that we all perceive colors differently, which affects our results. Also, a particular color may be more in tune with the operator's or subject's own energy aura at one time than another. Many factors that affect the results of crystal work can be taken into account only by our subconscious minds. If we use the higher power of our minds to choose our crystals, then we can't go wrong.

To help you in your choice of a particular color of crystal, we've outlined some of the qualities of each. You can use this list as a general guide, but don't let it restrict your vision of what you can accomplish with a particular crystal.

Smoky Quartz

Smoky quartz crystals are white or clear quartz that has been irradiated, either naturally by the Earth or artificially by people. Some crystal workers prefer the naturally occurring smokys; we prefer them for tools and crystal work because they feel more energetic and alive to us. On the other hand, we also like the toned-down energy of the artificially irradiated smokys for house crystals, and have kept a particularly nice twin around for years, where it makes a beautiful display while helping to neutralize and disperse negativity. Sometimes, the artificially irradiated smokys are a darker, more even black, making them easy to spot, but if you want to be sure what you're getting, ask the dealer if they've been treated.

Despite their black color, smokys radiate a white-light energy that's particularly intense. It's thought that they can be a powerful force for neutralizing negative thoughts and emotions. We find their intensity to be effective for many types of crystal work, but tricky to work with unless we're clear in our purpose. We like to use the lighter-colored specimens of smoky quartz in healing rods, with a clear quartz crystal in the other end to help balance the intense energy of the smoky. We also use smoky quartz crystals with amethyst, citrine, amazonite, or turquoise in rods, tools, or displays to establish a harmonious energy balance.

Doorways, phantoms, and rainbows, with either single or double terminations, can be found in lighter smoky quartz. We use them for channeling information and learning, or we mount them in power rods that require only one crystal.

Some of the very dark smoky quartz crystals can be used for crystal gazing to receive psychic impressions. This is especially true if they have a shiny, black, mirror-like surface. Black obsidian has also been used for this purpose, because of its mirror-like characteristics. Polished Apache tears fall into the same category.

Another use for smoky crystals, particularly if you have specimens that are broken or flawed, is to place them in potted plants. They stimulate the plant's growth, and the plant modifies the intensity of the smoky to produce a nice aura in the room.

In our society, the color black is often associated with negative emotions, and some people experience a sense of fear combined with fascination when they're confronted with dark crystals. Our experience has been that the fear is unfounded, but merely reflects our reluctance to face and release negative thoughts or emotions. So, even though the smokys occasionally make us feel uncomfortable during periods when we need to grow, we appreciate the fact that they're helping us accomplish our purpose.

AMETHYST

Purple amethyst crystals are among our favorites to use in combination with other crystals and stones, or by themselves. They provide a balanced and peaceful healing energy with a high spiritual quality. Amethysts aren't any less powerful or energetic than other colors, just more restful in their energy radiations. They work well in energy rods with both clear and smoky quartz crystals. Amethyst crystal clusters set around the home promote a harmonious environment, and also work well as car crystals, where peace and harmony are frequently needed. They are an excellent choice for personal crystals that are carried in pockets or purses, or worn as jewelry. By carrying them with us, their unique energy can help us in the achievement of peace, balance, and spirituality.

CITRINE

The gold or orange color of citrine crystals promotes practicality in everyday down-to-earth matters. They do this while inspiring the highest ideals, which provides a grounding base or foundation of energy that assists us in becoming more balanced. We, who are spiritual seekers, sometimes need a reminder that a good balance between physical and spiritual expressions is necessary. Although citrines are rarely used in energy rods, there's no reason why they shouldn't be, as they're particularly effective for dealing with matters of the body.

BLUE CRYSTALS

While natural blue quartz crystals are rare, you may have seen some bright aquamarine-colored crystals in the past few years. We're told that the bright blue color is produced by treating clear crystals with gold. These bright crystals are delightful, producing an energy that's calming, yet vibrant. We use them to help with communication problems, to make decisions, or for getting in tune with our higher selves. They also work well for healing confusion-related illness, such as a cold, chest flu, or congestion.

Rose Quartz

Although rose quartz rarely forms in individual crystals, or even in a cluster, you can easily find them as polished rocks or faceted for jewelry. Their aura of love energy makes them an excellent choice to include in crystal arrangements to make sure your home or office is filled with love. We have a large rose quartz boulder on our living room windowsill that glows whenever the sun shines, as love would look if we could see it. The rest of the time it projects a subtle aura of love into the room. We also make sure we include rose quartz near sleeping areas to provide a calming influence.

To keep that love energy with you when you're out and about, you can carry a polished rock or wear jewelry made from it. And it's always good to include rose quartz in any ceremony where you want love to be expressed. You've heard the saying that "love cures all ills," so wear it, hold it, or keep it nearby when you're doing healing work.

OTHER ROCKS FOR CRYSTAL WORKERS

The list of minerals used in conjunction with crystals in displays, as jewelry, or as decorations for rods is endless. Some of the more popular minerals include tourmaline, turquoise, amazonite, lapis lazuli, pyrite, carnelian, ruby, tiger's eye, apatite, aquamarine, topaz, opal, agate, magnetite, jade, malachite, onyx, tektite, and obsidian. All of these rocks, and many more, have special energy properties that blend well with quartz crystals. Choose any of the rocks that you use with crystals the same way you do your crystals—by color, feel, and intuition.

If you have a polished or faceted rock with an energy that feels good to you, consider adding it as a decoration to any of the crystal projects offered in this book. Its energy, combined with your crystal, may just provide the particular vibration you need to do your crystal work more effectively.

FOUR

The Crystal Experimenter

In order to communicate with crystals and other beings, we need to learn new languages.

In working with crystals, various questions arise regarding modifications of the tools we offer, materials that can be used, and methods of applying our techniques for using the tools. That's the way it should be in crystal work. We always tell readers that right brain creativity and intuition are the voices to heed first because the crystals and tools are going to be responding to your particular energy, not to a certain design, material, or technique.

Starting with the basic information we offer, many readers have come up with incredibly creative modifications using their own materials and design changes. The resulting tools were every bit as effective as the originals. Readers have also found uses for the tools that we never imagined when they were created. If a crystal invites a change in our design or you have different materials available, by all means use them. By inserting your own personality into crystal tools and experiments, you get results that are uniquely effective for you.

CLEARING AND CHARGING CRYSTALS

To quickly clear and charge our crystals, we simply hold them in our hands for a minute or two and think them clear. For additional clearing and charging, any type of jewelry, stone, or quartz crystal can be placed with another natural quartz crystal. Although we've designed a charging stand for you to use for this process, it's not essential. Your charging stand can also be much simpler than the one offered in the following experiment. In fact, we often just put our crystals and rocks in a dish together when they're not being used, which makes a nice display as well as charging the crystals and the room they're placed in.

When crystals and rocks are put together, they renew and communicate with each other through the interchange of Universal Energy. The results are the same as those that occur when jewelry, crystals, and other personal items are placed in the center of a healing circle to be exposed to blessings, good energy, and positive thoughts or feelings. If you have one crystal that works particularly well for you, put it with others that you want to program and you'll find they'll be easier to work with.

Charging and Clearing Stand for Faceted or Polished Crystals

This experiment came about because of differing opinions as to whether faceted or polished quartz crystals still retained the energy characteristics of natural, uncut crystals.

There's still a difference of opinion on this. Since each crystal has its own energy pattern, it's difficult to make direct comparisons, but we've found cases where a polished or faceted crystal provided an energy that suited our needs better than the uncut version.

We also found that when natural crystals are used to clear and charge polished or faceted crystals, the effects are beneficial. The following design is for an energy charging and clearing stand for your faceted and polished stones. As in all crystal experiments, use only natural quartz or stones, rather than those that are synthetic or leaded.

Materials:

A. 4" x 12" x ½" wood base with rounded corners

B. Two small screws and a copper or brass strap, 6" long, ½" or ⅜" wide, bendable, but sturdy enough to support the disk

C. Copper or brass disc, 2¾" in diameter, and two small screws to mount it

D. Cut, faceted, or polished natural quartz crystal

E. Natural quartz crystal, uncut

Construction:

1. Cut the ½" thick wood base 4" wide and 12" long. Round the corners to make a long oval.

2. Drill two holes at ¼" and 1" in from one end of the copper or brass strap. Drill two more holes at ¼" and 1¼" in from the other end of the strap. Drill two holes in the center of the wood base, about 4" in from one of the long ends, to match the first holes in the strap. Secure the strap to the base with two screws. Bend the loose end of the strap up at a 90 degree angle, then bend the other end of the strap out at another 90 degree angle to hold the disk. The distance between the base and the bent portion of the strap should be about 3". Drill holes in the disk to match those in the strap, and screw the disk on.

3. To use the stand, center an uncut quartz crystal under the disk and place the polished or faceted crystal to be charged on top of the disk.

4. *Optional:* ½" brass or copper strips can be attached to the edge or top of the base for decoration.

Shrink Tube Crystal Mount or Covering

Although shrink tubing was originally intended for covering computer cables and wires, we've found it effective for concealing flaws in the lower part of a crystal and for use as a shim when placing a crystal inside a fitting. Depending on what you're constructing, the shrink tube can even be left showing, or be used as a covering for the finished product.

Shrink tubing, which can be found at electronics stores, comes in various diameters and is designed to shrink to fit an object when heat is applied. An industrial heat gun can be used to shrink it. If you don't have a heat gun, a butane lighter will shrink short pieces, and the burner or heating element on a stove works for longer pieces.

CRYSTAL CHARGING STAND

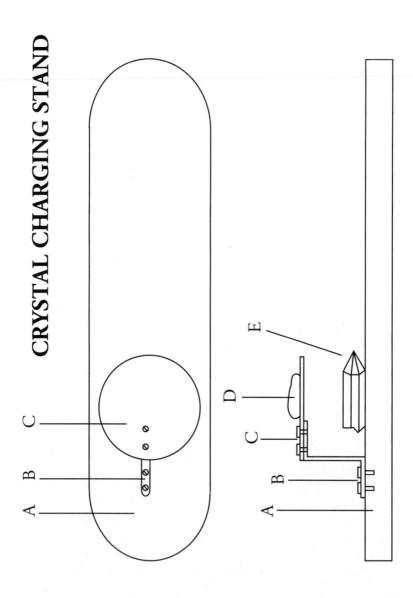

Materials:

Quartz crystal of your choice

A piece of shrink tubing with a diameter slightly larger than the crystal

Construction:

1. Fit the shrink tubing over the blunt end of the crystal.

2. Heat the shrink tubing until you get a snug fit.

3. Cut away extra tubing at the bottom of the crystal.

A variety of colors—red, blue, yellow—can be used in addition to the standard black shrink tube. We've also used shrink tubing as a covering for crystal tools when we want a futuristic, high-tech look. It has the advantage of being nice looking and much easier to apply than leather. Plastic electrical tape can also be used for the same purposes that you would use shrink tubing, but isn't as attractive for exterior use.

Crystal Charging Stand

SHRINK TUBE CRYSTAL MOUNT
OR COVERING

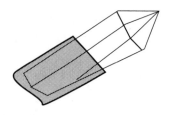

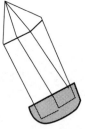

FIVE

Crystal Questions
and Answers

A crystal increases our ability to access information
that's always been available.

Since the first book in this series, *Crystal Power*, was published, it's
been impossible to answer all of the questions in the overwhelming volume of letters we've received. The best solution we've been able to find is
to answer them in this chapter. We'll also take this opportunity to fill you
in on what other readers are doing as they perform their own experiments
with crystals and crystal rods. Thank you all for your letters and the ideas
you've shared. As we're all learning and growing together, each shared
experience adds to the common fund of knowledge that will help all of us
evolve.

1. Where can I find quartz crystals?

In the United States, especially in urban areas, quartz crystals can
often be found at gem and mineral shows, in rock or mineral shops, metaphysical bookstores, and sometimes even in shopping malls. In fact, the
best clear quartz crystals in the world come from mines in Arkansas, right

here in the United States. Many crystals, especially the colored ones, are also imported from Brazil and other places around the world. If you aren't too picky about quality, crystals can often be found on rock hunting expeditions wherever you live.

2. What is the affect of glue on crystals?

Glue doesn't appear to affect a crystal's energy characteristics, probably because energy particles pass through most types of matter unhindered. We, and others, have used instant bonding, epoxy, or silicone glues to mount crystals in many projects with no decrease in the energy of the devices and no ill effects on the crystals or people. Generally, for aesthetic reasons, glue is only used on the lower part of the crystal, but even covering a crystal with glue shouldn't affect its basic energy properties.

3. How do I care for my crystals?

The main thing to avoid with crystals is rapid temperature changes, which can cause the crystals to crack or break, especially if you're using them with water or salt water. Sometimes, too, in harsh sunlight, crystals will turn cloudy. It's probably safest to keep your best crystals indoors and out of direct sunlight.

4. What kind of coverings can I use on my crystal rods?

Crystal rods were first wrapped with leather in the tradition of Native American crafts. We thought then that leather acted as insulation, but this turned out not to be the case. Uncovered crystal rods function as well as those that are wrapped. Wrappings other than leather have also been used with success. PVC shrink tubing, plastic and rubber electrical tape, foil tapes, cloth, and yarn, along with other materials, have been used in place of leather by us and our readers, with positive results.

Those who object to the use of animal skins can often find synthetic substitutes for leather or fur that work just as well, or better. And if yarn, jute, string, or brightly-colored cloth best expresses the way you want your rod to look and feel, by all means go ahead and use it. The wrapping used on a crystal energy rod is, most of all, a highly individual personal preference based on what feels right to you. Choose a color and type of wrap that fits your particular energy.

5. How can I decorate my crystal rod, and what affect will it have on its energy?

While decorations, especially stones, do modify the energy characteristics of the crystals, the effects are positive. The variety of decorations being used on rods is incredible, to say the least. Some rods have been built and decorated Native American-style with fur, feathers, and beadwork designs. Others have been built with bands of gold and silver. Often rods are built of copper, brass, or silver and left unwrapped.

Various stones such as amethyst, rose quartz, turquoise, lapis, rubies and many others have been used to adorn rods. Some of these crystal rods have become works of art, while maintaining their energy-working characteristics.

Science, art, and religion combine as one expression with the creation of crystal energy rods. The more your rod expresses your own personality and outlook, the easier it will be to work with it effectively.

6. Can materials other than copper be used to construct crystal rods and staffs?

Most of the rods we build are constructed of copper plumbing parts because they're cheap, serviceable, provide a smooth energy flow, and are easily available here in the United States. Readers from other parts of the world have written to say that brass or other metals are used for plumbing in their corner of the world. By all means, go ahead and use the metals you can easily acquire.

Copper, silver, gold, platinum, brass, and bronze, either used separately or in various combinations, are all popular metals that have been used successfully in the construction of crystal rods or jewelry. The choice of which metals to use are largely a matter of individual preference and economics. In fact, non-conducting materials like glass, wood, bamboo, and plastic have also been used to make extremely effective rods.

7. What kind of materials can be used inside crystal rods?

Most versions of the crystal energy rods are constructed using a hollow copper tube as an energy particle chamber behind the crystal. It was soon discovered that the copper tube could be loaded with a wide variety of materials and still function as an amplification chamber.

Round magnets or small pieces of lodestone placed in the copper tube add a complementary energy field to the quartz crystal in the energy rod. Rods also work well when loaded with smaller quartz crystals or crystal and quartz chips. Some have been filled with iron oxide and small crystals from mine beds in Arkansas. Many rods have been loaded with quartz crystals using spacers of lodestone or magnets to hold the crystals in place, an inch apart, throughout the entire length inside the energy rods.

Other types of crystals and gemstones can also be used inside crystal energy rods. Such stones as rose quartz, jade, turquoise, aquamarine, malachite, citrine, and amethyst, to name a few, have been used successfully.

The rods can be filled with anything your imagination and intuition can come up with. One of our favorite rods is a glass wand filled with colored particles suspended in a viscous liquid. To turn the wand into a healing rod, we mounted small rods on either end of it. Later, we discovered that watching the particles travel up and down the length of the wand was also an effective meditation tool to clear our minds before using it.

8. Are larger crystal rods and staffs more effective than smaller ones?

No. Practically every rod size imaginable has been built and used successfully since their introduction in the seventies. Some have been as small as 1" long by ⅛" in diameter with tiny quartz crystals. At the other end of the scale are staffs that are over seven feet long. Each person who builds a crystal rod seems to find a size suitable for their individual use, a size they feel comfortable with. Some crystal energy rods have even been constructed using telescoping tubes so the length can be adjusted for tuning the rod to the crystal or to the person operating the rod.

Many crystal experimenters have asked if a longer length, larger diameter, or larger crystal produces more power or energy output. When speaking of the Universal Energy that comes through quartz crystals, the "bigger is better and more powerful" theory doesn't hold true. Even a tiny grain of quartz sand is part of the energy field of the Universe. The perception and conscious awareness of the person is far more important than the size of the crystal or crystal energy rod. An aware, balanced operator will produce a more powerful energy flow through a small crystal rod than a less aware person could produce from a giant energy staff. Experiment to determine the size of the rod that "feels" right for you personally.

9. What should I look for when I'm choosing a crystal?

Choosing a quartz crystal is a very personal, individual process for both the person and the crystal. Often, a crystal chooses a person instead. More often, the person and the crystal "choose" each other, working together as they form a relationship of interacting energy fields.

While we sometimes try to find quartz crystals that are symmetrical with clear, unchipped facets for crystal power tools, it's only for aesthetic reasons. All crystals, regardless of what they "look like," have the particular structure that is actively energy-connected to the rest of the Universe. Likewise, all people, regardless of their degree of awareness, are energy-connected to the Universe.

Part of the confusion arises because crystal beings respond to human beings exactly the way we "think" they do. Some people think a crystal point or crystal ball projects a beam of Universal Energy; others think they send out a field of energy. The truth is, if a beam is visualized, that's what manifests; if it's a field you want, then that's what you get. The type of radiation depends on what you're programming and visualizing.

In the last twenty years, we've learned that a lot of our preconceptions about crystals were wrong. As our awareness increased and widened, so did the characteristics of our crystal friends, to the same degree. We now see from experience that all crystals, minerals, rocks, gemstones, and the Earth herself are working with us, not just for us. While we program and tune crystals they are, in turn, tuning us to a larger Universal Energy frequency. Each member of the mineral kingdom is open and receptive to the emotion of love and the energy of thought.

Some people advise using crystals with various facets and shapes for specific uses. While this practice works for many people, it tends to make a simple activity into a complex one. Choosing crystals by what "feels right" is the easiest process, even if you just hold the crystal without looking at it or intellectually trying to decide which one is right. As we become more aware of our relationship to our mineral friends, we're experiencing the fact that they all work with us.

When using more than one crystal in a rod, test them for compatibility with each other and with you by holding one in each hand. If the energy seems to travel up each arm and meet somewhere in the middle of your body, you've got a good match. Harmonious interaction of energy fields between crystals is as important as the relationships between individual people. In both cases, energy fields of conscious beings are involved.

Whether cloudy, milky, chipped, clear, cracked, double or single ter-minated, twinned, tripleted, clustered, angled, trenched, fused, or included, the crystals themselves will tell you by a feeling if you're right for them or they're right for you. If you listen to your intuition, quartz crystal beings will also tell you if they want to be used in a crystal tool; shaped into a ball, pyramid, or egg; polished, or mounted in jewelry.

Our crystal friends also tell us when they want to be left as they are in their natural state. The elementals of the mineral kingdom can be forceful when making their wishes known. Some of the ways they tell us to leave them alone are by disappearing or getting lost for periods of time, or even permanently. Being very difficult to mount in jewelry or a crystal tool is another method they use if we don't catch on right away. Some crystals fall off necklaces and earrings as well as out of crystal rods until we finally get the message.

Wherever there's a quartz crystal, there's an interaction and radiation of energy. At one time, people thought that quartz crystals below a half inch in diameter were much less powerful and shouldn't be used. Crystals smaller than this have since been used in many devices that worked just as well as the larger ones. Smaller crystals perform well in pocket-sized energy rods, in garden rods, and as shields. Tiny crystals (⅛" diameter and smaller) are also effective in miniature energy rods and jewelry.

The energy output of the crystal or tool depends on the operator's personal relationship to the crystal energy being. A weak or diffused energy projection reflects the individual's relationship to the crystal, not a flaw in the crystal's energy connection with Universal forces.

10. Can power boosters or amplifiers be built into crystal energy rods?

They can. Coils of copper wire with capacitors, resistors, and con-tact switches have been built into the Autoelectromags (For more infor-mation, see *Crystal Warrior* by the authors, available from Llewellyn Publications). However, a simple, effective way to increase the force of a crystal rod's electromagnetic particle field or beam is by loading the rod with round ceramic magnets. For a more down-to-earth boost, lodestone or magnetite can be used to provide a balanced electromagnetic force compatible with the crystal's energy field. Most crystals like this magnetic relationship since it helps them evolve and raise their own vibrations, consciousness, and awareness. A series of single or double termination crystals inside the rod also has an amplifying effect with or without magnetic materials.

11. How do crystal rods and staffs work?

The copper cap at one end of a crystal rod serves to define a particle or energy accumulation chamber, as well as direct the flow of energy one way through a crystal and out the point. This is true whether the crystal is a single or double termination one.

On the other hand, mounting a crystal in both ends of the copper tube also forms an accumulation chamber for energy. This was the form used for the original crystal healing rod. Many healers still prefer this model today for the healing energy flow in both directions, which also heals the healer.

Crystal staffs are usually constructed with a crystal in only one end, since the natural inclination is to rest the other end on the ground. However, we've built some with a crystal in each end to use in martial arts spiritual development, where neither end of the staff ever touches the floor or ground.

It's often been asked if wood can be used as the main body of staffs or rods. The answer is yes. Rods and staffs have been made of wood or bamboo, with a crystal on one end and a copper cap or another crystal at the other. Sometimes copper wire, carbon wire, or a copper spiral have been used to connect the crystal and copper cap. The bamboo wand in Chapter 16 uses copper tape on the exterior of the wand to connect crystal mounts on either end. All of these worked well, both with or without an insulating handgrip or covering. Even wooden rods or staffs with no connecting wire have performed well with energy projections. The "feel" of the operator has proven to be the determining factor time and time again.

12. What variations can I use to build crystal headbands?

Many variations of the crystal power headband are now in use. Some use the original design with the copper band going part way around the operator's head and a leather tie in back to make it easily adjustable. Other models use a copper band that completely encircles the operator's head.

Some have even been constructed using strands of copper wire wrapped around the crystal several times and then wrapped around the operator's head; others are made with only a crystal and leather. They all work.

Like other crystal tools, a number of ornately decorated or modified models have been constructed by creative individuals who wanted to embellish a personal headband. The solid silver headband is very popular. It makes this crystal device a beautiful jewelry item suitable for many occasions. Silver disks, crystals, healing stones, and gemstones have been mounted on both copper and silver bands. Sometimes only two or three stones, and at times, up to a dozen are equally spaced completely around the headband.

Crystals such as amethyst, smoky quartz, and rose quartz are popular for making headbands. Stones such as lapis, jade, agate, citrine, turquoise, and malachite have been used as decorations. Most members of the mineral kingdom work well together in a balanced field of harmonious energy.

Crystal headbands have been used for thought transmission and communication in both the past and present ages. Individual awareness and growth through meditation is also stimulated through the use of headbands. Wherever crystals are used, energy balancing usually occurs, making the headbands popular for healing. They have also been used in conjunction with energy rods, other crystals, and even black box-type radionic machines.

The standard headband uses an 1" wide copper strip, with a single termination crystal on a silver disk 1½" in diameter. Double termination crystals also work very well on headbands. Metal shapes, such as crosses, pyramids, and diamonds, have been used in place of a disk. Copper bands both wider and thinner than an inch have been made. Glues don't seem to affect the energy operation of headbands, although some people prefer to mount the crystal and silver by bending and shaping the copper band to hold them without the use of glue or solder.

13. Please tell me more about crystal communicator/generators.

A number of questions have been asked about the construction of the crystal communicator/generator, which is simply a large crystal in a copper cup, usually placed on a brass plate, in the center of a healing circle. The crystal can slide all the way into the copper cup so that it touches the bottom, but it doesn't need to. All that's necessary is that it should fit tightly enough to stay in position with the tip pointing straight up. Copper tape, copper mesh, or even silicone caulking can be used to make the crystal fit the cup with no adverse effects. If you plan to use the crystal for other purposes, don't mount it permanently in the cup. The copper cup can be mounted to copper or brass plates with either solder or glue, or they can merely be placed on the plate so that the crystal cup can be taken off and set elsewhere when the device isn't being used. The size of the plate or dish seems to make little difference.

Materials used for the cup and plate can also vary. Copper has been the most popular material so far, but brass, silver, bronze, and gold plates and cups have also been used. Various combinations of these materials are frequently used together, such as a copper cup on a brass or silver plate, or a silver cup and a copper plate. All combinations seem to work well with no material being better than another. Waves of energy, in color and heat, have been manifested with this device, but the phenomena is due to the operator's awareness, not the materials used.

14. What are crystal shields and how do they work?

Crystal shields are crystals that have been programmed to project an aura of protection around a person or place. Single crystals, various crystal devices, and crystal clusters have all been used for this purpose. Like other devices, it's the operator's programming rather than the shape, size, or conformation of the crystals that provides a protective aura.

Crystal clusters are frequently set inside the home for beneficial energy fields. The larger clusters sometimes radiate a wider field of energy and are used as artistic decorator pieces. Larger pieces don't create a stronger force field (that's determined by the person programming them), just a force field or shield with a wider area of energy inside it.

Clusters of clear quartz crystals of any size tend to radiate an intense energy field by themselves. When a crystal or cluster is glued to a white quartz rock base, the energy field broadens so it's not quite as intense. There are many other ways to mellow out a clear quartz crystal field without decreasing the strength. One of the most common ways is to intersperse amethyst crystals and amethyst clusters around the clear crystals in the house. Another way is to place rose or pink quartz rocks near or underneath clear crystals or clusters, especially if an unconditionally loving energy field is desired. Blue and green quartz rocks like adventurine also combine well to produce balanced energy fields. The color combinations of quartz crystals and quartz rocks cover a wide spectrum of energy combinations. It's best to experiment until you find one that feels right for a balanced shield.

Quite often, rocks and minerals are sawed into slices or plates and put under other crystals or clusters for a shield. A flat rock base can also be used. A crystal or crystal cluster can also be placed directly on the ground, floor, or table.

Double termination crystals have been used as personal energy shield projectors for quite some time. Some people thought any double termination crystal smaller than an inch or two in length wouldn't work as a personal energy shield. Now it's common for tiny double termination crystals (less than ½" long) to be programmed and carried as individual energy shields. All quartz crystals are of the same subatomic structure created by the Earth Mother, and all are connected to the Universal web of energy.

Likewise, single termination crystals of all sizes have been found to work well as personal energy shields, although many people report that the double termination crystals seem to radiate a more rounded and balanced energy field.

15. What relationship do crystals have to other natural forces, and can crystals be used to affect the weather?

Quartz crystals, natural forces, and weather conditions are electromagnetic in nature, with interrelated energy fields. Clouds are a good example of levitation (the term antigravity doesn't quite fit). Tons of water vapor float through the atmosphere through a balance of positive and negative ions. It may turn out that there's no difference between the forces that allow clouds to float and those used to float huge stones to build the ancient pyramids and other structures. Crystal workers soon learn to look to nature as our greatest teacher for learning about the energy changes Mother Nature uses to maintain her balance and nurture her life forms.

Electromagnetic interactions foster all life. Lightning above the Earth and quartz crystals below the Earth produce electromagnetic interactions. When an eagle soars upon the winds, both the wind and the eagle are one with the electromagnetic energy spectrum.

The Earth herself is a giant electromagnetic being, turning like an electric motor, or generator, on her axis. Her underground movements (earthquakes and volcanoes) are electromagnetic in nature. Piezoelectric crystals and minerals, and magnetic rocks like lodestone and magnetite, all function within her electrical system. The electromagnetic mineral kingdom lives in balance with her other electromagnetic beings; plants, birds, fish, animals, and people. All of her beings are electromagnetic in nature, functioning as switches, capacitors, resistors, transducers, transformers, insulators, and conductors.

The Earth lives in electromagnetic balance with other planets, the moon, asteroids, the sun and other stars. Galactic, solar, and earthly storms in the sea of Universal electromagnetic energy are different only in intensity and type of energy. The nature of weather is the same in any area, electromagnetic reactions in the subatomic realm.

Human beings, as electrical connections, have a great influence on the Earth Mother's weather, consciously or unconsciously. In this area all is one and intimately connected by the Universal Energy. The use of crystals for the conscious influence of the weather is a practice dating back to the beginnings of humankind. One of the easiest practices in weather modification involves using a crystal rod or a crystal by itself.

When rain or snow is needed for an area of the Earth, use the same process of balancing and healing the Earth's body and aura that you would for a person, plant, or animal. Begin by becoming one with and visualizing the desired effect. Picture clouds forming in the clear sky. Feel your oneness with the clouds. Visualize the clouds bringing the particles, electrons, ions, and water droplets together to form these giant "cells in the sky." With appropriate pictures in mind, an intense feeling of loving oneness with the crystal, the Earth Mother, and yourself, amplifies the healing manifestation. Crystal beings and the Earth being both want to work with you. It promotes life and growth, which is what the Earth Mother's nurturing is all about, whether we decide to be in harmony with it or not.

We're learning to be friends with the Earth Mother's crystal and mineral beings, her plant and animal beings, and her other human beings. Well, sometimes, anyway. If we want to change the weather, we need to start feeling a kinship with the Earth's weather beings. Seeing them as friends is a great way to establish this relationship. Friendly beings won't hurt us, so there's nothing to fear. It may be a bit disconcerting to try at-one-ness and unconditional love with a hurricane or a tornado, so try something easier at first. Cloud beings are nice. Thunder and lightning beings are always willing to put on a show while trying to get our attention. There's also the wind spirits who can be gentle or strong, warm or cold.

Our environment is composed of our own mass consciousness, thoughts, and emotions that are reflected back to us. The reason we can influence the Earth's weather is that we are already doing so, although we're not usually conscious of it. Humankind's mass consciousness, or thoughts and emotions, permeate the Earth Mother's aura and her geomagnetic field. Her weather beings are born, grow, change, and move within that aura. Mass consciousness is unconscious, undirected, and unfocused in its influence on weather energy patterns. By consciously controlling our own thoughts, little by little we influence and change the larger mass consciousness that forms and changes our planet. Since we're already connected to and part of the Earth's electromagnetic field maintained by our mass consciousness, we can focus our thoughts and emotions, with a feeling of unconditional love, on projecting the specific weather effects we need around the earth for balance and healing.

Throughout human history on our planet, individuals who are in tune with the Earth have used quartz crystals for influencing the weather. Druids, Atlanteans, Egyptians, witches, magicians, scientists, and medicine people have been influencing the weather for eons. One person or a group of people in a circle around a crystal can not only form clouds, but call upon the wind spirit beings to come and manifest themselves. In fact, with a crystal, one can call upon any kind of weather being. This is not so much a power (although people like to call it that) as it is a cooperation between electric beings as part of the same overall electromagnetic field of a larger being.

Learning to feel at one with the beings of Mother Nature is more a lifestyle than learning or knowledge. Thinking and feeling are more important than following anyone else's technique in this area. There are as many ways to do it as there are individual people. No one way is "right," but there are many ways that work. We can't give you a formula, like connecting part A to piece B, or following steps 1, 2, 3, and 4. Those procedures work in industry and business, but left-brain concepts don't apply to establishing a personal relationship with the Earth Mother and her friendly beings. In this creative area, you are your own best guide.

16. Why do authors of crystal books have contradictory statements about crystal usage, like what crystals will or won't do and how they do it?

Crystals and human beings are unique individuals. Some of each are similar, but no two are exactly alike. Crystal beings are very sensitive in response to human beings. They react to the way we think and feel on all levels. Our self-created world responds the same way. While it's easy for two people to elicit the same reaction from a crystal or crystals, it's just as easy to get two different and even opposite reactions from them.

17. What's the difference between personal and impersonal energy?

The energy of the Universe is, in essence, all the same. It appears different when minds form and direct it to new purposes for their own creations. Before this is done, the energy is impersonal and undifferentiated. Afterward, it can become personal in its focus.

18. What relationship does love have to energy work?

Love, like God, can be a highly misinterpreted word. It means different things to different people. The love we refer to is the conscious unconditional acceptance that we are all connected in the creative enterprise of living and being. For the word love, we could substitute the term creative force. We are all part of the whole of life, and each act or thought of an individual affects everything else to some degree. In order to be able to love and nurture ourselves, we have to love and nurture others. Our thoughts are things, and what we put out is exactly what we ultimately receive. That being the case, why would we harm ourselves by wishing harm on others?

Experiencing love is also the best way to tune into our connection to the Universal Energy and use it. If you find a person or condition impossible to love from your present perspective, maybe you could look at things differently. First, you could begin to see what we call evil as twisted love. We all want to feel love and loved, but sometimes we just don't know how to go about it and unspeakable acts can result. For example, take a look at the crusades and holy wars. Terrible acts were committed in the name of love. Wars between countries occur because people love their country but are unwilling to concede the same love to others. Throughout history individuals have fought and killed to preserve their own perceived good. These are all examples of twisted love. We need to see that our own good is tied up with everyone else's and there's plenty for all of us, before we can understand love.

When we see examples of twisted love in our personal lives or in the news, we can't let ourselves hate the perpetrators, because that fosters hatred in our own lives and adds it to the mass consciousness. Instead, we need to project healing love at the person or situation. That doesn't mean that criminals shouldn't be punished. Their punishment is the Karma they've created for themselves and is an opportunity for growth. If we project love into the situation, we can foster growth and healing in the criminal and victims that ultimately benefits everyone.

SIX

Power Rods

In order to use our power,
we have to realize that we possess it.

H ave you ever suspected that there's much more to you than is visible to the outside world? Or have you wished you could just focus and make use of the incredible power that you intuitively know exists in your own mind? Chances are, both thoughts have crossed your mind at one time or another. Well, there is much more to you than is visible, and the power of your mind is there just waiting to be tapped. The power rods were created to help you focus, amplify, and project that incredible power you possess by using the energy of your own thoughts and emotions to drive your thought forms in a one-way flow to the target.

While these rods are called power rods, crystals also produce an energy balancing or healing effect, as well as an amplification of energy. They project energy outward from the operator to any area of the world, which simply broadens the definition of healing to a much wider scale. You can use the power rods to channel or project a large flow of Universal Energy in an intense beam of blue-white light (sometimes visible but usually not) over longer distances than one would think of in relation to a healing rod.

TECHNIQUES FOR POWER ROD USE

Before using the power rod you may want to meditate for a minute or two to calm and focus your thoughts. You can also focus your own energy more intensely by cupping your palms a few inches apart. Concentrate on building up a ball of energy in the space between your palms. You can actually feel the energy build up in the sphere by moving your palms around it. It manifests as a tingling sensation, as if you were cupping a physical ball.

Hold the power rod as you would any other type of tool. Use whichever hand feels best to you with a comfortable grip, and visualize a beam of energy projecting from the point of the crystal and surrounding the target. The visualization of a white light shield or field of energy can also be used to protect you from a negative feedback reaction if you feel it's necessary. For instance, the shield visualization might be advisable if you're sending healing energy to a toxic chemical or radioactive area.

Your thoughts are directing the beam of energy from the crystal, and the emotions behind those thoughts are amplifying the beam. Both should be of a positive nature. For instance, rather than thinking about winning in a conflict while others lose, think about a healing taking place where everyone wins. As long as we continue to think in terms of winners and losers, we're going to be on the losing end at some point. There's no reason why we can't all be winners. If you can't visualize a particular solution where everyone wins, then project your intense desire and unconditional love toward the situation and let the Universal Mind decide the actual outcome. In many cases where the subject being healed is the Earth, the energy can be projected in an unqualified manner. This leaves the particular effect of the healing energy up to the Earth Mother herself to use in the needed areas.

Maybe the result you want to achieve with your power rod is personal: better health, a good job, a love relationship, abundance. That's okay. There's nothing wrong with wanting good things for yourself; in fact, it would be unnatural if you didn't. The trick is to focus your desire in positive terms.

Suppose it's a promotion you want, but you can't imagine getting it without removing the person who already has the job. Don't concentrate on getting that person out of the way; it's too likely to backfire, shield or not. Instead, imagine yourself having the job you want, doing what you like to do, and doing it well. It might turn out that another position will open up that's even more perfect for you than the one you wanted. Or the person who has the position you want might get promoted or move to another company so that you get his or her job. Maybe another company will offer you the perfect job. If someone's been standing in the way of your promotion, after using the power rod and surrounding your relationship in love, he or she could take another look at you and decide you're just the person to fill the position. The possibilities are endless if you keep an open mind and focus on the good you want rather than someone else's downfall. In many cases, just directing unconditional love at a situation will bring the result you want.

When using your power rod, you may want to try out various visualization techniques before you settle on the one that works best for you. The energy beam can be visualized as reaching out thousands of miles across the earth, or it can be seen as traveling through the earth's aura at about a six-foot altitude in the geomagnetic field that surrounds the planet. The beam of the power rod can also be seen as arcing from one point on the earth to another point, like a rainbow across the sky. In fact, remembering that the white light beam includes all the healing colors of the rainbow is a good practice for understanding the beneficial effects of the energy. The crystal energy beam can also be seen as traveling straight through the earth, since energy on a subatomic level moves through all forms of matter as easily as it moves through air or water.

It's also good to remember that the power rod's beam of energy is more than just a visualization of energy directed by thought. It's a perception of ourselves as the energy beings that we really are, that we're beginning to redevelop or reawaken. It's usually not long after projecting a beam of energy from a crystal rod that we begin to see, with our inner eye, the white-light beam coming out of our own brightened aura.

The egg-shaped aura around our bodies is not an illusion. When we see it surrounding ourselves and others, we can begin to understand the true nature of humans. We are eternal energy beings who temporarily inhabit physical bodies. This realization can lead to a better understanding of the fluid nature and relationships of all energy fields interacting within the energy field of the Universe.

Through the use of crystals and energy rods, the doors of our own minds and those of the universe continue to open or unfold between interpenetrating energy fields or dimensions.

CONSTRUCTING THE POWER RODS

In the following pages, you'll find six different variations on the basic power rod. Choose the one that best suits your purpose, and then follow these instructions for building the one you choose using whatever modifications suit you. For the specifications of the parts for each rod, refer to the diagrams.

1. Cut the copper pipe of the diameter indicated in the diagram to the specified length.

2. Use instant bonding glue or another glue suitable for metal to glue the end cap on one end of the copper pipe.

3. If the rod is to be filled with magnets, lodestones, crystals, iron oxide, or another material that you think might be appropriate, do so now from the open end of the rod. To keep the rod from rattling excessively, you can use leather or cloth to wrap the filling or pack the ends of the rod, without affecting its performance.

4. Mount the crystal into the copper coupler, or if no coupler is called for, make your slits in the end of the copper pipe.

5. Glue the crystal or crystal and fitting into or onto the open end of the pipe.

6. Use glue to wrap leather strips or the covering of your choice around the rod.

We've included some basic construction techniques below that will help you in building any of the rod variations offered in this chapter and elsewhere in the book.

1. Before gluing any of the pieces together, it's best to assemble most of the rod or tool first to make sure the pieces line up right and fit together easily.

2. To avoid getting glue where you don't want it when you're gluing copper parts together, run a line of glue around the inside of the larger piece to be glued, then slide the smaller piece inside to spread the glue to the interior.

3. *Mounting a crystal in the copper coupling:* Usually crystals won't fit perfectly into the coupling without some kind of shim material. To ensure a snug fit, wrap the base of the crystal with leather, cloth, copper tape, or copper mesh. The shim material will be visible when the crystal is mounted, so wrap it neatly. Next, insert the wrapped crystal into the coupling and squeeze drops of instant bonding glue onto the shim material. It will soak down to hold the crystal in place. As a final step, use the flat side of a knife blade to push the shim material down even with the edge of the coupling. Let the mounted crystal sit for a few minutes to dry before assembling it with the other copper fittings.

4. *Mounting crystals directly into copper pipe:* One of the rods in this chapter is made with the crystal mounted directly into the copper pipe. This method of mounting works well when you have a crystal with a larger diameter than the pipe.

   To mount the crystal, cut four slots in the end of the copper pipe at equally spaced intervals, using tinsnips or aircraft shears. The depth of the slots will depend on the size of the crystal to be fitted. Bend the cut portions outward with pliers until the crystal fits tightly into the pipe. Squeeze instant bonding glue down around the places where the crystal touches the pipe. It will drip down to form a bond. If the fit doesn't seem to be secure enough, cut small pieces of leather and poke them down around the base of the crystal for extra support; then squeeze glue over the leather where it will soak in to hold the crystal more securely.

5. *Cutting copper tubing:* We put a length of tubing in a vise to hold it steady, and then use a simple hand-held tube cutting device to make the cut. A hacksaw will also work. If you don't have the tools, you can usually get the tube cut to the length you want when you buy it at a hardware store.

6. *Buying copper fittings:* Copper fittings can be found at most hardware stores where plumbing supplies are sold. We try to buy fittings without sticky price tags on them, but it's not always possible. To remove the glue from the fittings, we usually rub the part vigorously to get the glue to form a ball, and then pick it off.

7. *Wrapping the rods:* Although all the rods offered here are wrapped with leather, you can use any material you want, or leave it unwrapped. For most wrappings, you'll need to cut the material in strips. We usually use strips ½" wide when we use ½" fittings, and ¾" wide for ¾" fittings. Cut the end of the strip at an angle to get started. Wrap carefully in a spiral pattern, overlapping the material a bit as you go and gluing the underside. If the strip you've cut isn't long enough to wrap the whole rod, cut the end off at an angle. Cut a matching angle for the new piece so the two pieces fit exactly together and continue wrapping. When you reach the end of the piece to be wrapped, cut the strip off at an angle and glue it down.

8. *To shine the copper fittings:* If the fittings are extremely dull, you can put them in a tumbler with jeweler's rouge. They can also be shined with a wire brush polisher, but it can leave brush marks. Although the fittings can be coated with a fixative or varnish so they won't tarnish, we've never done this. For the most part, we don't find a bit of tarnish on the rods unattractive. If you want to shine up the fittings on your rods after they've been assembled, you can use Brasso or another copper cleaner. A jeweler's rouge cloth will also do the trick, if the tarnish is minimal. The only problem with shining the copper occurs with spilled drops of glue. The glue will protect the metal from tarnish, leaving a shiny spot that never polishes to the exact color of the rest of the fitting.

MINIATURE MAGNETIC POWER/HEALING ROD

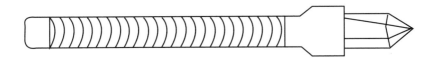

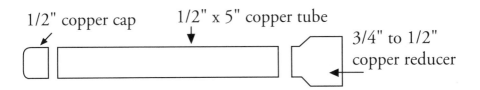

1/2" copper cap

1/2" x 5" copper tube

3/4" to 1/2" copper reducer

1/2" diameter ceramic magnets

(end view)

Quartz crystal 3/4" x 1 1/2"

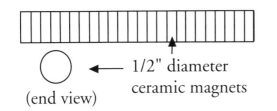

1/2" x 14" leather strip for tube wrap

Cutaway view of interior magnets from end cap to crystal

MAGNETIC ENERGY AND CRYSTALS

Magnetic energy is often used in healing and energy work. It's said to align the iron in the blood with the Earth's magnetic poles to enhance the healing of our bodies, and is often used in conjunction with Earth healing ceremonies. In addition, it's been used to enhance sleep or to help release the mind from the body along geomagnetic lines. The following two rods use magnets in combination with crystals to enhance the energy of power rods. While some people prefer the natural magnetism of lodestones (magnetite), we've also had good luck using manufactured ceramic magnets.

Miniature Magnetic Power/Healing Rod

This is a very popular model since it can be used as a healing or a power rod. It combines magnetic and crystal forces by loading ½" diameter ceramic magnets from the end cap to the crystal. The rod is small enough to be carried in a pocket or a purse, yet provides a powerful energy field.

Use it the same way as you would the rods with crystals alone. Visualize the desired result, amplified by the emotion of love.

Double Termination Lodestone Power/Healing Rod

Many people prefer the natural magnetic energy of lodestones (magnetite) to manufactured ceramic magnets. For those people, this rod combines lodestones with a double termination crystal for an especially powerful rod that's small and easy to carry in a pocket or purse, with an overall length of about 5¾". After gluing the end cap on, small lodestones are tightly packed into the hollow chamber of the pipe. For a tighter fit, you can use leather, cloth, or other packing material. Then the crystal is mounted in a ½" copper coupler and the leather wrap glued on, leaving the end cap and coupler uncovered.

The color of the leather wrap is usually chosen with your personal healing color in mind. Purple or green are popular colors, but pick one that feels right to you. While this rod was designed using a double termination crystal, you can also substitute a single termination crystal if the energy feels right to you. When choosing your crystal, you can use one

DOUBLE-TERMINATION LODESTONE POWER/HEALING ROD
POCKET SIZE

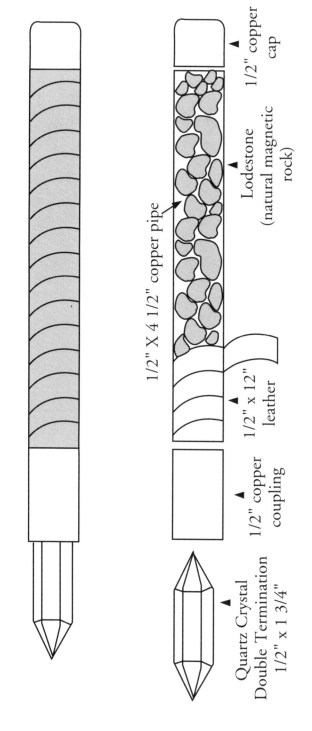

1/2" X 4 1/2" copper pipe

1/2" copper cap

Lodestone (natural magnetic rock)

1/2" x 12" leather

1/2" copper coupling

Quartz Crystal Double Termination 1/2" x 1 3/4"

QUARTZ CRYSTAL-FILLED POWER ROD

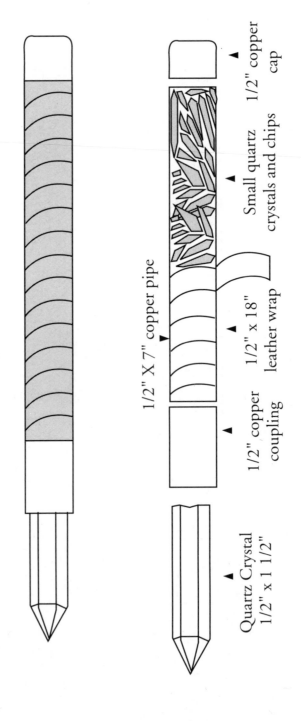

1/2" copper cap

Small quartz crystals and chips

1/2" X 7" copper pipe

1/2" x 18" leather wrap

1/2" copper coupling

Quartz Crystal 1/2" x 1 1/2"

that's visually appealing, but before deciding, hold it in your hand to feel its particular energy vibration, as some may feel more in tune with your own energy than others.

Quartz Crystal-Filled Power Rod

The filling of quartz crystals and crystal chips in this rod make it very powerful indeed. Remember that only the most powerful people can afford to be gentle healers. If you've done many crystal projects, you'll usually have tiny crystals and assorted chips left over. By loading them into the copper pipe of a rod and packing them tightly, you'll have a crystal rod—literally—that's about 8" long. The energy field or beam from this many quartz crystals is intense, and the crystals enjoy being next to each other rather than being discarded. If you want to muffle the rattling of the crystal pieces inside the rod, you can pack cloth, leather, or another material in the end of the rod without affecting its performance.

Iron Oxide and Quartz-Filled Healing Power Rod

This rod is similar to the quartz-filled rod, except that it's filled with the natural mix of small quartz crystals and iron oxide found in crystal mines. Many rock shops also have this left over as residue from cleaning their larger crystal specimens.

This is a healing power rod, and is used in the same way as the other rods. Like the other filled rods, no matter how carefully you pack them, there's usually a pleasant rattle and heavier feel to the rod that can enhance your use of it.

Short Large Crystal Power Rod

This rod was designed with the larger ¾" copper pipe, but is cut in a pocket-size length of 4½" that makes it easier to carry. The finished rod will measure approximately 6", depending on the length of the crystal that you use. One of the favorite colors of leather to use is black, since the contrast with the copper is so well defined, but any color may be used. The rod is a heavy-duty star warrior-type energy force rod.

IRON OXIDE AND QUARTZ-FILLED HEALING POWER ROD

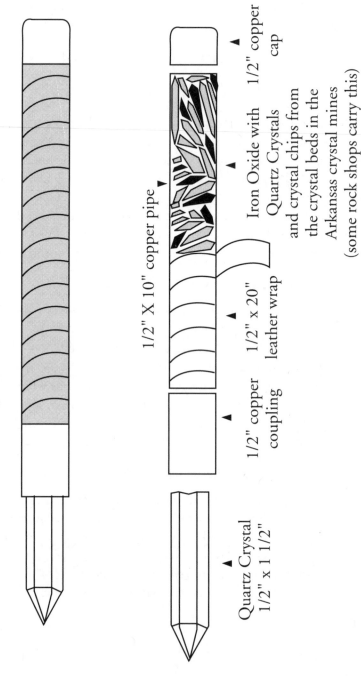

1/2" X 10" copper pipe

1/2" copper cap

Iron Oxide with Quartz Crystals and crystal chips from the crystal beds in the Arkansas crystal mines (some rock shops carry this)

1/2" x 20" leather wrap

1/2" copper coupling

Quartz Crystal 1/2" x 1 1/2"

SHORT LARGE CRYSTAL POWER ROD

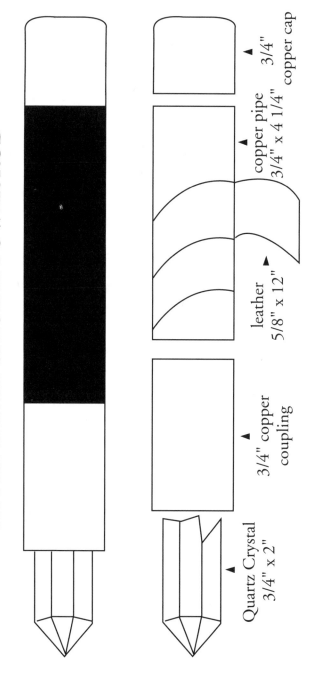

3/4"
copper cap

copper pipe
3/4" x 4 1/4"

leather
5/8" x 12"

3/4" copper
coupling

Quartz Crystal
3/4" x 2"

Large Amythest Power/Healing Rod

Like the early rods, this rod is constructed by cutting slots in the pipe to hold larger crystals than will fit in couplers. It's overall length can be up to 14", depending on the length of the amethyst used. The leather wrap is applied up to and around the base of the crystal. Green or red leather seems to be a favorite for this type of rod. Amethyst colors range from deep purple to light violet. The energy from the rod is calm, peaceful, and balanced. If you want a smaller rod, you can easily decrease the size by using a shorter piece of pipe or one with a smaller diameter. As with all the rods, if there is a change or modification you feel is right for you, follow your intuition and construct it exactly the way you want it for your personal use.

LARGE AMETHYST POWER/HEALING ROD

TRADITIONAL STYLE

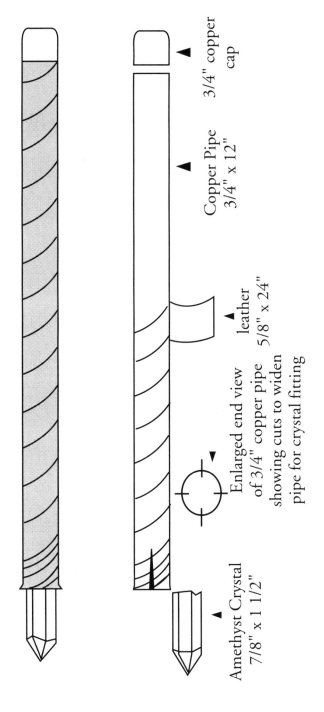

3/4" copper cap

Copper Pipe
3/4" x 12"

leather
5/8" x 24"

Enlarged end view
of 3/4" copper pipe
showing cuts to widen
pipe for crystal fitting

Amethyst Crystal
7/8" x 1 1/2"

Single Crystal Power Rods shown with a Double Crystal Healing Rod

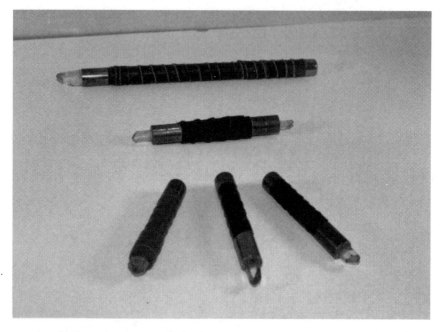

Single Crystal Power Rods shown with a Double Crystal Healing Rod

SEVEN

Through the Eye of the Crystal

Without intelligence, the eye is blind.
But vision sees beyond intelligence, into the infinite.

new future awareness:

> *A world at peace*
> *A world of health and prosperity*
> *A healthy planet*
> *Loving relationships*
> *Freedom and justice for all*

Do the above concepts sound like some unrealistic utopian vision that we can never hope to achieve? We believe that they are achievable—by us, and in our own time, rather than in some distant future. All we need do is decide we want it, believe that it is achievable, and take responsibility for ourselves to make it happen.

Visualizing and believing that a balanced world on Earth can be manifested is our first step when we take individual responsibility for bringing it about. The Earth herself can provide for all her children when they decide that a peaceful, abundant world is theirs. Ten percent of the world's population of over five billion people is enough to balance the scales. Peace and balance for the planet and its people must be radiated outward from the minds and hearts of strong individuals if it's ever to become a reality.

It is also necessary to understand the concepts of peace and balance. They aren't stagnant conditions, but a changing collage of manifestations that form a living work of art, harmonious in its diversity. At the Universal Energy level of subatomic particles, as at the human thought level, there is constant change and movement. Particles and energy fields ceaselessly gauge and rebalance the flow of creative energy fueled by our thoughts. The sum of this constant flux of interacting thought-energy is the Universal Mind, visualizing the moving picture of creation—the flow of life. Our spirits can be in harmony with this as we develop, beyond even thought, to the instantaneous Universal Mind picture. With our conscious awareness of our connection to the Universe, our spirit becomes one with the center of Love, Peace, and Harmony that flows through all life and material manifestation. At this point we experience our oneness, rather than just speaking or thinking about it.

Each person's thought energy radiates outward and inward through all of creation, instantly forming manifestations. By creating moving visualizations with a constant flow, unlike the static pictures we use to manifest a new car or house, we get in harmony with the Universal Mind. We see the past, the present, and the future blend together in a harmonious act of creation. This creative motion picture projection can also include vivid colors with sound, smell, and touch perceptions for a holistic dimension in balance.

The trick to creating moving visualizations is to focus on believing that there is a sense of "rightness" and perfection in all action that takes place at any given time. Rather than concentrating on a particular sequence of events or exact outcome, let your mind pictures range over a variety of ways the good you desire could manifest. Giving your creative mind this freedom can also give you new ideas as to how you might help the situation.

Remember when you're visualizing, though, to remove the negatives. If we think in terms of negatives, then we create the very things we're trying to avoid. To attain peace, we must positively project a moving picture of a world at peace instead of concentrating on a world without war.

Although our minds are the most important tool in achieving an evolved world, it would be foolish to ignore the tools our physical bodies provide us with, along with the unique talents we can bring to the task. Once we decide on evolution, our higher selves will guide us as to the right steps to take.

Suppose your mind refuses to provide you with peaceful scenarios, and you've taken every action you can think of to help yourself and others evolve. It happens to everyone at some time or another. At that point, we have only one option left if we hope to win. That weapon is faith. We've got to let go of the problem and turn it over to a higher power. Sometimes things aren't working because we haven't released them to let the Universe do it's job of manifestation. Once we've released the task of evolution, we can concentrate on believing that it's being accomplished. We do that by knowing that, despite surface appearances, what is happening right now will achieve it.

The last thing we need to do to manifest peace is to be at peace. The vision of a world at peace must include a vision of ourselves as peaceful. The nature or condition of peace includes pictures of good health, plenty, prosperity, planetary balance, love, freedom, and especially beauty. Are we working on being those things and granting them to others?

We manifest our vision through the eye of the crystal, by our own essence as co-creators. We seek peace in our world because we seek peace within ourselves. Yet by being at peace within ourselves, we radiate and project peace throughout the world. By being what we want and believing we have it, peace can be achieved.

PART TWO

Crystals for Modern Life

No matter what led to your interest in crystals, and the level of your technical expertise, the information in the next five chapters can enrich your experience of and participation in this exciting era of human evolution. We start you off with crystals that you can use in your car and home, where they'll have the most impact on your daily life. Next, our experiments with the effects of light, heat, and sound on crystals led to one of our most exciting inventions, the light rods. We offer you directions for these rods that range from the complex to one a child can build. Further explorations into the realm of hi-tech black box psionics culminated in the invention of the Psi-Comp, an astonishingly powerful twenty-first century tool that uses modern technology to help you boost the power of your mind and take control of your life. Humanity has reached a cross-road in its evolution. It's now within our grasp to reach out and create the world of our dreams. All we need do is learn about the power we all possess, and assume the responsibility for using it wisely.

EIGHT

Car Crystals
and Talismans

*Any rock or mineral can be used for any purpose
you can visualize or think of.*

The car crystal is important because most of us spend a considerable amount of time in our cars. We need the balance of energy we can achieve with a quartz crystal or cluster since our minds are usually concentrated on where we're going and when we need to be there.

A car crystal can be just one crystal, but, like crystals anywhere, it usually won't stay alone for very long. One crystal sitting on the console alone will soon be surrounded by other crystals and assorted rocks or minerals of various types, colors, and materials. This circle of crystal and mineral friends seems to come together miraculously from rock shops, riverbeds, and other places visited in the course of travel. The basic requirement for this arrangement, like all others, is that it feels right.

PROGRAMMING THE CAR CRYSTAL

To program the crystal initially, sit in your car and hold the crystal in your hand until you feel a tingle in your palm. You might feel it right away, or if the crystal is cold, it could take a few minutes. Once you feel a connection, take three or four deep breaths, then concentrate on visualizing an aura of white light emanating from the crystal and from your body. The visualization can be visual, or you can just feel the energy of the aura surrounding your body and the crystal. When you see or sense a strong aura, imagine it expanding to encompass your whole car. Within the space of this aura, know that there is protection, love, warmth, peace of mind, and safety. Place the crystal somewhere in the car, preferably, but not necessarily, where you can see it. If you don't smoke in the car, the open ash tray makes a good crystal holder. Then, without touching the crystal, sense the same aura emanating from it and yourself that you felt when you were holding it. When you can do that, the crystal is programmed.

After that, whenever you get in the car, while you're warming it up, visualize or sense that same protective aura.

As you're driving, you can mentally expand that aura to cover the road ahead of and behind you to help other drivers expand their own awareness. You can't force other people not to have accidents by your awareness, but they do seem to pick up on the vibrations and drive more carefully most of the time. At any rate, the aura will protect you. If you run into a situation on the road or highway where you're temporarily in a driver's blind spot and think he or she might pull over into your lane, you can expand the aura in the appropriate direction to tell him or her you're there. It's a little trick that's always worked for us. Occasionally, a driver will start to come into our lane, but as soon as we broadcast our presence with a thought, the driver immediately jerks back into his or her own lane, even when we know we haven't been seen. This reaction is probably due to a subliminal telepathic communication, enhanced by the crystal, that tells the other person that something is there.

Another trick you might want to try while driving sometimes works and sometimes doesn't, because it depends on the awareness of another. If you see someone driving badly or acting like an accident looking for a place to happen, expand your aura to that person and shoot thoughts of love, peace, and safety toward him or her. Often, the driver will immediately slow down or seem to become more aware of his or her driving habits. Even if it doesn't seem to have any effect, we like to detach a portion of our aura to encompass the other car, to help the driver get where he or she is going without harming anyone else along the way.

We believe that the reason we can't always help other drivers is due to the fact that we've each worked out major portions of our life's plan and major events before we were ever born. Of course, we're given free will so that plan can always be changed, but generally it seems best to follow the course we set when we were in a state of higher consciousness. The dangerous driver may need an accident to bring him or her to a higher plane of awareness and growth. Maybe you can, with your loving aura, help that person achieve the same awareness without the trauma of an accident. But ultimately, the choice of the path is his or hers and we can only try to help, not compel acceptance of the help.

Also, when our missions on Earth are completed, our bodies need to· die so that our spirit can go on to its next adventure. A car crash may be the way a person or persons have chosen to leave. Our aura and thoughts are probably picked up by the other driver, but are ignored because it would interfere with his or her agenda.

USES FOR CAR CRYSTALS

We've come up with a list of possible uses for car crystals. You can probably think of others.

1. As stated above, programming the quartz to radiate an energy shield or field to protect the car and occupants from harm is one of the first obvious uses.

2. Healing and balancing the automobile in the energy and sub-atomic particle spectrum creates more reliable operation with better gas mileage.

3. Car crystals can be programmed for guidance to get you to the right place at the right time. They'll help you find your way to appointments on time, and can even guide you to other rocks and minerals.

To use crystals for rock hunting, pick up a seed rock from the roadside and put it with your car crystals. Then pick up and hold a crystal, usually clear quartz or amethyst, while asking it to guide you to the kind of rocks or minerals you're seeking. Keep an open mind after asking for guidance. The crystal can lead you to a mountain road, a riverbed right beside your parked car, or even a rock and mineral shop in the next town. Listening to the voice within after asking for guidance is the key factor for being in the right place at the right time.

If you want to get somewhere specific but aren't sure of the way, or want to get there safely and on time, you can just put your crystal on your dash and focus your attention on it for a few seconds. Tell it where you want to go and when you want to be there. The crystal will nudge you into following the best route to get there safely and on time. Neither of the authors has much of a sense of direction. Occasionally when we use this guidance system, we take some unusual routes. But, so far, we've never failed to get where we wanted to be, exactly when we wanted to be there, even when we felt like we were hopelessly lost along the way.

4. A car crystal with its group of friendly crystals and rocks provides a constant connection, or ground, to the Earth Mother's source of nurturing. This in itself creates an automobile environment of healthy energy balancing, even if no specific programming for a purpose is involved.

5. Another very important benefit of car crystals is that they are pretty to look at and fun to play with while traveling.

THE SEEING-EYE CAR CRYSTAL

A car crystal can be as much or as little as you want it to be. For Lin, a crystal set her free from a paralyzing fear.

When I was three years old, my father was being transferred from military duty in Germany back to the United States. In order to get to the nearest airport, we had to travel by train. To my three-year-old mind, post-World

War II Germany was a depressing place of uncaring strangers who frightened me and spoke a strange language. Although I was eager to go "home," my parent's stress over accomplishing the hasty move made me nervous. As an Army brat, I was well aware that you went when and where they sent you, with no exceptions.

When we reached the train station on the first leg of our journey, Mom and Dad warned me to stick close because we couldn't risk missing the train. In the echoing chaos of the huge building, peopled with rushing giants, I intended to do just that. The crowds threatened to tear me from my father's side, so I grabbed his briefcase and held on for dear life while he pushed through a sea of legs and bags. To slow him down, I reached out and tugged on his trousers. He stopped, and I looked up at him. At the same time he looked down, and I realized my father had been transformed into a complete stranger who spoke a strange language. The realization hit me that I'd lost my parents and they would be forced to go to America without me. There was no hope of finding them when no one could understand me. I was doomed!

The stranger was obviously irritated and we couldn't communicate, but at least he didn't abandon me right away. Taking me to a huge counter, he left me with more strangers, who asked my name and then ignored me. I awaited my fate, glued to the floor in helpless terror, sure that my parents were on their way to America.

I've never in my life been so glad to see anyone, as I was my mother when she finally came rushing out of the crowd to collect me. At that moment I vowed to never get lost again.

Although the experience receded to the back of my mind, I never forgot my terror that day. In the wake of it, I developed a neurotic fear of being lost and wouldn't go anywhere unless someone was with me or the route was familiar. Sometimes, even as an adult, I'd look around when I was driving a familiar route, fail to recognize any landmarks, and the old terror would return as if I were again doomed.

To me, the fear was just a part of life. I couldn't understand why others didn't seem to share it, and thought maybe they did, but wouldn't admit it. I didn't admit it either. Instead, I learned to cope with it by never going to an unfamiliar place alone. When that wasn't possible, I made sure I had exact directions and tried to ignore the terror as best I could.

It wasn't until I was thirty years old and a man called me stupid for wanting exact directions to a meeting place, that I realized that others didn't share my fear and thought I was silly for having it. It was the first time I even considered the possibility that the fear wasn't necessary to my continued survival. Maybe I could even conquer it.

I remembered a story about a woman who lived alone. When asked if she ever got lonely, she replied, "How can I be alone when we're all part of each other and God?" I'd been studying metaphysics and realized that, in truth, I never was alone, but when the terror struck it was hard to remember that fact.

To remind myself that help was always nearby, I found a beautiful turquoise-colored amazonite with a round piece of smoky quartz embedded in it, just like an eye. I put the rock on the dashboard of my car and called it my seeing-eye rock. Whenever I was unsure of my direction, I'd glance at the rock and know that it would "see" the way for me. It worked, because I realized that my fear had been a kind of blindness and I trusted my rock to guide me, just as a seeing eye dog guides a visually blind person. The crystal eye in the rock also reminded me to open my eyes and see reality instead of the illusion of being lost.

CONQUERING FEAR

Many of us have fears arising from traumatic situations in childhood. Sometimes the fear comes from a specific situation, like Lin's, but often it's merely something that triggers the memory of terror. In either case, the fear can be faced and conquered. The first step is to take a look at what you're afraid of—spiders, snakes, dogs, thunderstorms, flying, driving, heights, enclosed places, being yelled at—admit the fear, and acknowledge it. You can't release the fear while you're trying to ignore or deny it.

Then ask yourself if you're reacting to a very real threat or if you're pretty much alone in your perception of danger. If other people don't see the situation as dangerous, chances are it's not.

Next, count up the times that the thing you fear has actually destroyed you. None, right? You wouldn't be here otherwise. Has your fear held you back and kept you from doing things you wanted to do? If the fear has kept you from living life to the fullest, then chances are the consequences of facing it will be much less painful than letting it wreck your life by avoiding it.

One way to conquer fear is to use our rational minds to decide how much danger there is in a particular situation. In Lin's case, getting lost is rarely fatal, but she acted as if being temporarily turned around were life-threatening. To rationalize herself out of the fear, she had to face the consequences of getting lost. When she realized that, at worst, she might be late for an appointment or have to stop and ask directions, she began to acknowledge how foolish her fear was.

That didn't conquer the fear, but it gave her a basis for judging whether the situation presented a real danger or not. Once she'd convinced herself that the danger existed only in her own mind and that it was holding her back from doing things she wanted to, she had the motivation she needed for finding a way to conquer it.

Lin took her battle with fear a step further. Suppose getting lost did result in her death? Would that be the end of her? No. She knew that despite whatever happened to her body, her spirit or essence would live on. She also believed that we aren't alone or powerless, and that she could call on that greater part of herself for help when she needed it.

Her fear didn't disappear overnight. It took a lot of hard work and she often turned to her seeing-eye rock for help, but she never again let the fear control her actions.

CRYSTAL TALISMANS

Sometimes we need a physical reminder of our power to direct our own lives, a talisman. Crystals have been used as talismans for centuries because they amplify our spiritual energy to the point where we can become aware of it. When facing your particular fear, pick out a crystal to help you. Hold that crystal in your hand and know that you are safe from harm. Take your crystal talisman with you when facing your fear. If your courage begins to waver, look at or hold it. The crystal will help you raise your vibrations to a level where you'll know that there is no death and that you are always going to be all right. With that knowledge comes an end to fears, small and large, rational or irrational.

NINE

Crystals for the Home

Home is a beacon in the dark.

Your home should be a place where you can go to renew yourself, the place where your creativity and spirit can blossom and flower out of the public eye. Surrounding yourself with crystals and rocks can help you nurture the divine part of yourself that is your source of inspiration.

In our own home, we are literally surrounded by crystals. There isn't a room, and hardly a surface, that doesn't contain one or more crystals. They live in containers, on stands, by themselves, and are incorporated into statues and pieces of art. The result of living with all these crystals is that the very air is alive with the energy of love, spirituality, and creativity.

In our search for containers for our crystals, we've run across quite a few that ordinarily wouldn't be used for that purpose, but make attractive and utilitarian stands. For example, we have a planter carved out of stone that supports a large smoky quartz crystal. Several stone elephants surround the edifice with their trunks raised in salute. A copper kettle holds the large quartz crystal we use in many of our circle ceremonies, a crystal ball rests on an antique silver medicine measure, a wise man carved out of wood holds a crystal staff, and a silver antique candy dish contains one each of our most powerful kinds of crystals and rocks. The possibilities are endless.

One type of stand we use, that's useless until it's filled with a crystal, is a brass shell casing. The type we used in the crystal light beacon that follows is a large antique shell casing that we found at a garage sale. But we have many more, of all sizes, that have become crystal stands. Some of these we acquired from a friend who enjoys target shooting and is happy to collect empty casings for us, some we bought new at a gun shop, and others have turned up at garage sales and antique stores. While people often look at us oddly if we tell them what the shell casings are for, they're generally pleased that we're using them for peaceful purposes.

Although the crystal light beacon diagram shows a base under the casing for more stability, the shells will stand on end by themselves, unless they're in a place where they'll be jostled. Construction of the various light beacons is simple. The crystal is fitted into the open end of the casing. If necessary, copper tape can be wrapped around the base of the crystal for a tight fit, or the opening of the casing can be crimped to fit the crystal. The casing can then stand alone or be used in conjunction with other items in a display. One way they might be used is to place several different sizes on a polished rock slab, using upright and prone crystals to break up the vertical lines. A small mirror could also be used as a base to reflect the different heights and angles. If the arrangement is to be permanent, the crystals and casings can be glued to the surface. For many groupings of wood, stone, ceramic, etc., a single crystal beacon can provide a nice vertical line. The beacon is often the item in a grouping that causes the viewer to stop and think a minute, which is what all good art should do. And in addition to functioning as art, the crystal is providing good energy to the room and can be used for healing, meditation, or in ceremonies.

NEW ENERGY

A word of warning about home crystals. The energy they provide is wonderful, but it can be overwhelming to the uninitiated. For example, when Lin met Michael, she had only one crystal, a necklace that she couldn't wear because it was programmed with the energy of the seller.

That energy wasn't bad, but it was incompatible with hers and made her nervous when she wore it. She decided it was useless, put it in her jewelry box, and forgot about it. After meeting Michael and handling some of his crystals and rods, which had a wonderful energy, she decided that she had just chosen the wrong crystal and gave the necklace to him. A few months later, she picked up the necklace again and it had the same good energy that all his crystals had. When he'd acquired the crystal, he'd automatically programmed it with his own energy, which was compatible with hers.

Crystals, particularly those used in jewelry, will often retain the energy of the person who made or handled them. The energy may or may not be compatible with yours, but it's easy to reprogram the stone if you want to buy a piece that looks perfect, but doesn't feel just right. The best way is to take the stone or jewelry in whichever hand feels best, let it warm up from the heat of your hand, then clear your mind and visualize the energy in the crystal radiating into your own aura until they merge and become inseparable. If that doesn't do the trick the first time, do it again at intervals. Also, the more you handle the crystal or stone, the closer the energy pattern will come to match your own.

Even compatible crystal energy can be uncomfortable at times. Shortly after Lin and Michael met, he gave her every crystal she admired. She was in a period of growth, and the influx of the crystals speeded up this growth something fierce. She was so pleased with the crystals' effect on her that she put most of them in a dish on her nightstand so she could maintain her rapid growth even as she slept. After a week of sleepless nights, she decided maybe she was pushing things a bit and moved the dish of crystals out to the living room. Eventually she became used to and caught up with the crystals' energy and moved them back to the bedroom, where they no longer disturb her sleep.

There's no doubt about it, crystals do promote growth—but their high energy can be upsetting. If you find their effects disturbing or feel overwhelmed at first, you can add your crystals a few at a time, or move the crystals gradually closer to the places where you spend the most time. Programming each crystal as you acquire it can help, but sometimes the energy they've picked up on their travels can be beneficial, and you might want to gradually let them blend their energy with your own over a period of time.

Some people are more sensitive to crystals than others, and find their effects more disturbing. Some aren't disturbed at all and just experience an added feeling of well-being, or don't notice a difference. Whatever your personal reaction to the presence of crystals, be assured that they are working to tune you to a higher vibration even as you program them with your own thoughts and energy.

THE CRYSTAL LIGHT BEACON

The crystal light beacon shown here is made from a large antique shell casing. Any metal cylinder with a similar shape can be used, or the shell casing and crystal may be larger or smaller. The beacon can be used for psionic experiments, and double as a home decoration. It's an excellent way to use crystals that aren't suitable for rods, but are still of too high a quality to dismiss. For example, the one we used in the beacon is cloudy all the way through with dirt embedded in its striations. It's not especially pretty, but it's a perfectly shaped double termination crystal with hundreds of tiny attached crystals pointing toward one end. When we look at it, we're reminded of Indian ceramic dolls with children overflowing from the mother's arms, and it exudes the energy of abundance and fertility.

Using Crystal Light Beacons

Crystal light beacons lend themselves to various uses: meditation, sending and receiving white light energy, or transmitting and receiving energy from the Universe itself. They can also be used as energy beacons to send and receive messages between sentient beings throughout the Universe, or for sending mental and emotional messages to people on our planet. They're particularly effective for sending healing energy to the Earth Mother. One of their most positive uses is to send a blessing to the the spirit, mineral, plant, winged, and water people, including our four-legged and two-legged brothers and sisters. We can all benefit from this energy, whether we're the senders or receivers.

Constructing a Crystal Light Beacon

Materials:

A. Single or double termination quartz crystal, clear, cloudy, or smoky, 2" in diameter, 4" long (or a size that fits the opening in the casing)

B. *Optional:* Copper tape, copper mesh, leather, or other material to use as a shim

C. Brass shell case or copper cylinder, 2" in diameter by 12" tall (or the size of your choice)

D. *Optional:* Round base: brass, copper, or wood, slightly larger than diameter of container, up to 1" thick

E. Instant bonding glue

Construction:

1. Although the shell casing used here is large, any size can be used. Another kind of metal cylinder can also be substituted. The construction can be permanent or temporary.

2. Fit the crystal into the opening of the shell casing or cylinder. Wrap shim material around the base of the crystal for a better fit, if necessary; the top of the cylinder can also be crimped with pliers to accommodate the shape of the crystal. For a permanent fitting, squeeze instant bonding glue onto the shim material and/or crystal once it's in the cylinder.

3. If a base is used, it can be any circular piece of metal or wood you find attractive. The thinner and lighter the base, the larger the diameter you'll need for stability. If you don't have anything suitable around the house, a small round wooden plaque from a craft store can be stained or finished attractively. A hardwood plaque often needs only several applications of lemon oil to give it a rich, finished sheen. Once you've chosen the base, use instant bonding glue to attach it to the bottom of the shell casing or cylinder.

4. As a finishing touch, if the cylinder or base is tarnished or stained, rubbing it with a jeweler's rouge polishing cloth or Brasso will restore much of its luster.

CRYSTAL LIGHT BEACONS

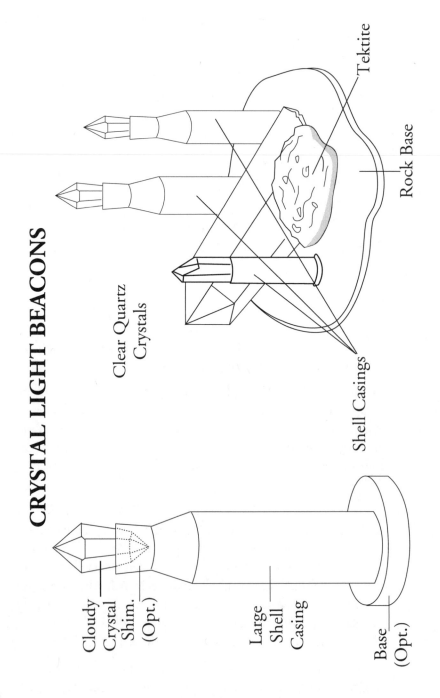

Tektite

Rock Base

Clear Quartz Crystals

Shell Casings

Cloudy Crystal Shim. (Opt.)

Large Shell Casing

Base (Opt.)

TRI-CRYSTAL PSIONIC AMPLIFIER

This crystal device provides a way to use three smaller crystals as you would a large communicator crystal. The larger quartz crystals have become more expensive in the last few years, so in order to make it affordable for everyone, it's necessary to find ways to keep crystal work economical.

Actually, when you're working with crystals, the consciousness of the operator is more important than the size or type of crystal used. This can't be emphasized too much. As the operator grows in spiritual consciousness, so do the results of his or her crystal work. The crystals only amplify the operator's awareness, they can't amplify what isn't there.

USING THE TRI-CRYSTAL PSIONIC AMPLIFIER

The tri-crystal psionic amplifier is an especially high-powered supermind amplifier, similar to the beacon, and can be used the same way. We find ours works really well for a circle of two, four, or six people acting in unison for a very powerful sending or receiving. If it's nicely put together, it also makes a good household decoration when it's not being used. It energizes the atmosphere while pleasing the eye.

Constructing a Tri-Crystal Psionic Amplifier

Materials:

A. Quartz crystal, ¾" diameter, 2" long

B. Brass or copper crystal holder (can use the cup portion of a candlestick holder, fashion your own out of sheet metal, or use any cup-shaped metal)

C. 4 bolts: 1 to mount crystal holder on copper dish, and 3 to attach the dish to the three support struts

D. Copper dish, inverted, 5½" diameter

E. Copper support frame, three struts or straps, ½" wide, 9" long, and at least ³⁄₃₂" thick

TRI-CRYSTAL PSIONIC AMPLIFIER

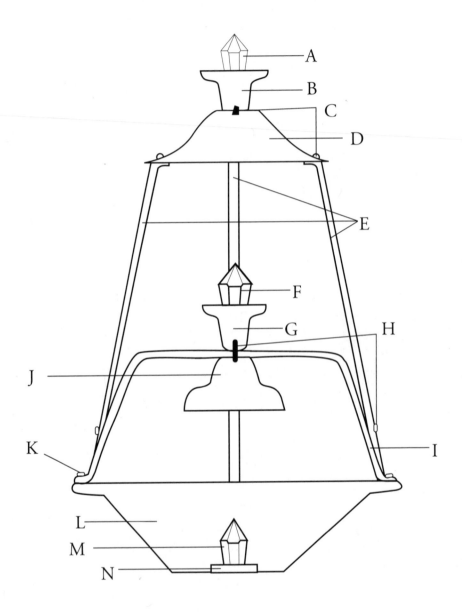

F. Middle quartz crystal, 1" diameter, 2" long

G. Brass or copper crystal holder

H. 4 Bolts: 1 to mount crystal holder to support straps and inverted dish, 3 to fasten top struts to lower ones

I. 3 copper straps, 12" long, similar to (E) bent at slightly more than 90 degree angle to hold middle crystal and attach to base dish (copper corner brackets can be used)

J. Copper cone-dish, inverted, 4" diameter (the base of a candlestick holder or an inverted copper bowl will work)

K. 3 bolts to mount lower struts to base dish

L. Copper or brass base dish, 10" to 12" diameter

M. Base quartz crystal, 1¼" diameter, 2" long

N. Brass or copper base crystal holder (can use metal napkin ring or bend brass or copper strap, at least ½" wide, in a circle)

Construction:

The parts used in the tri-crystal psionic amplifier were all scrounged from copper dishes, candleholders, straps, and brackets that we found at home or at garage sales. When you build your own model, chances are the parts you come up with will be slightly different. We tried to give you ideas about what kind of parts will work.

Bolt the frame, base, and crystal holders together as shown in the diagram. The crystals can be mounted permanently using shims and glue, or if you use candlestick holders for the crystals, they won't need shims or glue to sit upright. The ring that holds the base crystal can be glued to the dish or just set in the middle of it. When looking for the parts for the amplifier, keep in mind the basic structure and use whatever metal parts are available. Many variations are possible and the device will still be workable. The model in the diagram has a base dish of 11½" diameter, with a total height of 17".

Tri-Crystal Psionic Amplifier

TEN

Crystal Light Rods

Crystals, like people, react to stimulation.

The lighted force rods we saw in the *Star Wars* movies made us wonder about the effects of light, and the heat it produces, on crystals. To find out, Michael designed some lighted rods for experiments. The results we got with these rods were even better than we'd hoped for.

To begin with, we knew that when the crystals were exposed to light and heat, the subatomic energy structure within would become excited. When we used them, we discovered that the energy output of the rods intensified to the point where it seemed almost as if the molecules inside the crystals were dancing. That intense, lively energy, combined with the crystal's response to our own biomagnetic auras, produced some very powerful crystal rods.

As a side benefit, we discovered that the light also let us explore deeper into the visible structure of crystals during meditation. We saw otherworldly scenes, recordings of history on Earth, and something of ourselves. It was as if the crystals pulled us deep into themselves, where we caught glimpses of whole new worlds.

When we placed the tip of a light rod on our third eye, we could feel the light illuminating our minds. High order ideas, positive and hopeful, flowed with extreme clarity, as if the lighted crystals were clearing away all the confusion and darkness. Our auras strengthened and expanded in the light.

We urge you to build one of the rods we offer here and discover for yourself the power of lighted crystals. The rods vary in complexity, but the last one is so easy that even a young child could build it. For those of you who are interested in color therapy, colored pieces of plastic can be used in any of the rods to produce the color of light that you desire. Regardless of your resources and abilities, you can build one of these rods and discover its power for yourself.

LIGHTED CRYSTAL DISPLAYS

Since the invention of the crystal light rods, Michael has devised many complicated set-ups that added color, lights, and music to crystals, with awe-inspiring results for meditation. Our favorite display used Christmas tree lights placed in large shells and covered with crystals. The lights were wired into the stereo system so that different tones caused the colored lights to flash on and off independently. With its wide range of tones, the music of Kitaro really made the lights react.

We had a gathering to show the system to our friends, inviting them into the garage to experience it in groups of two or three. Although conversation had been lively earlier, when our guests emerged from the experience, they seemed almost stunned by the spiritual energy generated when lights and music vibrations stimulated hundreds of crystals. Afterward, we found ourselves thoughtful, with a heightened awareness of the sounds of the night, the rhythm of life, and our role in the whole of existence. That lighted display marked a turning point in our evolution, where we found it necessary to withdraw from public life to discover who and what we had become. When we emerged two years later, we found that others at the gathering had also made startling steps of growth that led them on wonderful new paths.

That display no longer exists and is too complicated to explain here (assuming we could recreate it). But we wanted to share the concept with you in hopes that it would inspire those of you with a knowledge of electronics to try your own lighted displays.

Another particularly effective use of lights, color, and music with crystals is much simpler. If you have, or can acquire, one of the fiber optic devices that were so popular a few years ago, you can simply remove the fibers and insert a crystal in the opening. Usually, a lighted color wheel inside the device will rotate through four colors, lighting the crystal from below. Playing an inspirational tape of music and watching the crystal light up with different colors produces a higher state of consciousness that leads to leaps of growth.

CRYSTALS FOR LIGHT RODS

When you're choosing a crystal for your light rod, you'll find that some reflect light better than others. Flaws and cloudy areas in the crystal often produce better light reflection than a perfect specimen. You can test your crystal by wrapping a piece of aluminum foil around its base. Push the lighted end of a penlight into the foil in a darkened room. If you have a lot of crystals to choose from, chances are you're going to want to test them all before making a choice. In fact, we ended up testing crystals we couldn't possibly use for rods because each was more wonderful than the last in the light. If you're going to buy a new crystal for your light rod, you can take along your penlight and a piece of foil to try out crystals in a lighted store.

USING THE CRYSTAL LIGHT RODS

Light and the small amount of heat generated by a penlight or small flashlight gives power/healing rods a real boost of energy. They're especially effective when used as healing rods in a darkened room. The lighted crystal gives off just enough light to illuminate the part of the body being healed, and helps the healer concentrate by eliminating extraneous visual distractions. The low light level is also effective for helping both the healer and the patient relax.

Before you start your healing, build up a ball of invisible energy between your cupped hands. Then hold the rod an inch or two above the area being healed, and concentrate on sending energy into the body. You might want to grip the rod up near the crystal so that you can rest your index finger on one of its facets. Visualize the energy clearing blockages and illuminating each cell in healing light. Think of yourself and the subject as being perfect, whole, and complete while you perform the healing.

When the rods are being used as power rods, they add a real energy boost, especially when they're used at night or in a darkened room. We like to use light rods in the circle ceremonies described in Part Four of this book. The leader can hold or pass the rod, or it can be placed in a container in the center of the circle to illuminate the symbolic items placed there and add energy to the whole proceeding. If each person holds a light rod, it produces a visible circle of spiritual light for the ceremony. In fact, light rods can be used to boost the energy of any ceremony, rite, or ritual, as well as to energize the individual user. Once you've used one of these, you'll probably find they're indispensable.

Constructing Crystal Light Rods

Use the directions we offer as a guideline or starting point. Any type of flashlight will light up a crystal. If an exact type of penlight isn't easily obtainable, use one that is. There are many models of penlights on the market, but larger lights will still do the most important thing, which is to light the crystal.

When you're constructing the rods, fit all the pieces together several times before they're glued, to make sure the lights will still work and you can change the batteries.

For those of you who aren't mechanically inclined, the last crystal light rod only requires three simple materials and five or ten minutes construction time. This is a crystal device that anyone who has a crystal can make and use.

Constructing Crystal Light Rod 1

The first light rod is the most complicated to build, as the only part of the penlight left showing is the pushbutton switch on the end. It's also the most impressive when it's finished.

Materials:

> Quartz crystal, ¾" diameter, 3" long
>
> Copper mesh, tape, or leather for shim
>
> Copper reducer, 1" to ¾" diameter
>
> Copper coupler for lightbulb guard, ½" diameter
>
> Silver foil tape or aluminum foil
>
> Copper pipe, ¾" diameter, about 6" long (finished length approx. 9-10")
>
> Copper end cap, ¾" diameter
>
> Copper or other tape, ¼" wide
>
> Penlight, about ½" in diameter, with a pushbutton switch on the end (takes 2 AA batteries)
>
> Leather wrap, ¾" wide
>
> Instant bonding glue
>
> *Optional:* Color filters (thin pieces of colored plastic) can be used to create different colored light rods

Construction:

1. Wrap the base of the crystal with copper mesh, tape, or leather shim material. Insert the crystal into the large end of the copper reducer. Squeeze glue down onto the shim material, where it will soak down and form a permanent bond. Use the flat part of a blade to push the shim material down even with the end of the reducer for a neater look.

2. Line the interior of the ½" copper coupler with shiny foil tape or glued aluminum wrap for better light reflection. Glue or tape the coupler onto the lighted end of the penlight.

3. Run a bead of glue around the inside of the small end of the reducer with its crystal. Slide the copper pipe in it to spread the glue and form a firm bond.

4. Drill a hole in the center of the copper cap large enough to accommodate the pushbutton of the penlight (approx. ¼").

5. Fit the penlight with its coupler into the copper pipe. Cut the copper pipe so that the coupler on the penlight rests snugly against the base of the crystal, and the copper cap fits over the pipe. Make sure before you glue or tape the pieces that the switch will still work when it's put together. If you're building a colored light rod, cut a circle of the filter and fit it over the end of the coupler on the penlight, so it's between the light and the crystal.

6. When you're sure everything fits, glue the parts together and use ¼" wide copper (or other) tape to secure the copper cap on the pipe. Try the pushbutton switch again to make sure it's working. The copper cap is taped rather than glued so that the end of the penlight can be unscrewed to change its batteries.

7. Cut a leather strip ¾" wide. Wrap and glue it on the copper pipe, leaving the copper cap and reducer bare.

Constructing a Twist-Light Rod

The twist-light rod is fairly easy to build, using only a mounted crystal and leather wrap. Also, twist-on penlights are probably easier to find in stores than those with push-buttons on the end. The flashlight model we used for this one is a high intensity penlight with a halogen bulb that is bright enough so that the light rod doubles as a flashlight. But any twist-on penlight with a face diameter of ½" will do the trick. The finished rod measures about 7", and is small and light enough to be easily carried in a pocket or purse.

Materials:

Quartz crystal, slightly less than ½" diameter, 1½" to 3" long

Copper coupler, ½" diameter

Silver foil tape or aluminum foil, and electrical tape

Penlight, ½" in diameter at face, with a twist-on switch (uses two AA batteries)

Soft leather or suede wrap, ⅞" wide, 2 strips (approx. 15" and 10" long)

Instant bonding glue, rubber cement, 2 rubber bands

CRYSTAL LIGHT ROD 1

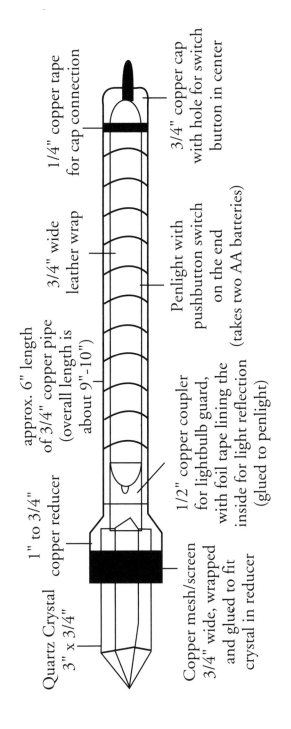

1/4" copper tape for cap connection

3/4" copper cap with hole for switch button in center

3/4" wide leather wrap

approx. 6" length of 3/4" copper pipe (overall length is about 9"-10")

Penlight with pushbutton switch on the end (takes two AA batteries)

1" to 3/4" copper reducer

1/2" copper coupler for lightbulb guard, with foil tape lining the inside for light reflection (glued to penlight)

Quartz Crystal 3" x 3/4"

Copper mesh/screen 3/4" wide, wrapped and glued to fit crystal in reducer

TWIST-LIGHT ROD

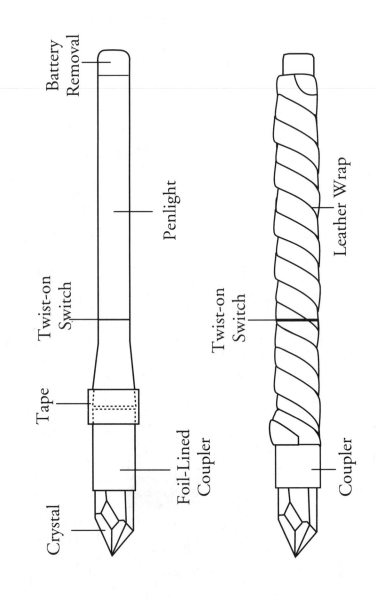

Battery Removal

Penlight

Twist-on Switch

Tape

Foil-Lined Coupler

Crystal

Leather Wrap

Twist-on Switch

Coupler

Optional: Color filters (thin pieces of colored plastic) can be used for a colored light rod.

Construction:

1. Mount the crystal in the copper coupler after lining the interior of the coupler in silver foil tape or glued aluminum foil, shiny side showing. If you need shim material to get the crystal to fit snugly, you can wrap aluminum foil or foil tape around the base of the crystal before inserting it into the coupler. Squeeze glue down into the shim material or around the base of the crystal for a more secure fit, if necessary.

2. If you're building a color light rod, cut a small circle of plastic and place it over the lighted end of the penlight.

3. Use a small strip of tape to connect the coupler and the face of the penlight. (The face of the penlight and coupler should be the same diameter. If they aren't, use more tape.)

4. Use the longer piece of leather to wrap the lower portion of the rod. Start just below the point where the light twists on and wrap to just above the screw-off cap. Leave the cap uncovered so you can replace the batteries. A rubber band will hold the leather in place temporarily. Use the shorter piece of leather to wrap the upper portion of the rod. Start so the leather overhangs the first piece of leather about ⅛", and wrap upward toward the crystal until about half of the coupler is covered. Hold that piece of leather in place with another rubber band. When you're sure the middle portion of the rod is attractive and will still allow you to twist on the light, glue down the loose ends of the leather at the top and bottom of the rod with rubber cement. If you've wrapped it tightly, it shouldn't be necessary to glue down the whole length of leather. When you need to replace the bulb, the rubber cement bond will easily pull loose.

Constructing an Easy Crystal Light Rod

We designed a simple version of the light rod for those who don't enjoy complicated construction projects, or who want a quick, easy light rod to try out before deciding to build something more complicated. The rod works the same way as the others and you can have it finished almost instantly. You can also use small flashlights of almost any size and design.

Materials:

> Crystal, same or slightly larger diameter than face of penlight
>
> Penlight
>
> Aluminum foil
>
> Electrical tape, black or the color of your choice

Construction:

1. Wrap the base of the crystal in a rectangular square of aluminum foil, letting the foil extend out beyond the base.

2. Push the face of the flashlight up into the foil until it almost touches the end of the crystal.

3. Wrap electrical tape over the base of the crystal, covering the aluminum foil, and back along the length of the flashlight to the point where it turns on or unscrews for battery replacement.

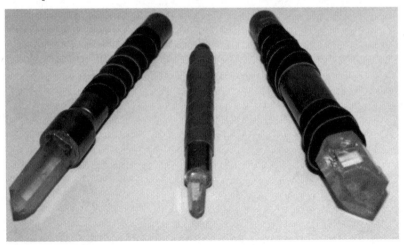

Various Crystal Light Rods

ELEVEN

The Black Box

Miracles are an everyday affair when we
understand how the Universe works.

Although we're all aware of the rise of technology in the twentieth century, a technological revolution that falls in the gray area between the psychic sciences and electronic technology has been quietly taking place. The black box, powered by the mind rather than an electrical current, is a prime example of this psychic technology. Black boxes have been known to heal people and crops, transmit thoughts, determine the presence of valuable minerals in ore samples, and influence people and events. The use of black boxes and other mind-powered devices was first called radionics or psychotronics. Now, it's better known as psionics. The key to psionic devices is the mind of the operator, tuned to the frequency of the object being influenced.

In Chapter 12, with the Psi-Comp, we've taken psionics a step further. Based on the principle that the energy black boxes use is also found in crystals, heat, light, magnets, living cells, and chemical reactions, we've wired a crystal and a computer into the circuit of the black box, along with a control box to provide more accurate tuning. But first, you'll need to read this chapter and build the black box used in the Psi-Comp.

HOW THE BLACK BOX WORKS

To define the black box for those of you who may not be familiar with it, we have to explain that there is nothing physical per se in the physical world. Matter is just another form of energy at a lower frequency vibration. All energy is part of the electromagnetic spectrum. If we think of matter as slowly moving energy and thought as more swiftly moving energy, then we can see that the swift energy of thought is capable of moving and transforming matter. In other words, "Thought creates form."

The black box transmits mind waves, or thought signals, through a solid-state electronic device using an energy field that allows the mind to perceive and influence matter. It's a mind over matter machine that tunes into the source of energy. Since matter is produced by stepped-down vibrations of energy, when the black box is correctly tuned, matter can be manipulated.

Energy can be sent along a wire, like electricity, or it can be sent or received on light waves. This energy is the Universal Force that manifests itself in many diverse forms, including thought and matter. You can manipulate matter by tuning in to the energy.

The black box functions as an amplifier for the intensity of emotion that powers thought energy. It works like sympathetic magic. The symbol of the thing to be transformed (called a witness) used in the black box is the object's past, present, and future state. Since magic depends on form or pattern rather than substance, whatever you do to the symbol also is done to the object. The electronic circuit provides a pattern of relationships. As long as the pattern is intact, it will work.

For a more thorough introduction to psionics and black boxes, you might read *Psychic Power* (formerly *Psionics 101*) by Charles W. Cosimano, published by Llewellyn Publications. The black box we used for our Psi-Comp is similar to the design he offers in his book.

OPERATING THE BLACK BOX

A black box consists of three or more dials, a stroker plate, and a sample well, all connected by electrical wiring. It may or may not have an on/off switch. Rather than being connected to an electrical source, the power is provided by the mind of the operator.

To operate the box, the dials, which are calibrated from zero to ten, are set on zero. Say your cat is sick and you want to cure it. You first need to get a rate for the cause of the illness on the dials. To do this, put a representation of the cat, called a witness, in the sample well. The witness could be a few hairs, a picture, or even the cat's name written on a piece of paper. Next, write on a piece of paper, "Cause of cat's illness," and put that in the sample well with the witness.

Now you'll need to get what is called a *rate* for the cause of the cat's illness by setting the dials. In order to set them, rub your thumb across the stroker plate while turning each dial. Your thumb will stick, as if glue is holding it back, when you get the correct setting for each dial. It may take some practice before your thumb will stick, so don't give up if it doesn't happen right away. Meditating to concentrate your psychic energy before you begin will help if you're having problems.

Once you have the rate for the cause of the illness (for example, 8, 3.5, 4.2) deduct each of the rates from ten to get the rate for the cure. (10-8=2, 10-3.5=6.5, 10-4.2=5.8.) Set the dials on the black box to the rate for the cure (2, 6.5, 5.8), and leave them there until the cat recovers. Be sure to back up your efforts with medical attention for the cat. You don't want to put the animal at risk to test your ability to operate the black box.

Suppose instead you want to be accepted into a particular group or organization. In that case you would put something that represents that group as a witness in the sample well (i.e., a picture, letterhead, etc.). If your acceptance is dependent on one person, you can use a representation of the person, such as a picture, signature, business card, or his or her name written on a slip of paper. Next, write what it is you want on a slip of paper. For example, "Acceptance into the organization." Put the slip of paper into the sample well with your witness. Get the rate for your acceptance by using the stroker plate to set the dials, as you did above, and leave the dials set until the decision is made.

Constructing the Black Box

A variety of black boxes and black box designs are used by psionics practitioners. The elements they all have in common are dials, a stroker plate, wiring, and a sample well. But there are infinite variations on the number of dials, the material for the boxes, the material used for the stroker plate, and whether the sample well is cuplike or flat. Some of the fancier models have on/off switches and antennas. We chose a model that's similar to the one Charles Cosimano offers in *Psionic Power* because it's the least complicated. In fact, you can even use a shoebox to contain it, plastic cut from a coffee can lid for the stroker plate, and a tin can for the sample well. Our model is fancier, but feel free to substitute the parts you have on hand or can acquire easily. It's the pattern, rather than the materials, that's important.

Materials:

> Plastic box with detachable lid, 7½" long, 4½" wide, 2¼" deep (available at electronics stores), or a cardboard or wood box large enough to accommodate hardware and wiring
>
> 3 dials (volume control type—any kind)
>
> Calibration knobs for dials, preferably 0-10 (or cut a circle of paper or plastic and write the numbers 0 through 10 around the perimeter)
>
> Copper plate or sheeting, 2" by 2" for stroker plate, insulated with wide clear tape, plastic, or verathane coating—or you can use soft plastic or rubber (i.e., coffee can lid)
>
> Small metal dish or flat metal plate for a sample well, about 2¼" diameter (or a size that fits your box)
>
> 2 small nuts with bolts to attach sample well
>
> Insulated copper wire, about 24"
>
> Bare copper wire, about 12"
>
> Electrical tape
>
> Glue

Construction:

1. Drill 3 holes in the top of the plastic box to accommodate the shaft of the dials. They should be evenly spaced along the long side about 1½" in from the edge. Drill two more holes, large enough for the bare copper wire to be pulled through, under the space where the stroker plate will be. Drill two final holes for the nuts and bolts that will hold the sample well in place.

2. Install the dials (volume controls). You can scrounge them from old appliances or buy them at electronics stores. If they don't have calibrated knobs, you can easily make your own by cutting a circle of paper or plastic with a hole in the center and writing the numbers 0 through 10 around the perimeter. Glue the calibration to the top of the box so it's centered over the hole for the dial shaft, with 0 at the bottom. As an alternative, you can use a permanent marking pen to write the numbers directly on the box around the dial.

3. Bolt the sample well in place with the two nuts and bolts. Even if you use a flat piece of copper or metal for the sample well, you'll need to use bolts, rather than glue, to complete the wiring.

   Wire the box as shown in the diagram, leaving two loose ends under the stroker plate. Twist all connections together and fasten them with electrical tape or solder them. (*Note:* Be precise with the wiring. On one model, we fastened the wires to the two outer connectors on the dials. When we tested it with a circuit tester, it didn't work. Fastening the wires to the two right-hand connectors, as shown in the diagram on page 102, produced a current.)

4. Use the bare copper wire to make a coil small enough to fit under your stroker plate. Thread the two ends down through the holes in the top of the box. If necessary, you can hold the coil in place with electrical tape. Connect the bare wire ends to the two free insulated wires inside the box, and tape or solder the connection. Before you glue on the stroker plate, test it out by holding it in place over the coiled wire with one hand and asking a question with a "yes" answer. Rub the plate with your thumb while asking the question. It should feel like the plate is grabbing your thumb.

BLACK BOX

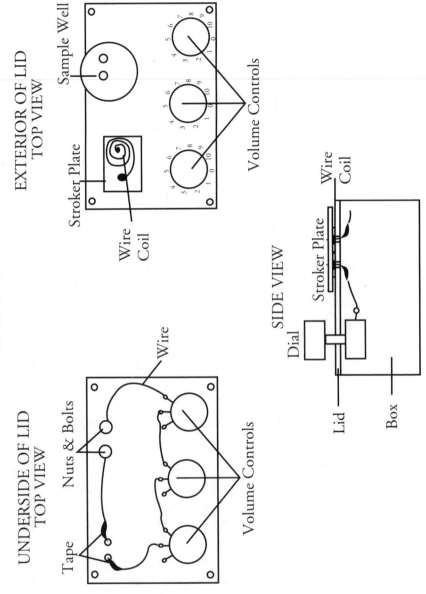

EXTERIOR OF LID
TOP VIEW

Sample Well

Stroker Plate

Wire
Coil

Volume Controls

UNDERSIDE OF LID
TOP VIEW

Nuts & Bolts

Wire

Tape

Volume Controls

SIDE VIEW

Dial

Stroker Plate

Wire
Coil

Lid

Box

If you'd asked a question with a "no" answer, your thumb would have glided over the plate without sticking. Another test is to write out three possible answers to a question on pieces of paper. Fold them and mix them up. Put the answers one at a time into the sample well. Your thumb should stick at the best answer. If you don't achieve a stick, cut a square out of a plastic coffee can lid and try again. Glue the stroker plate that works best for you in place over the wire coil.

TWELVE

Psi-Comp

In order to remain on the cutting edge
we need a good grounding in the basics.

Now that you've built a black box and understand how it works, you're ready to bring in the big guns and build the Psi-Comp to boost the effectiveness of your psionic work. The Psi-Comp is a quartz crystal amplified copper transfer screen for a home computer interface with a black box psionic generator. The Psi-Comp works on the same principle as the black box, and is operated in nearly the same way. Use it for the same purposes. By interfacing a crystal, a computer, and a control box with the psionic circuit of the black box, you can increase the accuracy of your rates and amplify its capabilities.

When you use the Psi-Comp, instead of placing your directions (such as acceptance into a group or rate for an illness) in the sample well with the witness, you type them in on the computer screen. Since you'll need to leave the Psi-Comp in operation and the characters visible on the computer screen until the decision is made or the cat gets well, an obsolete computer model or one you don't need every day should be used. The only requirement for the computer is that it has a software program that allows you to type in the instructions. The instructions themselves should be as precise as possible, taking up no more than one screen of characters; they should be erased as soon as the experiment is completed, rather than putting them in stored memory. The extra dials provided on the control box allow for more accuracy of your tuning rates. Be sure that you keep a notebook of the rates (dial settings) you get for various things, as you may need to use them again in the future.

Successful operation of the Psi-Comp is dependent on your ability to concentrate, combined with sensitivity, practice, and experience. The Psi-Comp serves to enhance and augment your abilities to an incredible degree with the most advanced synthesis of ancient and modern techniques.

Using the Psi-Comp

Let's assume you want to analyze an ore sample to see if it contains gold. Your Psi-Comp is set up and in place, as shown in the diagram. All tuning knobs and switches on the black box and control box are turned off. The computer should be turned on and set up so that you can type sentences on the monitor screen. (For instance, you can set up a file in a word processing program. If you don't have word processing, you can even type sentences in your utility program since the material won't be stored.) Type in the command, "Register the presence of gold."

Place an ore sample that might contain gold in the sample well of the black box. Switch on the control box. Start with the black box and rub your thumb over the stroker plate while turning each dial. When your thumb sticks to the stroker plate, you know you have the right dial setting. If your thumb doesn't stick at all, you know the sample has no gold and you can quit here.

If you did achieve a stick, set the other two black box dials. Then set the control box dials by using the stroker plate on the black box. The combined settings on the control box and the black box dials are the rate for gold, and you know that your sample contains gold. Write down your rate in case you need it again, erase your computer instructions, and turn your control box switch to off. Return the dials on the black box and control box to zero.

Another way to determine the presence of gold in an ore sample with the Psi-Comp is to put a piece of gold or a sample that contains gold in the sample well. Type "Rate for gold" on the computer screen. Tune the dials as above to get the rate for gold. Write down the setting of each of the dials. Set all the dials back to zero and remove the gold.

Place your ore sample in the well. Tune the dials as you did for the gold. If you get the same settings for your sample, you'll know there's gold in it.

Constructing the Psi-Comp

Control Box

Materials:

> Plastic or wooden box, at least 7½" x 4½" x 2¼" deep, with detachable lid (we used a plastic box identical to the one used for the black box)
>
> 6 dials (volume control type) with knobs calibrated from 0-10 (or make your own calibrations, as for the black box)
>
> On/off switch
>
> Insulated copper wire, 6-8 feet, and electrical tape or solder

Construction:

1. Drill 6 holes large enough to accommodate the shafts of the volume controls, evenly spaced across the lid of the box.

2. Drill a hole in one short side of the box for the on/off switch and another on the opposite end where the wires will emerge.

3. Install the volume control dials on the lid of the box and the switch on the side.

4. Wire the dials and the switch together as shown in the diagram on page 110, and tape or solder the connections. The wires attached to the two dials nearest the end of the box without the switch should be long enough for one to reach the top of the monitor screen and the other to reach to one screw on the black box screen. Their length will depend on your set-up. Leave them a little longer than you think you'll need to give your set-up more flexibility.

5. Screw the lid onto the box.

CONTROL BOX WIRING
UNDERSIDE OF LID

TOP VIEW

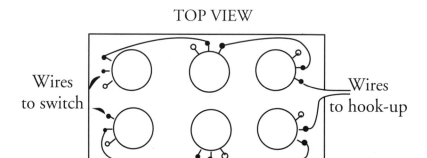

Wires
to switch

Wires
to hook-up

SIDE VIEW

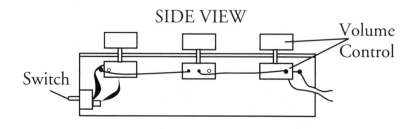

Volume
Control

Switch

Monitor Screen

Materials:

> Wood frame, approx. 1" x 12" x 12", sized to fit in front of the screen of a computer monitor
>
> Thin copper wire, approximately 500 feet, for ½" grid screen
>
> Thin piece of plastic or wood for stand, approximately 4½" x 12"
>
> 4 small screws, 2 for attaching wiring and 2 to attach stand to frame
>
> *Optional:* Copper wire, paint, or stain for frame

Construction:

1. Out of 1" x 1" pieces of wood, construct a frame that is 12" square, or a size that matches the size of your computer monitor screen. The two screens don't touch, so the sizing doesn't need to be exact.

2. Drill approximately 20 small holes ½" apart, from the exterior to the interior, through all four sides of the frame.

3. Use a single length of small-gauge bare copper wire to lace through the holes, from top to bottom and side to side, as shown in the wiring pattern, to form a ½" grid screen. If you run out of wire before you're through, or the wire breaks, twist a new piece on the end and keep lacing. You should have two loose ends when you finish.

4. Insert a screw at the top of the screen and one on a lower side (or wherever the loose ends of wire are), leaving about ⅛"-¼" of the head protruding. Twist one loose end of wire around each screw.

5. Use the other two screws to attach the stand to the frame so it will sit up by itself.

6. We used wide copper tape to cover the wooden frame for a high-tech look, but you can leave the frame bare, paint, or stain it as you wish.

MONITOR SCREEN

SIDE VIEW

WIRING PATTERN

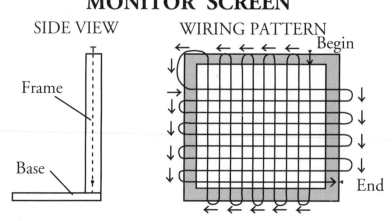

BLACK BOX SCREEN

TOP VIEW

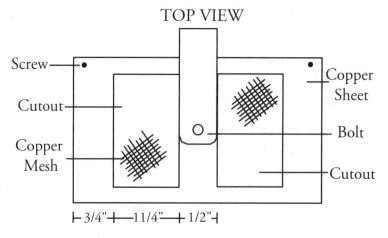

⊢ 3/4" ⊣ 1 1/4" ⊣ 1/2" ⊣

SIDE VIEW

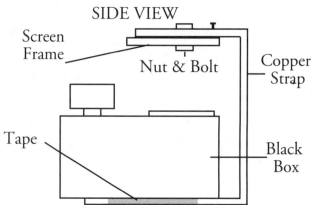

7. When the monitor screen is placed in front of the computer monitor, it interfaces with the typed words through radiations in the electromagnetic spectrum.

Black Box Screen

Materials:

>   Small wooden or copper frame, at least 4½" by 2¼" (could use small picture frame, copper switch plate, copper plate)
>
>   Small gauge copper wire, or copper mesh or screen
>
>   Copper strap, approximately ½" wide, 13" long
>
>   3-4 small screws (and bolts if necessary)
>
>   Duct tape

Construction:

1. If you use a small picture frame for your screen, construct this smaller screen as you did the monitor screen (before adding the stand) with the two loose ends of the wire twisted around protruding screws. As an alternative we used a copper switch plate with all but a center brace cut out, then taped copper mesh across the open portion.

2. Drill 2 holes and partially insert small screws at each edge of one of the long sides of the black box screen. Use bolts to hold them upright, if necessary.

3. Bend the copper strap in an uneven U shape, with a bottom measurement of 5", the center 5", and the upper portion 3" long. Use a screw to attach the shortest side of the copper strap to the center of the black box screen. (If you used a picture frame, cut the strap longer, extend the short side of the "U" and use screws to attach the strap to the frame at both edges.) The opposite end of the "U" can be screwed or taped to the bottom of the black box so that the screen is centered about 2¾" or more above the sample well.

Crystal with Optional Dome and Stand

Materials:

> Clear quartz crystal, approximately 1¼" diameter, 2" long (or larger) with a fairly flat base
>
> Insulated copper wire, approximately 6 feet
>
> Copper or electrical tape
>
> *Optional:* Stand for crystal: block of wood 5½" square, 1½" thick; block of wood 3½" square, 7" tall; or any stand you choose
>
> *Optional:* Dome for crystal: any plastic or glass dome with or without a bottom (we used a plastic dome, 3½" in diameter, 4" tall, with a plastic base)
>
> *Optional:* Heat sink or ring to hold crystal upright

Construction:

1. You can get as fancy as you want with this part of the Psi-Comp, but all you really need is a crystal with a wire (long enough to reach the black box screen) taped to a facet on the side of the crystal, and another wire (long enough to reach the bottom screw on the monitor screen) taped to the base. Before you tape the wires to the crystal, scrape the insulation off the ends so the bare wire is in contact with the crystal.

2. If you want to build a stand like ours, nail the two blocks of wood together. Drill a hole for the wiring down through the center of the tall block. Drill another hole that meets the first hole at an angle through the side of the block. Place the wired crystal in a heat sink or a ring that keeps it upright. Thread both wires down through the block and out the side hole. Use a hook or staple on the lower side of the long block to attach the wires for a neater appearance.

3. If you use a plastic dome similar to ours, after you've wired the crystal, drill a hole for the wires through the base of the dome. Place the crystal in a heat sink or ring with the wires feeding through the base of the dome. Thread the wires down through the stand, and glue the dome to the base.

CRYSTAL STAND

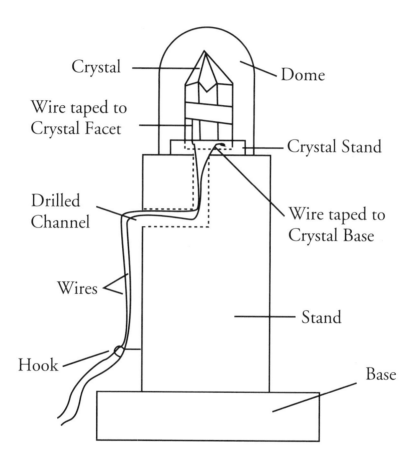

Crystal — Dome

Wire taped to Crystal Facet

Crystal Stand

Drilled Channel

Wire taped to Crystal Base

Wires

Stand

Hook

Base

PSI-COMP SETUP

Set up your Psi-Comp in any way that's convenient for you to use, as long as you follow the wiring instructions on the diagram. For more flexibility, rather than attaching the wires permanently with tape or solder, we use alligator clips to complete the connections. If your black box screen is made of copper, you can attach alligator clips directly to the screen.

PSI-COMP SET UP

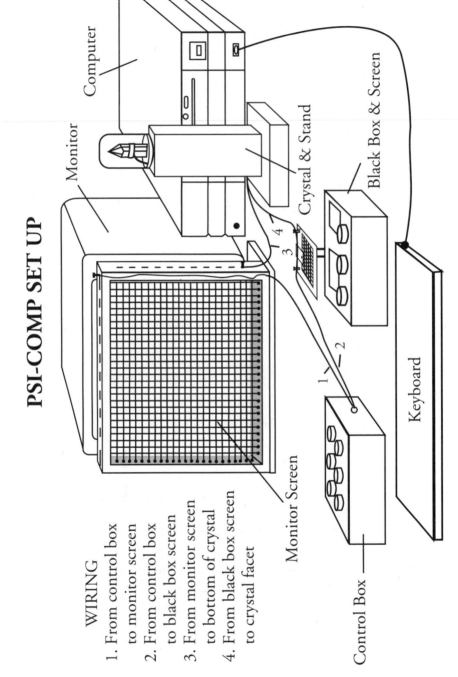

WIRING

1. From control box
   to monitor screen
2. From control box
   to black box screen
3. From monitor screen
   to bottom of crystal
4. From black box screen
   to crystal facet

Computer

Monitor

Crystal & Stand

Black Box & Screen

Keyboard

Monitor Screen

Control Box

PSI-COMP SET UP

PART THREE

Ancient Crystal Archetypes

Human evolution is a process that has taken us many lifetimes to accomplish, and will take us through many more. In this section we'll talk about some of the tools and archetypes, or symbols, that have helped us along the way and are still influencing our lives. We believe that in order to understand who and what we are, it's essential that we get in touch with where we came from. Sometimes our actions, attitudes, and relationships in the present only make sense in light of past events. If we're aware of our successes and failures in the past we can accept that they are part of who we are, appreciate them for the lessons we've learned, and go on to new adventures, knowing that we have grown beyond what we were.

The tools in this section are made from archetypes, or symbols in our genetic consciousness, that have helped us to evolve. In fact, despite the antiquity of these symbols, they are still, or again, helping us evolve into the consciousness of our spiritual essence. With these tools we can develop our inborn talents and use our potential to achieve something better for ourselves and the whole human race.

Left to Right: Trident Krystallos (Chapter 15),
Atlantean Crystal Cross (Chapter 13),
Crux Crystallum (Chapter 14), Ankh Crystallos (Chapter 17)

THIRTEEN

Atlantean
Crystal Cross

*There are many writings, both ancient and
modern, about the secrets of the Universe. None
contain all of what you seek. Only you contain
all of what you seek.*

THE CROSS AND THE SWORD

Thousands of years ago, when Universal Energies were better understood, the Atlantean crystal cross was widely used. The four equal arms
of this cross breathed, as if alive, with the force of the Universal Creator.
The cross, which represented the life-giving waters of the crossed rivers
that sustained the main continent of Atlantis, channeled the energy of
the four powers of the winds when it was placed on the Earth with its
arms pointing to the north, south, east, and west. Through misuse and
loss of knowledge, one arm of the cross was replaced with a long blade
that became the crystal sword. After the fall of Atlantis, the other two

ATLANTEAN CRYSTAL CROSS

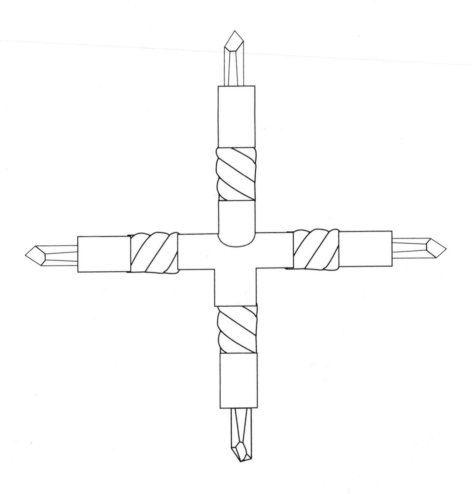

crystal arms disappeared and the crystal sword became the sword of magic used in battles that divided humankind. The last of these swords was called Excalibur. Later, the Excalibur became merely a sword, with no crystals or stones.

Through Michael's memories of past lives, the crystal force knife and Excalibur sword were remanifested. Now the sword has been replaced by the Crux Crystallum, symbolic of Christianity for the last two thousand years. Despite the religious significance of the cross, swords have been used more often than the cross in the short history of Christianity. As we strive toward a new era of peace, the Crux Crystallum is once again in use. But, even now, the long arm of this cross is sometimes shortened to become the equal and balanced Atlantean crystal cross of the four spirit forces of creation.

THE ATLANTEAN CRYSTAL CROSS

The Atlantean crystal cross is a powerful archetype from ancient history. Its four equal arms provide a balance that radiates healing Earth energy. Surrounded by a circle, it becomes the symbol of Earth. When four smaller circles are centered in the four sections of the cross and circle, it is the Hopi sign for land and good life. Alone, it balances the energy of the Universe with the energy of the Earth Mother. The cross is alive at all times as soon as it's constructed. In fact, all power/healing rods are active during use, and passively radiate energy the rest of the time. The cross emits high-intensity energy for healing and balancing when it's used in the center of a healing or meditation circle of light workers. It can be used by itself or with a large generator crystal to expand the sphere of spiritual energy to encompass the whole planet.

USING THE ATLANTEAN CRYSTAL CROSS

Before using the cross, you can clear it by touching each of the crystals and visualizing white light energy emanating from them. The cross can be gripped in the palm of your hand or placed on the ground with the crystals pointing in the four directions. In most cases, when the cross is being used for healing the Earth, the energy is not visualized for a specific healing use, but the results are left up to the Earth, who knows best how to heal and balance herself. Crystal work often involves bringing in energy from the rest of creation for the Earth to use and disperse. The nurturing, healing energy the cross emits supports the balanced life force of all the beings on our planet.

When using the cross, you should cultivate a feeling of universal love and sense your connection to all of creation. Consciously realize that you are an expression of the creator; not just connected to the creator, but expressing and projecting the source of Universal Energy. You'll get a better energy flow if you're relaxed and joyful. Spontaneous toning or chanting is effective when the cross is used in a ceremonial circle.

Some crystal healers hold the cross in their right palm while using a flowing motion of spiraling the cross through the energy field of the being they are balancing and harmonizing. Others prefer the same motions with the cross in the left palm. While crystal workers often use the right hand for transmitting and the left for receiving energy, there are also people who prefer the opposite. This may have to do with a person being right- or left-handed, or right- or left-brained. You're the best judge of what feels right and works for you. Experiment and determine the best methods for yourself, regardless of what others are doing.

You can also work with two crystal crosses, one in each palm, to balance and complement each other. When you're using the cross, keep in mind the importance of polarity; balance the positive/negative, male/female energy within yourself as the Universal Energy flows through you.

PAST LIFE RECALL

In addition to using the Atlantean cross or other tools from the ancient past for healing, power, or ceremonial work, you can also use them to trigger past life memories. We believe that most, or all, of us have lived many times before. You may even recognize one of the tools in this section from a past life, or feel a curious affinity with it.

But even if you don't remember other lives or believe you've had them, you can use crystals to explore the past. All thoughts, feelings, ideas, and memories remain long after those who had them have gone on to other experiences. We like to think of the information as residing in a giant library that we can tap into whenever we want. Why not try it for yourself? Whether the memory you recall is your own, someone else's, or a total fantasy, you're bound to find yourself entertained and learn something about your current attitudes. Don't worry about where the memory comes from, just enjoy it and accept what you learn without judgment.

To get ready to do your past life recall, sit down in a comfortable position somewhere where you won't be disturbed. To make sure you don't forget what you've remembered, you can use a tape recorder or write down the information as it comes. Choose whichever method feels most natural to you.

When you're comfortable and relaxed, form a ball of energy between your palms, then pick up the crystal tool you've chosen in the hand that feels best to you. If you don't have a crystal tool, even a plain crystal will work for this experiment. Next, use any relaxation technique you like, making sure your breathing is slow and deep. When you're ready, ask about a past life. If you're using a tape recorder, your questions and answers can be spoken out loud while holding the crystal or tool. If you're writing, lay down the crystal or tool while you're writing, and pick it up again if you get stuck for an answer. Usually you won't need the tool once the process has begun. Your first question can be about a specific time period, for instance, "Have I lived in Atlantis in a past life?" Or it can be general, such as, "Tell me about a past life that I've lived," or even, "Tell me about the life of someone who lived in the past." After you ask the question, write down or record the first thing that comes to mind, no matter how silly it sounds. Often, the information will make perfect sense later.

You can also recall a past life with a friend or a guide to help you relax and ask the questions. To give you an idea of what you might find out from one of these sessions, we've reprinted a past life Lin discovered while being regressed by a friend. Notice how she progresses from a feeling of viewing someone else to actually being that person.

Past Life in Atlantis

Q: Go to a lifetime you may have had in Atlantis.

A: It's a party. Everyone is dressed in colorful toga-type silks. I'm dressed in red, I think. I can't see myself.

Q: Look into a mirror.

A: I'm having a problem telling if I'm a man or a woman, as if I'm seeing more than one life. I think I'll go with the man. He's got light-colored hair, curly. There are laurel leaves embroidered on my outfit. It's not silk, though, it's more like a cotton. Short.

Q: What kind of work do you do and what are you interested in?

A: I want to say crystals. There's a big red one in the floor with a railing around it. It's huge and it's a source of power for the city. I'm standing looking at it.

Q: Do you know how it works?

A: I'm not sure. There's some sort of apparatus below it that you can't see. Copper and wires. I don't think I understand it well enough to explain it.

Q: Are there a series of metal plates?

A: Yes, but they're around the wires and stuff—erect double plates on four sides. And more plates underneath—double plates held apart by some sort of screws or metal things. The plates form a three-sided box under the crystal.

Q: Does this mechanism require the sun to produce energy?

A: No. It's geothermal. Something to do with the Earth, drawing up the energy through grid lines in the earth. There's another kind with disks to catch the sun, but not this one. I'm there as a sight-seer rather than having any scientific connection with crystals. I don't really know how they work.

Q: How old are you?

A: 18.

Q: How many years did you live in that body?

A: 36. I think I became involved in politics.

Q: Go to age 36.

A: I'm having an argument. It has to do with the crystals—power and misuse of the crystals. We aren't using them right. We're abusing the natural forces that power them. I think we're programming ourselves for destruction. I'm very angry and arguing with people, trying to convince them.

Q: What are they doing with the crystals?

A: I'm not sure exactly, but we're drawing too much power too fast so that a rebalancing doesn't have time to take place, and I'm afraid it's going to blow up.

Q: How do you know this?

A: Well, some of our scientists said that it will happen; have warned us. And I believe them, but most people don't. They think the scientists are just being alarmists. We've had some accidents. There've been minor blow-ups. They need to listen!

And then there are people who don't care—power seekers. There's one in particular, who's very influential. He kills me—stabs me with a knife. It's at night and we're alone. No one knows we're together. He said that he wanted to meet me so that we could resolve our differences, and I hoped that I could get him to listen. But he didn't want to talk, he just wanted to get me out of the way.

Q: Is that person someone you know now?

A: Maybe, but I can't ... No, I don't think so.

Q: What lesson did you learn in that lifetime?

A: I learned about politics, about trying to shape the world and about power. Not that I had much power, but I observed the abuse of power.

Q: How could those people have used the crystals better?

A: They could have remained in tune with their world. They were more interested in temporary comfort and pleasure, rather than being close ... they got too far away from the Earth and their source. They weren't bad people, but it was such a good life and they screwed it up.

Q: What kind of things did you see that were built with crystals that could help people?

A: I see a helmet with crystals in it. It's hooked up to the various areas of the brain for direct learning. It was powered by a mild electric current. The crystals picked up and resonated the current and resonated with each other—it all had to do with resonance. The helmets were made of copper. Inside the helmet were crystals and copper wires—titanium. Maybe the wires were titanium. It was very low-powered; if you touched it, you'd just feel a slight tingle. The crystals were attached with some sort of sticky substance. People could learn languages or the history of the world from tapes. The tapes would be put in a machine and run through the helmet.

Q: Anything else about that lifetime?

A: I was too judgmental. I wanted people to be the way I thought they should be, and they weren't. I could have accomplished more had I been less angry and outspoken. Instead of trying to shame people into doing things, I should have tried to help them see what needed to be done. If I'd been more accepting of people, they might have listened to my ideas.

Constructing the Atlantean Crystal Cross

The Atlantean crystal cross, sometimes known as the Earth cross, is fairly compact, measuring only about 7" from point to point, depending on the length of the quartz crystals used. For a larger cross, ¾" pipe and couplings can be used and the copper pipe can be cut in longer lengths. The model we've given you is a prototype that can be adjusted to fit your personal needs. The relationships of energy fields are in a constant state of change and expression, and our creations reflect this moving balance of harmony. Follow your own intuition for modifications or additions.

Materials:

Copper tee, ½" diameter, with ⅜" hole drilled in top of tee

Solder

ATLANTEAN CRYSTAL CROSS

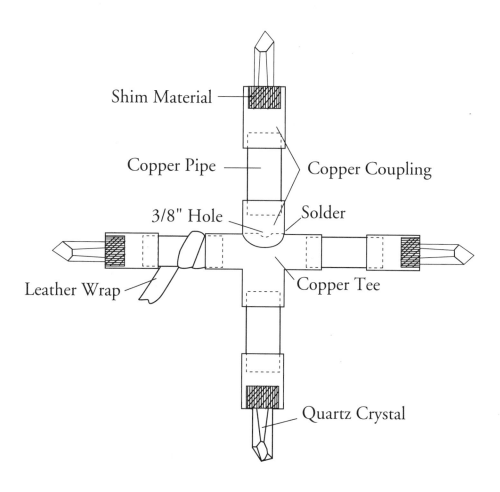

Shim Material

Copper Pipe

Copper Coupling

3/8" Hole

Solder

Leather Wrap

Copper Tee

Quartz Crystal

Copper coupling, ½" diameter, notched to fit top of tee

4 copper couplings, ½" diameter

4 pieces of copper pipe, ½" diameter, cut 1¾" long

4 quartz crystals, ¼" to ½" diameter, of desired length

Shim material to wrap crystals—copper mesh, copper tape, leather, etc.

4 pieces leather wrap, ⅜" wide by about 4" long

Instant bonding glue

Construction:

Before gluing anything, prefit the pieces to make sure they're properly aligned. It's a simple matter to make adjustments before they're glued, but practically impossible afterwards. To glue copper parts together, run a bead of glue around the inside of the larger piece, then fit the smaller piece into the larger. This will push the glue up into and over both pieces for a secure fit with no mess.

1. Drill a hole, approximately ⅜" in diameter, in the top of the copper tee to allow an open flow of energy inside the device.

2. Notch the first copper coupling to fit over the hole in the tee and solder it in place, forming an cross with four equal arms. Sand or file the soldered area to create a neater, more uniform surface.

3. Glue the four pieces of copper pipe onto the four arms of the cross.

4. Wrap the four crystals with shim material, if necessary, then fit one in each of the four copper couplings. Squirt glue down into the shim material. It will soak down and hold the crystal securely in place. Let the glue dry for a few minutes.

5. Glue the couplings with their crystals onto the four pieces of copper pipe.

6. Wrap and glue leather over the four pieces of copper pipe, leaving the tee and the copper couplings bare.

FOURTEEN

Crux Crystallum

The cross symbolizes both love and a rejection of love.
Which is it to be this time?

The Crux Crystallum was originally a Pleiadean tool, but it's more familiar to many people as a powerful religious symbol and archetype. As an individual, hand-held, crystal energy rod, the cross radiates a strong pattern of Universal light for healing and balance. When it's used in groups or circles of light workers, the cross can be placed upright in the Earth for manifesting the spiritual and material projection of energy. While supported by the Earth, the top three crystals of the trinity emit energy for human spiritual development.

This tool from the Pleiades sets a standard for personal growth, balance, self-healing, and attunement to the Universal Creative Force. In fact, its form radiates the most powerful force there is—the force of love. Let yourself experience the heart's spirit of love in this tool's white light energy and you can make some incredible discoveries. Often people also experience a sense of reverence and oneness with the Christ Consciousness while using the crystal cross. It radiates an energy that encourages our highest ideals, while reminding us of our eternal nature.

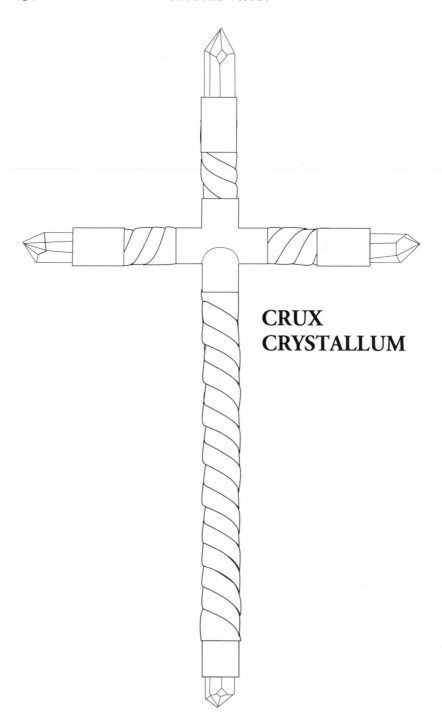

**CRUX
CRYSTALLUM**

People's experiences with the Crux Crystallum vary widely, depending on their particular perceptions and beliefs. Chances are that how you choose to use it will be determined by its symbolism for you, along with your sensitivity to the patterns and relationships of constantly moving fields of Universal creative energy. A good place to begin is with self-healing, balance, and love that then radiates to the energy fields of all the beings around you. Let intuition and guidance from your inner connection with spirit lead you on an exciting path of discovery with this tool. Words can't fully describe the powerful feelings of unconditional love most people experience while using the Crux Crystallum.

Many quartz crystal tools have been associated with the ancient past or the far future, but the reality is that they are tools for *right now*. Before you use it, it may be wise to meditate on the crystal cross and what it means, or how it feels to *you*, personally.

USING THE CRUX CRYSTALLUM

There are several ways to use this crystal tool. The obvious way is by holding the long arm at the bottom while visualizing or sensing a loving, peaceful energy field of white or golden light radiating outward in an expanding sphere of life energy.

The cross can also be held with its center in the palm of your hand, and the long arm parallel to your forearm. Beams of healing energy can be visualized as radiating from the three shorter arms of the cross, while the long arm feeds energy into your own body.

Another position that can be used, particularly for healing, is to hold the shorter top arm in your hand like a sword grip, with the energy beam emitting through the crystal at the end of the long arm, and energy from the three short arms surrounding you. It's probably more than coincidence that a reversed or upside-down cross becomes a sword. There's a lesson in both symbolism and polarity here for you to explore. The Crux Crystallum is one of the finest self-healing, self-teaching tools you can build.

PAST LIFE MEMORY

Lin, who felt a real connection with the Crux Crystallum, had a strange experience after handling it. In the chapter on the Atlantean cross, we reprinted one of her past life memories, recalled with the help of a guide and a tape recorder. This particular memory was triggered by several factors, including the Crux Crystallum, and involved a series of visual images that prompted her to write down the following questions and the answers that came to her.

Although her memory was spontaneous, you can recall past memories by relaxing and meditating with the cross and then asking questions about your own past lives.

One morning in 1987, a coworker dropped by my office to chat. We discovered a mutual fascination with archaeology and he offered to lend me a recent National Geographic article on an ancient Mayan site, called Mirador. Although I was busy doing accounting work on my computer, I couldn't resist taking a quick peek at the article. When I saw a fold-out drawing of the excavation, I gasped in recognition, knowing that I'd lived there before!

Shaken, I reluctantly put the magazine away and went back to work. But my mind refused to leave Mirador; images and words started flowing through my mind. In order to keep track of what was happening, I grabbed a note pad and began scribbling my impressions on one page after another. The following is what I recorded then, along with questions I later asked at home, using the Crux Crystallum.

A Mayan in the Pleiades

My first visual impression was of being in a home made of stone blocks in the jungle. It was steamy outside, but within it was cool and dim, the only light a bright swath from the open doorway. The sparse furnishings were invisible except as shapes in the shadows. I was a teenage boy, wearing a brief garment, and my feeling was one of terrified horror at being all alone.

Q: What am I seeing?

A: You once lived in Mirador. It was then called Capezidos. Thus, your recognition of the ruins triggered by the National Geographic article.

Q: What happened to the ancient Mayans?

A: They were taken away. You were among their number, and lived out your life on a planet much like Earth in the Pleiades. While there, you were taught many of the things that you are now remembering. You were told that you would use the information at a later date, and it is soon to be that time. You will have ample opportunity to use it in the near future.

Q: How did the Mayans acquire the advanced information discovered in their ruins?

A: Much of it came from your hosts in the Pleiades.

Q: Why were we removed from Earth?

A: Many had died from a plague, and the rest of you were invited to go with the Pleiadeans to their home. At the time you were a lad of 17, eager for adventure. The plague provided the impetus for you to accept the invitation; with all the members of your family dead, you no longer had ties to the Earth.

I saw myself climbing high on a mountain and then tumbling off a rocky outcrop. While the fall was an accident, it was my impression that I'd planned the death subconsciously so that I could return to Earth in another human body.

Q: Tell me about my death.

A: Thirty years later, you died of a fall while searching in the mountains for an esoteric mineral, native to that planet. Since you had gone out alone, without your wrist monitor, the sophisticated medical equipment of your hosts couldn't be employed to prevent your death.

Although life was good for you there, you frequently felt awed and insignificant. You never really adjusted to the sophisticated culture of your hosts and longed for your old life. As a result, you became interested in nature and spent much of your time in wilderness areas on that planet.

Next, I saw a short stocky woman with long black hair and wise, knowing eyes.

Q: Was I married?

A: Yes. Your wife was a Mayan called Lona. You were rather happy together, but she objected to your spending so much time away from her in the mountains. You were proud of the fact that she was far ahead of you in learning, but her assimilation into your host's culture added to your feelings of inadequacy and alienation.

Q: Does the Crux Crystallum or crystal cross have anything to do with the people in the Pleiades?

A: Yes. The crystal cross was used by them for healing and was brought to earth by some colonists in the days of your pre-history. The cross, as both a symbol and a tool, has been passed down from generation to generation since that time. The tool, with its four crystals, emits a field of low frequency vibrations and was used by trained healers to clear blockages in the body and enhance the workings of the immune system by creating a balance of hormonal and enzyme activity.

Constructing the Crux Crystallum

Materials:

Copper tee, ½" diameter, with ⅜" hole drilled in top of tee

Solder

Copper coupling, ½" diameter, notched to fit top of tee

4 copper couplings, ½" diameter

1 piece of copper pipe, ½" diameter, cut 7" long

3 pieces of copper pipe, ½" diameter, cut 1¾" long

4 quartz crystals, ¼" to ½" diameter, of desired length

Shim material to wrap crystals: copper mesh, copper tape, leather, etc.

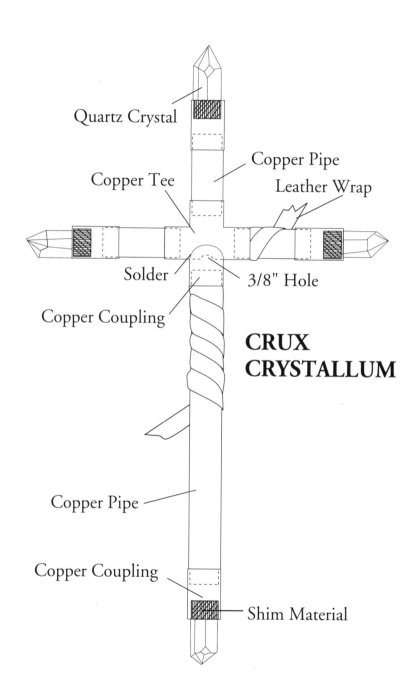

Quartz Crystal

Copper Pipe

Copper Tee

Leather Wrap

Solder

3/8" Hole

Copper Coupling

CRUX CRYSTALLUM

Copper Pipe

Copper Coupling

Shim Material

4 pieces leather wrap, ⅜" wide, long enough to wrap 4 arms of cross

Instant bonding glue

Construction:

Before gluing anything, prefit the pieces to make sure they're properly aligned. It's a simple matter to make adjustments before they're glued, but practically impossible afterwards. To glue copper parts together, run a bead of glue around the inside of the larger piece, then fit the smaller piece into the larger. This will push the glue up into and over both pieces for a secure fit with no mess.

1. Drill a hole, approximately ⅜" in diameter, in the top of the copper tee to allow an open flow of energy inside the device.

2. Notch the first copper coupling to fit over the hole in the tee and solder it in place, forming a cross with four equal arms. Sand or file the soldered area to create a smooth surface.

3. Glue the four pieces of copper pipe onto the four arms of the cross.

4. Wrap the four crystals with shim material if their diameters are smaller than ½", then glue them into the four copper couplings by squeezing glue down onto the shim material, where it will drip down to form a secure bond.

5. Glue the couplings with their crystals onto the four pieces of copper pipe.

6. Wrap and glue the leather over the long and short pieces of copper pipe, leaving the tee and the copper couplings bare.

The Crux Crystallum is a very powerful tool, employing the creation energy of the Universe. It's a projector and radiator of the loving power of the Christ Consciousness in action. It's also an awesome thought/feeling amplifier. This device and a light-being operator express the kind of loving energy that the Earth is much in need of at this time. It's also quite a learning experience tool, as you'll discover for yourself.

FIFTEEN

Trident Krystallos

Today, we are living in New Atlantis.

T he Trident Krystallos has often been associated with Neptune, or Poseidon, as well as the lost island of Atlantis. While building the first model, Michael experienced this memory.

Amid the earthquakes and volcanic eruptions of the last Atlantean battle between the forces of light and darkness, a group of white-robed warrior priests emerged from an underground installation. All of the light warriors were armed with crystal tridents. Blue-white beams of energy flowed from their tridents as they sought to neutralize the destructive energy reactions within the huge domed crystal powerhouses of Atlantis. The night sky was filled with blue-white beams of energy clashing with red-white energy flashes from within the domes.

The trident-armed warriors succeeded in delaying the final destruction long enough for their brothers and sisters to flee the island in ships of both sea and air. The warriors themselves stayed behind to hold the massive energies in check, sacrificing their lives so that those they had sworn to protect could escape to eastern and western colonies of Atlantis. When they could hold out no longer, all of the warriors and their crystal tridents disappeared, with Atlantis, beneath the seas.

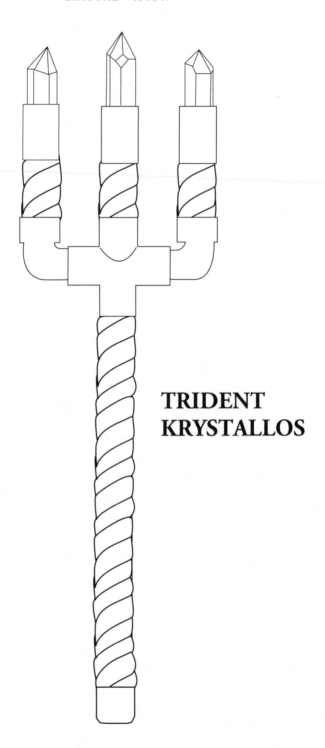

**TRIDENT
KRYSTALLOS**

Thousands of years later, warrior-priests and priestesses would inhabit new bodies and once again take up crystal tridents to neutralize the forces of negativity. That time is now!

USING THE TRIDENT KRYSTALLOS

In the past, the trident has been associated with the sea god Neptune, or Poseidon, but today the trident is more likely to be related to the seas of Universal Energy. It's most often used to project separate beams of white light energy in contrast to the field radiations of the crystal crosses. The trident starts radiating a field of energy as soon as it's constructed, but its most startling application is as an energy beam and ray projector. Most people see it as another form of the power rod for disarming or neutralizing worldwide negativity to bring about a healing peace and balance. It appeals to people who understand the nature of the healer as warrior and the warrior as healer—people whose motivating force is the power of light and love. The trident reaffirms the truth of the saying, "Only the most powerful people have the strength to be gentle."

To use the trident, hold it by its handle while visualizing the crystal's projection of three parallel beams of white light energy. Or, you can perceive the three beams as merging into one from an energy cone emission point. Although it's not often used that way, the trident will also radiate a field of Universal Energy.

The trident's trinity of crystals represents a powerful archetype of strong spiritual light-energy for our world. As with the other crystal tools, your ultimate guidance for use and responsibility will come from within. This tool may sometimes surprise you, and many feel an important kinship with it. The trident is one of the tools whose capabilities we are just now starting to learn about.

Interestingly enough, with its high intensity energy pattern and dramatic appearance, it can still be used as a tool for healing and balance in the same way that we use crystal healing rods. This type of tool tends to widen the definition of healing more than is usually perceived. While it can be set in the ground for a healing circle, this is very rarely done. Most often it's used as an individual, hand-held crystal energy device for helping the planet and her beings.

PAST LIFE RECALL

Although recalling past lives is only one of the things the trident can be used for, the results are usually so interesting that we've chosen to tell you about Lin's findings when she used the trident to ask if she'd shared any past lives with a friend and business associate. She not only found out about their past connection, but got information that would explain certain aspects of their current relationship.

Lin used the trident by holding it in both hands while she relaxed into a meditative state, and then asked her first question. After that, she laid the trident down while she wrote out her questions and answers, and focused her gaze occasionally on the trident to strengthen the energy connection when information was slow in coming. The results follow.

Q: Have my friend and I known each other in a previous life?

A: Of course you have, my dear, or you wouldn't feel the mystical connection with each other that you do.

Q: Tell me about it, please.

A: Your shared lifetime took place in the days of old Atlantis, before corruption set into that society. You lived as sisters on an island called Cosmos in the Atlantic Ocean. Actually, Marda was not your biological sister. She was found floating in a small boat on the ocean when she was two years old, having previously come from an island of primitives. Her family had too many girls and Marda was chosen to be given to the gods in this manner. Your parents adopted her and you grew up together.

Although Marda was part of your family, she was dark-haired and dark-skinned, unlike the rest of you, who were blond-haired, blue-eyed, Nordic types. Although she was accepted as part of the community, she always felt at a disadvantage because of her looks and the fact that one of her legs was shorter than the other, causing a slight limp. You were a few years older than her and fiercely protective, jumping to her defense with little or no provocation.

When you were 14 and Marda was 11, you both went to serve in the temple of Athena to learn healing. Life there was rather restrictive, and one night you decided to sneak out of the temple and borrow a boat to meet two boys you had grown up with on the far side of the island.

Marda, who was terrified of the water but would loyally follow you in all your exploits, went with you reluctantly. While you were out in the small sailboat, a sudden squall came up. Marda panicked and let the sail hit you, knocking you into the water. Then, despite her fear, she jumped into the water to rescue you.

Q: Don't stop there. What happened?

A: You were unconscious when she found you. She grabbed your hair to keep your head afloat and tried to swim back to the boat. You woke up and panicked, striking out at her. In the meantime, the boat had floated out of reach. You were both drowned.

Q: So what are we dealing with in our present relationship?

A: You feel guilty for leading her into danger and want to be careful not to do so again. You know that spiritual growth can sometimes cause stress and are worried you might inadvertently harm her. Don't be. The relationship will be good for both of you. She, on the other hand, feels guilty for knocking you out of the boat and is afraid her fear might hurt you again. This will not happen, either. Currently you have been relating to each other as you did in your past life together, but shortly this lifetime's realities will come to the fore and the past will fade away.

Q: What was my name in that lifetime?

A: Peradoe.

Q: What was the date?

A: 10,003 BC, in your years.

Q: Were we related to the gods, Geb and Nut, who, according to Manetho and Herodotus, ruled during that time?

A: You had a distant relationship to the star people. That is why both of you were allowed to serve in the temple.

Q: If Marda was an orphan, how could they tell she was related to the star people?

A: Through certain physical characteristics that all the direct products of interbreeding shared (i.e., a lack of body hair, different bone structure and eye sockets).

After discovering this interesting past life, Lin said that she makes no judgment, one way or the other, as to the accuracy of the information she received, but that it explains some of the peculiarities in her relationship with her friend and has helped them relate to each other on a more realistic basis.

Constructing the Trident Krystallos

Materials:

Copper tee, ½" diameter, ⅜" diameter hole drilled in top of tee

Solder

Copper coupling, ½" diameter, notched to fit top of tee

2 copper elbows, ½" diameter, 90 degree angle

3 pieces of copper pipe, ½" diameter, cut 1¾" long

1 piece of copper pipe, ½" diameter, cut 7½" long

3 copper couplings, ½" diameter, to hold crystals

2 quartz crystals, approximately ½" diameter, 1¼" long

1 quartz crystal, approximately ½" diameter, 1½" long

Shim material to mount crystals (copper mesh, leather, copper tape, etc.)

1 copper end cap, ½" diameter

Leather wrap, ⅜" wide strip, long enough to wrap handle and 3 arms

Instant bonding glue

Construction:

Before gluing anything, prefit the pieces to make sure they're properly aligned. It's a simple matter to adjust the pieces before they're glued, but practically impossible afterwards. To glue copper parts together, run a

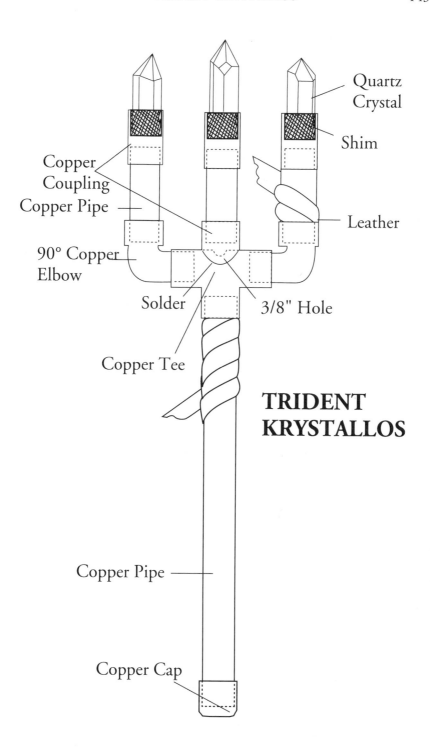

Quartz
Crystal

Shim

Copper
Coupling

Copper Pipe

Leather

90° Copper
Elbow

Solder

3/8" Hole

Copper Tee

**TRIDENT
KRYSTALLOS**

Copper Pipe

Copper Cap

bead of glue around the inside of the larger piece, then fit the smaller piece into the larger. This will push the glue up into and over both pieces for a secure fit with no mess.

1. Drill a hole approximately ⅜" in diameter in the top of the copper tee to allow an open flow of energy inside the device.

2. Notch the first copper coupling by cutting, grinding, drilling, or filing it to fit over the hole in the tee. Solder it in place, forming a cross with four equal arms. Sand or file the soldered area to create a neater, more uniform surface.

3. Fit the two copper elbows onto the two arms of the tee. Before gluing, they should be lined up vertically with the center coupler on the tee.

4. Glue the two 2¼" pieces of copper pipe into the two copper elbows, then glue the third into the center copper coupler, forming a trident.

5. Glue the 8" piece of copper pipe into the bottom of the tee for the handle.

6. Mount the three crystals into the three copper couplers, using the shim material of your choice for a tight fit. Wrap the bottom of a crystal with the shim material, fit it into the coupler, then squeeze instant bonding glue onto the shim material. It will soak down and hold the crystal securely in place in the coupler. Let the glue dry for a few minutes.

7. Glue the three couplers with their mounted crystals into the three arms of the trident, using the longer crystal in the middle arm.

8. Glue the copper end cap onto the handle of the trident.

9. Wrap and glue the leather over the long and short pieces of copper pipe leaving the tee, elbows, end cap, and the copper couplings bare.

10. Choose the color of covering that you feel comfortable with. The Trident Krystallos, especially when covered in black leather, is startling and disarming, literally. It's frequently used to send white light energy to military and political decision-makers to ease tense international situations.

SIXTEEN

Ancient
Martial Arts

Ki or Chi is the essence of the Universe.

Crystal hands and crystal wands are usually used in self-development practices to help us experience the extension of our energy into the larger world where we become one with the energy of the planet and Universe. We are then able to tune into our higher, all-encompassing self that goes beyond human limitations.

The hands and wands lend themselves to use in a wide variety of martial arts forms, as well as for healing. Using the Chi energy of T'ai Chi Chuan, the Ki energy of Aikido, or any of the terms you prefer from your particular martial arts practice, you are still using the same Universal Energy of healing and quartz crystals.

When you're using these tools, feel the Earth's life energy flowing up through the soles of your feet while experiencing the Universe's energy pouring downward through the top of your head. The energy follows a path outward through your arms and hands, continues through the crystal tool, and is projected outward from the tips of the quartz crystals. The best way to learn how to use these tools is by practicing with them, while allowing creative ideas a free rein. You'll probably discover original ideas of your own that far surpass those already in existence.

CRYSTAL HANDS

Your can adapt the crystal hands to many martial arts techniques by letting your intuition guide you into creative uses that accurately project your individual personality. Most practitioners of the martial arts are more in tune with the Universal Energy than they give themselves credit for or accept. While most martial arts are by their nature in harmony with the Earth Mother, some practices, such as the animal and bird forms used in some techniques, lend themselves especially well to the crystal hands.

Now is a time for growth, a time when we can expand on and enhance the traditional practices or harmony of an earlier time in preparation for the future. Keep that which is good from tradition, and add something more that will make it better. We can use this time period to expand the growth of traditions to come, insuring inner and outer peace and harmony that will result in peace and balance for the planet. The moving energy of our future on Earth is now being created and the present is the only time we have to do it.

The crystal hands manifest the positive and negative as a balance of the male/female energy rather than a judgment of good or bad. This balance shows up in some of the martial arts forms patterned after the movements of birds and animals. The forms often resemble a dance of nature, as in the following scenario describing Michael's martial arts interpretation of a confrontation between an eagle and a baby hawk.

As the man and woman moved into position, facing each other, the crystal hands were held with the the crystals pointing back along their wrists toward their bodies. Their fluid, slow-motion movements focused on one another as they moved closer. The woman brought one crystal hand out first, her right arm extended with the crystals pointed downward like the beak of an eagle. Her left arm bent at the elbow as she pointed the other crystal hand outward to represent the eagle's left foot and claw.

Her male opponent dropped into a crouch, perfectly balanced and centered, as a baby hawk on the ground will do when threatened. With arms bent at the elbows, the crystals in his hands pointed straight up at his opponent. His form resembled that of a baby hawk on its back, with its legs in the air and claws pointed upward for fast defensive action. After the opponents feinted and parried for some time, the eagle learned it couldn't penetrate the baby hawk's outstretched claws and retreated to find easier prey. As the eagle discovered, it takes more than brute strength to compete with cunning.

Constructing the Crystal Hands

Materials:

> 2 quartz crystals, approximately ⅜" diameter, 1½" long
>
> Shim material of copper mesh, copper tape, or leather
>
> 4 copper couplings, ½"diameter
>
> 4 copper elbows, ½"diameter, 45 degree angle
>
> 3 pieces copper pipe, ½"diameter, cut in ¾" lengths
>
> Leather wrap, ¾" wide strip, long enough to cover tool from crystal to crystal
>
> Instant bonding glue
>
> *Note:* The crystal hands are usually constructed in pairs. Double the materials listed to make two hands.

Construction:

Prefit all parts, to make sure they're aligned and fit properly, before gluing any of them. If you're making two hands, do them both at once. The pieces can be put together loosely or tightly, giving you two different sized hands if you're not careful.

1. Mount the two crystals in two of the copper couplings. Wrap the base of each crystal with the shim material of your choice, fit it into a coupling, then squeeze instant bonding glue onto the shim material. It will soak down and hold the crystal securely in place in the coupling. Let the glue dry for a few minutes.

2. Join two of the copper elbows with one piece of the copper pipe, which fits inside the two pieces. Join the other two copper elbows and the last two copper couplings in the same manner.

3. Fit the elbow joint assemblies on either end of the center copper couplings. This should give you a shallow U shape.

4. Fit the crystal-mounted couplings over the open ends of the elbow assemblies. You should now have the basic shape of the crystal hand in the diagram.

5. Once you've made sure everything fits together and lines up properly, take the pieces apart and glue them. Run a bead of glue around the interior of the larger piece, then push the smaller part into the glued piece. This spreads the glue up into and over both pieces for a firm seal with no mess.

6. Use the leather strip to wrap all the copper parts, leaving only the crystals bare. Glue as you wrap the leather in a spiral around the copper parts.

CRYSTAL WAND

Little is known about the tradition of the crystal wand, except that the original Chinese wands were approximately four-foot lengths of bamboo—not staff length, and not short like the T'ai Chi Ruler, but somewhere in between. The complement of quartz crystals in copper reducers connected by the spirals of copper tape amplifies the wand's crystal energy. Single or double termination quartz crystals can be used. Like the crystal hands, your judgment as to how to use the wand is the ultimate guide. You are the key.

When the wand isn't in use, it makes a good decoration. We've hung ours over the entrance to a special meditation room in the garage. It can also be hung on a mantle or displayed on a wall. If space is short, hooks can be screwed into the top shelf of a bookcase to display the wand out of harm's way.

An excellent book for reference is *Aikido and the New Warrior* by Richard Heckler, available from North Atlantic Books, 2320 Blake Street, Berkeley, CA 94704.

CRYSTAL
HANDS

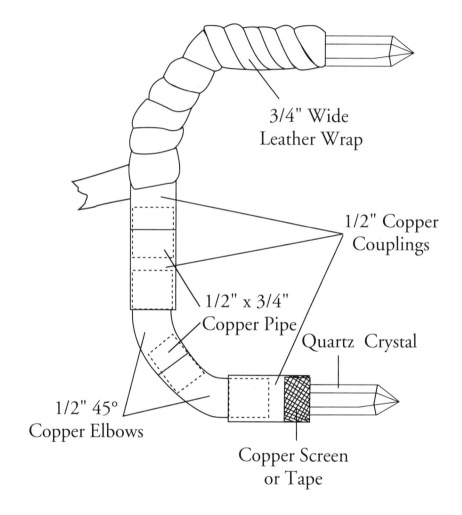

3/4" Wide
Leather Wrap

1/2" Copper
Couplings

1/2" x 3/4"
Copper Pipe

Quartz Crystal

1/2" 45°
Copper Elbows

Copper Screen
or Tape

Constructing the Crystal Wand

Materials:

> 2 quartz crystals, approximately ½" diameter, 1½" long
>
> Shim material of copper mesh, copper tape, or leather
>
> 2 copper reducers, 1" diameter down to ¾" diameter
>
> Bamboo staff, 48" to 56" long, approximately 1" diameter (available at import stores)
>
> Copper tape, ¼" wide, approximately 30 feet long (available where stained glass supplies are sold)
>
> Instant bonding glue

Construction:

1. Mount each of the crystals in the small end of one of the copper reducers. Wrap the base of the crystal with shim material before fitting it into the reducer. Squeeze instant bonding glue onto the shim material, where it will soak down to hold the crystal securely in the reducer. Let the glue dry a few minutes.

2. Cut your piece of bamboo to the length you want, making sure your reducers will be mounted at least two inches away from any growth knots.

3. If the bamboo is too large for the reducer, sand or file it down. If it's too small, use shim material wrapped around the end of the bamboo to bring it up to the right size.

4. Use copper tape to wrap the bamboo in a loose spiral wrap in one direction. Then wrap the tape in the opposite direction so it crosses the first tape.

5. Mount the large end of the reducers, with their crystals, on each end of the bamboo and glue them in place. Copper tape can be wrapped around the base of the reducer, a short way down onto the bamboo, for a smoother look.

CRYSTAL WAND

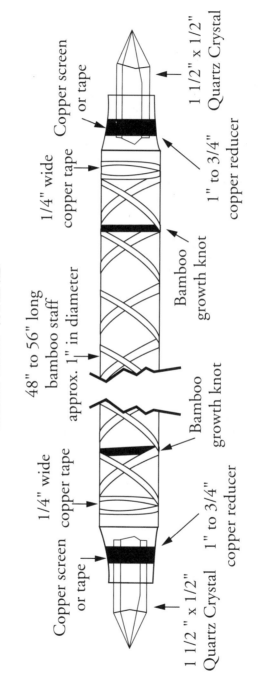

Copper screen or tape

1/4" wide copper tape

48" to 56" long bamboo staff approx. 1" in diameter

1 1/2" x 1/2" Quartz Crystal

1" to 3/4" copper reducer

Bamboo growth knot

Bamboo growth knot

1" to 3/4" copper reducer

Copper screen or tape

1/4" wide copper tape

1 1/2 " x 1/2" Quartz Crystal

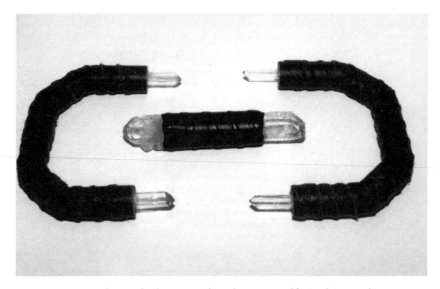

Crystal Hands shown with Palm-Size Self-Healing Rod

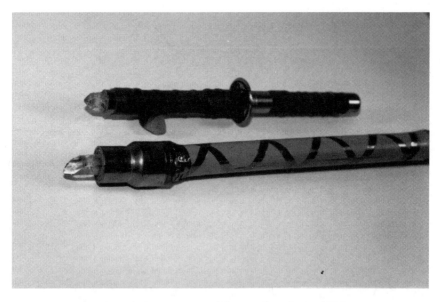

Top: Crystal Container Rod featured in Crystal Warrior
Bottom: Crystal Wand

SEVENTEEN

Ancient Egypt

*The past plays an important part in shaping
our current attitudes and beliefs.*

The Ankh Crystallos is familiar to us as the Egyptian symbol of eternal life. Study of the ankh reveals that this archetype, or symbol in our genetic or mass consciousness, activates a deeply emotional feeling. By inserting a double termination quartz crystal in the top loop of the ankh, you can turn it into a powerful tool for balance, healing, and the expression of life.

We believe that Atlanteans originally acquired the ankh from members of a civilization in the Pleiades. Healers in Egypt learned of this tool while Egypt was still a colony of Atlantis. After Poseidon, the last island of Atlantis, sank beneath the ocean, ankh-bearing Atlanteans found refuge in Egypt and the ankh became more widely known. Today, this symbol of the eternal life force can be a powerful tool for people dedicated to preserving and improving all life. It radiates the energy necessary for the peace that makes a long life possible, while eliciting the joyous expression of the life force in the user.

ANKH
CRYSTALLOS

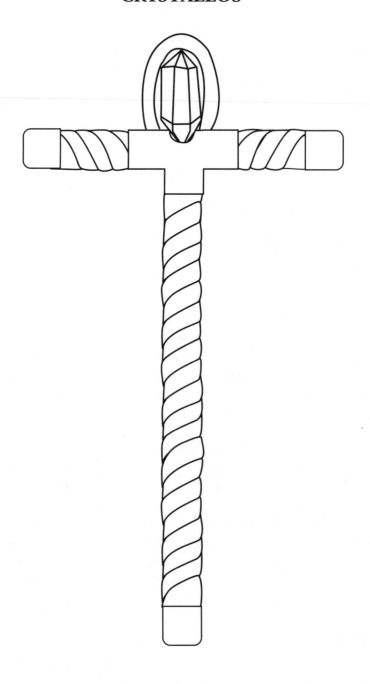

Using the Ankh Crystallos

The looped cross, as a symbol of life, also radiates the energy of peace, love, trust, health, and abundance. It serves as an example of the balance of polarity: male and female, or positive and negative. Some of its uses include healing, blessing, and meditation, individually or in groups. Due to its pattern, shape, and form, combined with the crystal, the ankh is active at all times after it's constructed.

During outdoor circles or ceremonies, the ankh can be set upright in the ground for a harmonious Earth contact. It's especially powerful for radiating light-energy to help human beings maintain balance, and can help us raise our level of consciousness when we're tuning into the Source.

Larger versions of this tool are becoming popular, along with small jewelry-sized creations set in silver instead of copper. Use your intuition to determine the size and color of your own Ankh Crystallos. Your intuition is also your best guide for using this life-giving reinvention.

Usually the ankh is held by the long bottom arm of the cross. However, an unusual technique is used by some crystal healers for the purpose of projecting a beam. They hold the ankh with the crystal loop and cross arms in one hand, with the long arm pointing outward through the fingers. The operator can then visualize and project a beam of energy through the copper end cap in the same manner as he or she would a healing power rod. Try both methods to see which works best for you.

PAST LIFE RECALL

The ankh, as an ancient tool, can also be useful in exploring past lives. Long ago, Lin dreamed about a past life in Egypt. In this vivid dream, she was a pharaoh's daughter who was in love with a minor member of the nobility. Her handmaiden arranged a secret meeting between her and her loved one. During the tryst, Lin realized that it was her social position rather than herself that attracted her lover, but since she sincerely loved him, she agreed to ask her father's permission to marry him. The dream ended with the pharaoh's refusal.

Later, she used the ankh to elicit more details of that intriguing lifetime, pinning down the date to 1472 BC, and learning that she eventually married a warrior her father chose for her. She lived a pleasant life and came to love the man she married. At age 29, she died in childbirth.

Lin found the past life interesting, particularly since a lifestyle that was considered opulent then was pretty primitive compared to current standards. But the most significant thing about the dream and later information was that every person in that life was someone she knew in the present. The dream helped her understand why an old love had deserted her, and prodded her into trying to create a more balanced relationship with a current friend. She also gained insights into the dynamics of two other relationships that had been puzzling her.

When asked whether she thought her dream and later sessions with the ankh were true memories of a past life, she replied, "They felt very real, but even if they were only a product of my imagination, they helped me deal with issues in this lifetime." This is a healthy attitude. During your own explorations into the past, rather than worrying about whether or not they actually took place (perhaps they even occurred in another dimension), take what you learn from them to deal with your current lifetime.

Constructing the Ankh Crystallos

The finished ankh measures about 10" long by 5½" wide.

Materials:

> Copper tee, ½" diameter, ⅜" diameter hole drilled in top of tee
>
> Copper pipe, ¼" diameter, approximately 4" long
>
> Solder
>
> 2 pieces of copper pipe, ½" diameter, cut 2" long
>
> 1 piece of copper pipe, ½" diameter, cut 8" long
>
> 3 copper end caps, ½" diameter
>
> 1 double termination quartz crystal, approximately ¾" diameter, 1½" long
>
> Leather wrap, ⅜" wide strips, to wrap handle and arms
>
> Instant bonding glue

ANKH
CRYSTALLOS

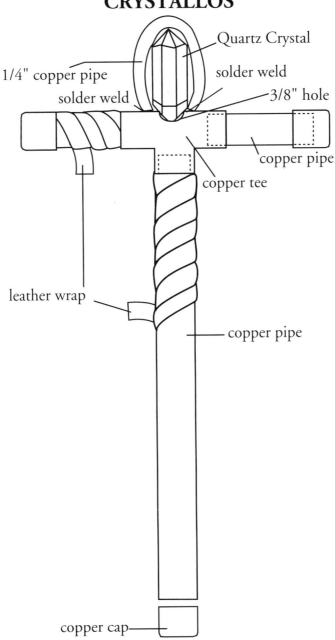

Quartz Crystal

1/4" copper pipe

solder weld

solder weld

3/8" hole

copper pipe

copper tee

leather wrap

copper pipe

copper cap

Construction:

1. Drill a hole approximately ⅜" in diameter in the top of the copper tee to allow an open flow of energy inside the device.

2. The ¼" piece of copper tubing (pipe) is used to hold the crystal in the loop of the ankh. Bend the tubing around the crystal and cut off any extra. After you're sure you have a good fit, the ends of the copper tubing are soldered to the top of the copper tee. One side of the loop should be soldered in place without the crystal to avoid exposing it to too much heat. When one side is securely soldered, the crystal can be fitted inside the loop with one tip in the hole at the center top of the tee. Clamp the crystal in place while the other side is soldered securely. This forms the main unit of the ankh. Sand or file the soldered area to create a neater, more uniform surface.

3. Fit and glue the two short pieces of copper pipe onto the two arms of the tee.

4. Fit and glue the 8" piece of copper pipe into the bottom of the tee for the handle.

5. Glue the three copper end caps onto the open ends of the copper pipe.

6. Wrap and glue the leather around the long and short pieces of copper pipe leaving the tee, tubing, and end caps bare.

    Note: Before gluing anything, prefit the pieces. It's easy to file, sand, or adjust before things are glued, but practically impossible afterwards. To glue copper pieces together, run a bead of glue around the inside of the larger piece, then fit the smaller piece into the larger. This will push the glue up into and over both pieces for a secure fit with no mess.

    If your favorite crystal is too large for the ½" diameter pipe, you can make the ankh of ¾" diameter copper pipe and expand the length of the arms and upright. The arms are at a ratio to the upright portion of approximately one to four.

EIGHTEEN

Pyramid Power

The new interest in pyramids is a sign of the ancients reborn.

CRYSTAL ENERGY DOORS

A brown-skinned man moved silently through the jungle, rays of sunlight through the trees highlighting his feathered headdress. The headdress, which appeared to be blue, was actually an iridescent blend of many colors. It had been passed down to him from his great-great grandfather who, it was said, had come across the water from the land where the sun rose. He carried another treasure that had belonged to his great-great grandfather. In a fur-skinned bag slung over his shoulder was a shiny copper pyramid with a clear quartz crystal on the top. The sacred object had always been treasured for its copper, which was more valuable than gold or silver. But now he knew the copper and crystal cap were even more valuable than he'd thought. A few weeks ago, acting on his father's deathbed instructions, he'd learned that placing the cap on a stone pyramid in the jungle caused strange things to happen.

The man, who was both priest and healer, reached the pyramid and reverently set the cap in place on top of it. After that he sat at the base of the pyramid and waited, playing haunting melodies on his carved wooden flute.

159

When early evening approached, he began to beat on his sacred drum with a rhythm that echoed like heartbeats of the Universal Creator.

As night darkened the jungle around the pyramid, the crystal on the copper cap began to glow with a blue-white light. Soon the pyramid itself shimmered with an aura of light that reflected all the colors of the rainbow. A bright star appeared in the dark sky above the pyramid. As the star came lower, reflecting light brighter than the sun, it became day-bright in the jungle around the ancient stonework.

Later, when rays of morning sun pierced the thick foliage, the gray stone structure sat silent—darkened and abandoned. No sign remained of the man with blue feathers, his flute, his drum, or the copper crystal cap. It was as if they had never been. Yet, after more than five thousand years, the man would return to awaken the sacred pyramid's energy with his jungle-shaking drumbeat.

Meanwhile, in another time …

A young lady in a white lab coat gazed at an invisible pyramid. The device that produced the pyramid form had a square copper base with angled crystals pointing toward a central crystal on a copper column.

She thought she detected a fine line of bluish light being emitted from each crystal, but she wasn't sure. Her gaze followed the faint lines of light to where they intersected at the point of the center crystal; they formed a perfect energy pyramid, invisible and visible at the same time. It couldn't really exist, and yet it did. Surprisingly, the plants sitting within the pyramid were growing just fine. She hadn't expected that result because her earlier test plants had been mummified in the pyramid. Two opposite reactions to the same test were puzzling. More was going on in the experiment than she'd first suspected, and she would continue exploring the energy phenomena until she understood its secrets.

THE MYSTERY OF THE PYRAMIDS

Throughout the ages, people have been intrigued and confounded by the enigma of the pyramid. Archaeologists have found ancient pyramids all over the world: in Egypt, Mexico, Central and South America, China, Cambodia, the Himalayas, Europe, and possibly Siberia. Even in the

United States, pyramid markers and mounds have been found in Montana, Arizona, Illinois, Alaska, and Florida.

Although many of the pyramids that exist today have been used as tombs, markers, living quarters, and temples, we wonder if that was their original purpose, or if some of them were abandoned by their builders and later used or copied by primitives. It's hard to believe that a structure such as the Great Pyramid, which is built of perfectly carved and placed mortarless stones weighing two to seventy tons, could or would have been built by the ancient Egyptians. Moving the seventy-ton granite blocks used in the King's Chamber of the Great Pyramid all the way from the Aswan Dam area, some five hundred miles away, just doesn't make sense unless the people who built the pyramid had the technology to cut, move, and place the giant stones easily.

Another curious fact about the pyramids is that many of them are missing capstones. Although we can only speculate, we believe that some of these pyramids were built by cultures long forgotten who used them as energy generators. When they abandoned them, they took along the capstones that powered them, along with anything else they might have contained. That would explain why, when the Great Pyramid at Giza was first entered, it was virtually empty. Otherwise, why would the ancient Egyptians, who supposedly built the huge pyramid, seal it up and abandon such a monumental project that we would find difficult or impossible to duplicate today?

The concept of using pyramids and crystals as energy generators isn't as fanciful as it may seem. Modern researchers have experimented with small pyramids and found them to be effective for drying foods and seeds without spoilage; sharpening razor blades, scissors, and knives; curing headaches; as meditation or healing chambers; for converting thoughts into physical manifestations; and as hothouses for sick or dormant plants. Obviously the pyramid shape in itself has curious energy properties. But we believe that in order to fully energize the pyramid into its full potential as an energy generator, quartz crystals, already known to have electrical properties (i.e., in quartz digital equipment, solar cells, etc.), were used in both the capstones and the interiors of the pyramids to focus the resonating energy of the pyramid shape. The following seven models of pyramids are made of copper and quartz crystals. By experimenting with them, you may discover the secret of the pyramids for yourself.

Using Pyramids

Different types of energy have been detected at different points in the interior of pyramids. For instance, when sharpening razor blades, the razor is placed at the one-third height level of the pyramid with its head facing north and the blades facing east and west. Curing headaches and meditation is often done inside people-sized pyramids with the head near the apex. A sense of peace or inspiration is sometimes found by lying with the head facing north. In addition, there seems to be a strong energy field above the top of the pyramid, extending upward quite a distance.

People have also used pyramids under beds and chairs as energizers. Any of the smaller crystal pyramids in this section can be used in this fashion. We use some of our own small pyramids as room energizers and in the center of ceremonial circles. To use the pyramids as energizers that turn thoughts into form, we write out the thing we want to manifest on a piece of paper and put it inside the pyramid, on and between different types of metals and crystals. Although very few people who have experimented with pyramids doubt any longer that they create strange energy fields both inside and outside, the nature of that energy and how it can be directed to specific purposes has yet to be fully explained.

In most pyramid experiments, the placement of the pyramid and the objects within is said to affect the outcome. Most experimenters agree that one side of the pyramid and the objects within should face north, but they disagree as to whether the direction should be true north or magnetic north. We believe that geomagnetic forces are at work within the pyramid and place them towards magnetic north. In your own experiments, you might want to try both and see which direction produces the best results.

When you're building and experimenting with any of the following pyramid projects, use the designs we offer as a take-off point for your own creativity and intuition. Although the pyramid form in itself produces energy, it's probably thought that directs and controls the energy and only you know how to make that energy work best for you.

For those of you who aren't mechanically inclined, there are numerous manufactured pyramids, large and small, available commercially, including pyramids cut out of solid quartz. You can substitute commercial pyramids to try out any of the experiments we suggest in this chapter, and you may come up with new experiments of your own that will allow you to explore the energy capabilities of pyramids and crystals.

THE DOUBLE PYRAMID

The double pyramid shape of this device forms two pyramids from tip to tip, which means that the crystal sphere in the center is constantly building up a charge of energy. We suggest that the crystal sphere (or other crystals) be removed when not in use to avoid a build-up of too much energy.

Although the exact use and limits of this double pyramid haven't been determined, we can suggest several experiments you might try. Place the side of the pyramid opposite the copper upright toward the north. Then remove the center crystal sphere and place a small glass or dish of water on the wooden center tray to charge for twenty-four hours. The water can then be used for washing for healthier skin, for drinking to produce greater health and vitality, or for watering ailing plants.

If you have some special desire, the double pyramid can be used for wish fulfillment by writing out your wish or goal on a piece of paper and folding it in half. Build up a ball of energy between your hands and hold the paper while concentrating on what you've written. Place the paper under the crystal sphere with the top and bottom of the wish facing north, and release the thought with the idea that it will come about. Once a day, focus your thoughts on the wish and know that it's being taken care of for you.

In addition, other experiments for a single pyramid can be performed with this device. They include drying food, energizing a room, sharpening a razor, and meditating with the pyramid above, below, or next to you.

Constructing the Double Pyramid

Materials:

A. Wood rectangle for the base, 9" x 10", ⅜" thick, stained, oiled, or finished

B. 2 1¼" bolts with nuts for attaching copper caps to pyramid apexes

C. 2 copper caps, ½" diameter, for pyramid apexes

D. 2 natural quartz crystals, ⅜" diameter, 1" long, and shim material of leather, copper mesh, or copper tape

E. 2 copper or brass straps, ½" wide, approximately 14" long, and 4 small wood screws

F. Wood square, 6" x 6" x ⅜", stained, oiled, or finished

G. Natural quartz crystal sphere, 1" diameter or larger

H. Copper cap, ½" diameter, for hanger

I. Copper pipe, ½" diameter, cut 5½" long, for hanger horizontal

J. Copper elbow, ½" diameter, 90 degrees

K. Copper pipe, ½" diameter, cut 10" long, for hanger upright

L. *Optional:* Backing for bottom of base

Construction:

1. Drill a ½" diameter hole 2" in from one of the 9" sides of the wood base (A).

2. Insert the 10" length of pipe (K) into the hole in the wood base, and attach the copper elbow (J) to its other end.

3. Drill a ³⁄₁₆" diameter hole for a bolt ¾" in from one end of the 5½" length of copper pipe (I). Drill the hole through both sides of the pipe. Insert the undrilled end of the pipe into the copper elbow and put the copper cap (H) on the other end.

4. Drill a ³⁄₁₆" diameter hole for the other bolt in the base (A) directly under the hole in the copper pipe.

5. Take the 6" square of wood (F) and measure ¾" in on each of the corners. Cut the corners off so you have flattened edges instead of sharp corners. Drill a ¾" diameter hole through the center of the square.

6. Drill a ³⁄₁₆" diameter hole in each of the two copper caps for the pyramid points (C). Drill a matching hole in the center of each of the copper or brass straps (E). Insert one of the bolts through the copper cap, through the center of each of the two straps, and

DOUBLE PYRAMID

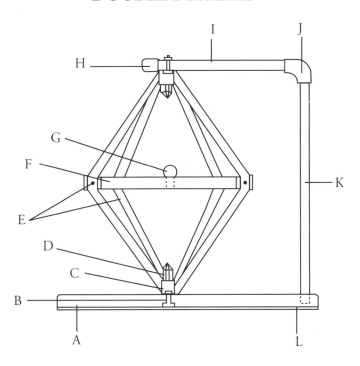

through the 5½" piece of copper tubing (I). Attach the bolt with a nut.

7. Center the wood square (F) halfway between the wood base and the underside of the top support (I), and put books or wood blocks under it to hold it in place. Bend the straps down and drill a hole through the straps and the center of all four flat corner areas in the wood square. Attach the strapping with the small wood screws. Your top pyramid frame is now formed.

8. Remove the supports and bend the strapping down over the hole in the wood base to shape the lower pyramid. Flatten the ends of the strapping down over the hole and cut off any excess strapping. Drill holes in all four ends of the strapping where they line up over the hole. Put the remaining bolt down through the copper cap, the four ends of the straps, and the base. Attach the nut to the bolt on the bottom of the base. The double pyramid frame is now complete. *Note:* If you want a smooth bottom for your base, countersink the nut or use a backing on the bottom of the base (L).

9. Wrap the base of the two crystals (D) with shim material and insert one in each of the copper caps (C) at the pyramid points.

    Put the crystal sphere over the hole in the wooden square (F). The double pyramid is now ready to use. For some experiments you can place four small crystals on each of the corners of the center platform, with their tips pointing toward the crystal sphere. Remove the loose crystals and the sphere when the device isn't in use.

INVISIBLE ENERGY PYRAMID

A pyramid doesn't necessarily need to be a physical form, as illustrated by the stories at the beginning of the chapter. Energy that emanates from the crystals on the base of this device form the vertical lines of the pyramid. The physical shape is usually visualized by the operator, although people who are sensitive to energies can sometimes see the pyramid form outlined in blue-white or other colors of light.

Using The Invisible Energy Pyramid

The configuration of this unit forms an invisible energy grid that produces a significant amount of energy. The psi energy can be used for a variety of purposes, including those suggested throughout the chapter.

We often use ours for producing a peaceful aura (room-sized or larger) for meditation and receiving or sending information. To use it this way, align one side of the pyramid north (either magnetic or true north). Sit on the south side of the device so you, too, are facing north. Imagine your thoughts flowing down into the top crystal, then gaining energy by reflecting off the four base crystals and emerging once again from the top crystal in a cone shape that expands as it rises. If you're using the invisible energy pyramid with a group, align it in the same way and stand or sit in a circle around it. Use your combined mental energy in the same manner to achieve a common purpose.

Constructing the Invisible Energy Pyramid

Materials:

A. Sheet of copper, 18" square

B. Copper cap, ½" diameter, with mounting bolt and nut

C. Copper pipe for upright, ½" diameter, 15¼" long

D. Copper reducer, ¾" to ½" diameter

E. One quartz crystal, less than ¾" diameter, 2" long, and shim material of leather, copper mesh, or copper tape

F. Four quartz crystals, ½" diameter, 2" long, and copper or electrical tape

G. 4 copper straps, about 3" long and 1" wide, bent to mount and hold base crystals, with 4 nuts and bolts

Construction:

1. Drill a ¼" hole 1" from the edge in each corner of the copper sheet. Drill a fifth hole in the center of the sheet.

2. Drill a ¼" hole in the bottom of the copper cap. Bolt the cap to the center of the copper sheet with the nut inside the cap.

3. Bend one end of each of the copper straps in a half circle to form a trough to hold a crystal. Remove the crystal and place the other end of the strap flat on the corner of the copper sheet. Bend the trough portion upward, facing the center, about 1½" in from the end. Drill a hole in each of the flat ends of the straps, and bolt a strap to each corner of the sheet.

4. Mount the center crystal in the large end of the reducer by wrapping copper tape, leather, or copper mesh around the base of the crystal to form a shim and sliding it into the reducer. Fit the reducer with its crystal over one end of the copper pipe and place the other end of the pipe into the bolted-on copper cap. (To build a multipurpose device capable of holding either a crystal point or crystal sphere, don't glue the crystal or the pipe into the reducer or the pipe into the copper cap.)

5. Place one of the crystals in each of the trough ends of the mounting straps. Wrap tape around the crystal and the strap to hold the crystal in place on the strap. To make sure the crystals point exactly toward the tip of the center crystal, tape a piece of string to the underside of each of the straps and hold the other end at the top of the center crystal. Then adjust the angle of the straps until you have the exact angle that will form your invisible energy pyramid. Remove the string.

To create different angles of invisible pyramids, vary the length of the copper pipe and angle of the crystals. You can also replace the center crystal on the pyramid with a crystal sphere or egg. Some say the spheres produce a slightly different type of energy, although the exact nature of the difference is often hotly debated. While some say that a crystal point projects a beam and a crystal ball radiates a field or aura of energy, others take the opposite viewpoint. Our personal experience is that a crystal ball or a crystal point can produce either a beam or a field of energy, depending on the person using the crystal or crystal device.

INVISIBLE ENERGY PYRAMID

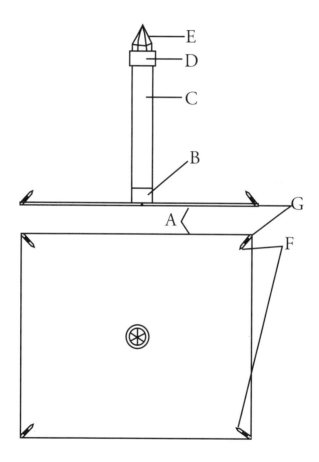

PYRAMID ENERGY AMPLIFIER

If you're not mechanically inclined, or are and want to try out one of the large pyramids sold commercially, the following project is for you. The large pyramid frames are usually manufactured in three-, five-, and six-foot sizes. Although the pyramid energy amplifier is usually made with the six-foot size, any size will do.

Uses for the Pyramid Energy Amplifier

Chances are if you purchase a pyramid, the manufacturer will furnish you with experiments to perform. Any of those experiments can also be enhanced with the crystal amplifier. Larger pyramids are nice because you can actually go inside them and feel the beneficial energy for yourself.

You might try meditating in your pyramid. Alter your position by sitting on a chair, sitting on the ground, and lying on the ground on three successive days, to see which height level is the most beneficial. Spend about twenty minutes on your meditation. Once you're in a comfortable position, take several deep breaths. Inhale and imagine that you're drawing white light down from the crystal into the top of your head, or into your forehead if you're lying down. Visualize the light filling your head, shoulders, arms, fingers, etc., until it's filled every part of your body and is coming out of the ends of your fingers and toes. On the exhalations, imagine the excess light surrounding your body in a halo. Once you've reached this state, you can concentrate on healing yourself or another, do a past life recall, or become a crystal channel. If you like, you don't even have to do anything but enjoy being surrounded in light and energy. Leave the positive effect up to the Universe to create what's best for you. If you have a headache, try different positions inside the pyramid to cure it.

Another use for the large pyramid is to suspend it over your favorite chair so your head is inside it while you relax. Or you can hang it over your bed while you sleep. Water can also be energized in larger amounts in the large pyramid, and plants can be healed.

Constructing a Pyramid Energy Amplifier

Pyramid with Base and Fixed Double Termination Crystal

Materials:

A. A prefabricated pyramid with a six-foot base (or a homemade model). The prefabricated models are manufactured with or without a clear plastic covering. Either variety will do. These come without the base frame section shown in the diagram

B. Copper wire (insulated or bare wire), 4 long pieces to wrap the legs of the pyramid, plus a bare piece to wrap around the crystal

C. Quartz crystal, double termination, with copper wire wrapped around it to connect it to the pyramid apex

D. *Optional:* Base frame section: 4 5½-foot pieces of wood to connect corners of pyramid

Construction:

For a sturdier base, you can use pieces of wood to connect the legs of the pyramid. Then wrap the copper wire clockwise, starting at the bottom of each leg of the pyramid and ending at the apex. Wrap the crystal securely in the bare copper wire and attach the ends of the wire to the wires on the legs of the pyramid. One tip of the crystal should just touch the apex of the pyramid, and the other should point straight down.

Pyramid with no Base and a Single Termination Hanging Crystal

This version of the large pyramid with no frame around the base has been used in recent experiments for energizing cars. The apex of the pyramid and crystal should be centered over the engine on the hood of the car on the principle that, if pyramid energy can rebuild the molecules of a razor blade, it can also work on larger objects. Reports of other psionic machines actually materializing new parts in large electrical systems also tend to reinforce this idea.

If you're a gardener, place the uncovered pyramid out in the sun and put trays of food to be dried inside. The drying ability of the pyramid coupled with the sun should make your food dry in record time.

When using either of the above pyramids, the process is so simple and the materials required are so basic, that the main challenge is to free

PYRAMID ENERGY AMPLIFIER

Pyramid with
base and fixed
Double Termination
Crystal

TOP

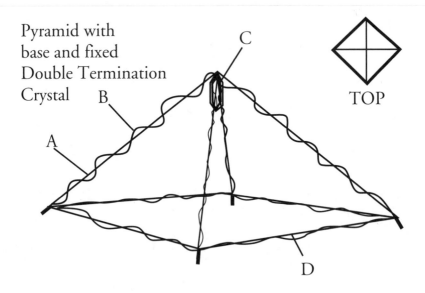

Pyramid without
base with hanging
Single Termination
Crystal

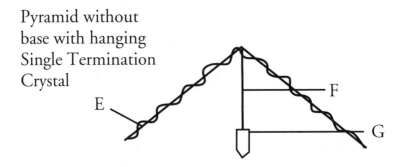

our minds from the preconceived notion that something has to be complex to work. Once we free our minds of that idea, the pyramid energy amplifier can produce some wonderful and unexpected results.

Materials:

    A.   Open frame prefabricated pyramid without base frame

    B.   Copper wire, any size, 4 pieces, each long enough to wrap one leg of the frame, plus one piece of thin bare wire at least 2½ feet long to wrap the crystal and suspend it from the apex

    C.   Quartz crystal, single termination

Construction:

Assemble the frame of the pyramid and then use the copper wire in a clockwise spiral to wrap each leg of the pyramid, starting at the bottom and wrapping until you reach the apex. Wrap the thin copper wire around the crystal to hold it securely, then attach it to the apex of the pyramid so that the crystal hangs tip down at one-third the height of the pyramid. In other words, if you have a six-foot pyramid, the tip of the crystal should hang four feet above the ground.

ENERGIZER PYRAMID

The energizer is one of the more popular combinations of pyramids and crystals. Its large open area makes it ideal for placing a variety of objects, such as crystals, pieces of paper, water, seeds, small plants, etc. Yet its size (approximately 10" square and 17" high) is small enough to use for a room energizer. It can also be used for meditation, crystal, and psi experiments. In addition, the rod extension on the top can easily be lengthened or shortened to meet your needs and perception.

One of the nicest benefits of this pyramid frame is that its center is open and visible, allowing you to monitor your experiments without disturbing the pyramid or anything in it. Since an important part of pyramid experiments is getting the pyramid and the objects within lined up exactly and keeping them that way until the experiment is over, being able to see inside is a real advantage.

Constructing the Energizer Pyramid

Materials:

A. Quartz crystal, ¾" diameter, 1½" length, and shim material of copper mesh, copper tape, or leather

B. Copper reducer, ¾" to 1" diameter

C. Copper pipe, ¾" diameter, 2" long

D. Copper cap, ¾" diameter

E. Bolt to attach cap to apex

F. Four copper straps, 11" long, ½" wide, about ³⁄₃₂" thick

G. Pyramid base: copper sheet, 10" square

H. 4 bolts and nuts to attach straps and legs to copper sheet

I. 4 legs: copper straps, 6" long, ½" wide, ³⁄₃₂" thick

J. 4 leg supports: ½" wide copper strap, 10" long

K. 4 bolts to attach leg supports

L. Instant bonding glue

Construction:

1. Wrap the base of the crystal with shim material (A) and fit it into the large end of the copper reducer (B). Squeeze drops of glue onto the shim material, where it will soak down to seal the crystal into the reducer. Set it aside to dry.

2. Drill a ¼" hole ¼" from the edge of each corner of the copper sheet (G). Drill ¼" holes ½" from the end of each of the four 11" copper straps (F). Drill a ¼" hole ½" from the end on one end of each of the legs (I), and another hole in the middle of the length of each. Drill a ¼" hole ½" from each of the ends of of the leg-frame supports (J). Drill the last ¼" hole in the bottom of the copper cap (D).

3. Bend 1" of each end of the legs (I) at a 90-degree angle as shown in the diagram. Bend the last inch of each of the 11" copper straps (F) at an acute angle.

ENERGIZER PYRAMID

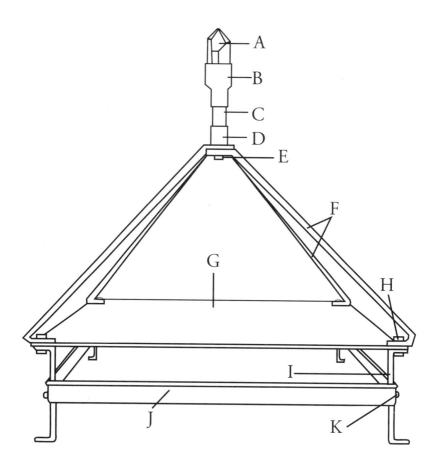

4. Insert a bolt through the hole of the bent end of the 11" strap, one corner of the copper sheet, and one end of one of the legs. Fasten with a nut. Repeat for all four corners.

5. Bolt the leg frame supports to each of the legs. (They will overlap more than shown in the diagram.)

6. Put a bolt (E) through the copper cap and the loose end of each of the 11" straps to form a pyramid. Fasten with a nut. For clarity, the diagram shows the copper straps as square but the wide part will actually face the center of the copper sheet.

7. Insert the copper pipe (C) into the copper cap. Fit the small end of the reducer with the crystal (A and B) over the pipe. These pieces can be glued in place, or just fitted on if you want to be able to remove them for use on other devices. If you glue them, squeeze glue around the inside of the copper cap and the reducer. When you push the copper pipe into each of these pieces, it will spread the glue and prevent leakage.

COPPER WIRE PYRAMID

It's been noticed by practitioners in the pyramid field that pyramid shapes in both two- and three-dimensional forms tend to accumulate and radiate energy. The copper wire pyramid shown here provides an easy-to-build pyramid for your experiments. It can be used for charging crystals, manifesting wishes, or other experiments in this chapter that are appropriate for its size.

Constructing the Copper Wire Pyramid

Materials:

A. 2" x 6" block of pine, cut into a 5½" square; can be stained, oiled, or finished

B. 4 copper nails or thin copper tubing, 3½" long, ³⁄₁₆" to ¼" diameter

C. Copper nail, 6" long, or thin copper tubing

D. Small gauge bare copper wire

COPPER WIRE PYRAMID

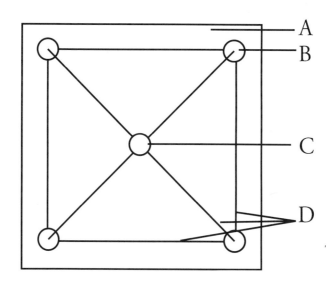

TOP VIEW

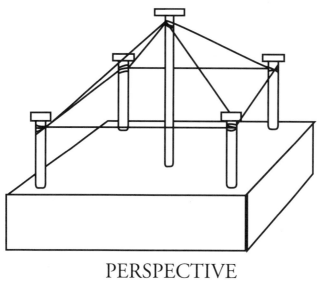

PERSPECTIVE

Construction:

1. Drill holes a little smaller than the short nails (B) ½" in from each corner of the wooden block. Drill another hole slightly smaller than the large nail (C) in the center of the block. Pound the nails (or tubing) into the block until they're secure.

2. Wrap wire around each of the outside nails, and from each corner to the center until you have two or three thicknesses of wire. (Chances are you'll have 2 thicknesses in some places and three thicknesses in others if you use a single strand of wire.)

CRYSTAL PYRAMID CAP

We believe the pyramid cap, used to complete and operate the giant stone pyramids around the Earth, was one of the most important secrets of the ancient pyramid builders. The pyramid cap shown here works as a unit by itself or acts as a super energy accumulator and amplifier when placed on a larger pyramid. It can be used as a room energizer, put in the center of a ceremonial circle, placed over or under chairs and beds to heighten energy or inspiration, and small objects can be placed within it.

Constructing the Crystal Pyramid Cap

Materials:

A. Quartz crystal, about ½" diameter, shim material for crystal (leather, copper mesh, copper tape), and glue if crystal is to be mounted permanently

B. Copper cap, ½" diameter

C. Small bolt, 1" long, and solder

D. Four sturdy copper sheets cut in triangles with 6" base, 5⅞" sides, and 5" height

E. 4 copper straps, 2" long, about ½" wide, and 8 copper rivets or small bolts

PYRAMID CAP

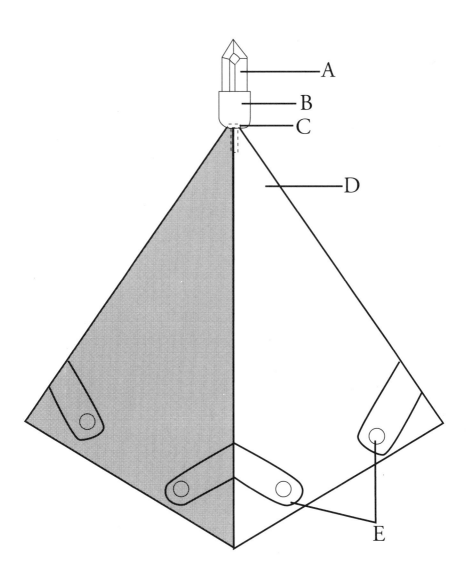

Construction:

1. Drill a hole large enough to accommodate your bolt in the bottom of the copper cap. Stick the bolt down through the copper cap with the end sticking out of the bottom.

2. Cut four triangles out of a copper sheet, with bases of 6", height of 5", and sides of 5⅞". *Note:* If you measure out the base and height, the sides will automatically be 5⅞" long.

3. Cut off the tip of each triangle so that when the four pieces are put together there will be a hole big enough for the bolt.

4. Drill two holes in each of the copper straps, then bend them to hold the sides of the pyramid together as shown in the diagram (E). Drill eight holes in the triangular pieces to match and fasten the straps on with the copper rivets or bolts.

5. Take the copper cap with its protruding bolt and stick it into the top of the pyramid. When you're sure it's in straight, solder it in place.

6. Wrap the base of the crystal in shim material, if necessary, and fit the crystal into the copper cap. If the mounting is to be permanent, squeeze glue down onto the shim material to hold the crystal securely in place.

PART FOUR

Crystal Shaman

A shaman, as the authors define it, is a spiritually-oriented seeker of truth who goes beyond the realm of common knowledge to gain wisdom and help others. Although different cultures and religions have specific requirements for the shaman, we believe that we are our own best shamans. We don't need priests or miracle workers to tell us what to do or believe. What we really need is to discover the truth, whatever that may be, for ourselves.

Most of us have wasted time thinking someone else had all the answers, when all along they were within us. In order to evolve we must take responsibility for ourselves, for it's only by realizing that we are in charge of our own lives that we can change them for the better.

Do you automatically accept the dictates of so-called experts (including the authors of this book), or do you search within yourself to see if their ideas are your truth? If we each create our own reality, as the authors believe, then our truth may not be yours. That's why it's important for you to follow your own intuition in the experiments and projects we provide. The real knowledge and wisdom lies within each of you, and our only goal is to share what we've learned in the hope that it will provide a springboard for your own inspiration. We strongly believe that it is within the abilities of all of our readers to be shamans.

In this section we've provided some of the tools, ceremonies, and methods various shamans, wise people, healers, etc., use to help themselves and others. It takes hard work, practice, and dedication to gain wisdom, and we hope that some of the material we present will help you along that road.

We also hope that you'll keep your mind open to possibilities you may not have considered before. That quality of open-mindedness is essential to growth and wisdom. A friend, who was in the Southwest visiting a Hopi shaman, told us a story that illustrates our point. Our friend noticed the shaman was using a quartz crystal in his sacred circle. He was surprised, and asked the wise man if crystals were traditionally used in Hopi rituals. The shaman said, "Heck no. I read about crystals in a book and found out these suckers really work." That story got a chuckle out of us, but we applauded the shaman's wisdom in realizing that there's always something more to be learned. This realization allowed him to adapt and use new knowledge to enhance and revitalize his traditions. Perhaps something you read here will allow you to do the same.

NINETEEN

Crystal Channels

All music, song, and dance, is, by its nature, channeled.

You may have been awed by people who seem to be able to channel information from a higher source, and maybe you've sought out these gurus to help you with your own life. There's no denying that some of the channeled information in circulation comes from a higher source, but why depend on someone else to get it for you? Each one of us has the ability to tap into our higher selves to get our own information. It's actually one of the easiest forms of so-called occult practices, and doesn't take any particular psychic ability. All channeling does take is the willingness to believe that your connection to the creator is as good or better than someone else's.

There's a part of each of us that lives purely in the spiritual realm; the authors refer to it as our higher self. Some people don't feel comfortable taking that much responsibility, and credit the information to a guardian angel, guiding spirit, ghosts, or beings in another dimension. It doesn't really matter where we think the information comes from, except that when we place it on causes outside ourselves, we face the possibility of retarding our growth by depending on others for wisdom. We don't deny that information could come from any of those sources, and have even channeled information from different entities, but the information that is most dependable comes from our own higher selves.

Another point to remember when channeling is that any information we receive has to come through what we call our own personal computer, which is a combination of our minds, beliefs, and egos. It's possible for our computer to distort information, so like any other source of information, it should be taken with a grain of salt. For instance, if you channel instructions to sell all your worldly goods and move to the top of a mountain to await the end of the world, or find out that aliens will be attacking tomorrow, the chances are pretty good that you're distorting or your information isn't coming from a higher source. For one thing, the future is never entirely predictable because we all have free will. Your future may be heading in a direction where a certain outcome is likely, but you can always change that direction and change the future.

Another good reality check for your channeling is time. Time doesn't exist as a reality in the spiritual realm. If you channel that you're going to meet your true love or get a raise soon, don't hold your breath because soon to your higher self may be years down the road, and in that time you may be heading in an entirely different direction. In short, although trying to predict the future is irresistible for most of us, it's the area that's least likely to be accurate.

That's not to say that information about the future is necessarily wrong. Lin channeled not only that Michael and she would meet and marry, but the actual date and the fact that they would do spiritual work together. She also saw him in a dream before they met. The whole scenario seemed so implausible at the time that she discounted it until it actually happened. On the other hand, while none of her subsequent predictions have been proved wrong, they certainly haven't happened as quickly as her channelings indicated. Perhaps they never will happen, as her life and goals change. It's possible that some events in our lives are more or less inevitable, because we planned them before we were born as part of this particular life journey. Other events aren't crucial to our personal missions and are probably decided on a day to day basis by our choices in life.

On the other hand, if you channel information on spiritual questions, particularly if you don't have a preconceived idea of what the answer should be, chances are you're going to find out some interesting things that make a lot of sense. We've found that often our answers run counter to our beliefs, but they always have the ring of truth.

The most accurate type of personal information to channel is the answers to questions such as, "How can I improve my chances for a promotion? ... How do I get along better with my mate? ... What do I need to know to help me deal with a stressful situation? ... Is a certain path right for me?" Chances are when you channel the answers to those kinds of questions, you'll be able to see the truth in them right away, even when they're not what you wanted to hear. Lin proved this for herself in the following example.

Before I met Michael, I channeled that my relationship with another man was over, and that I'd soon be telling people that the breakup was the best thing that ever happened to me. Although I recognized that the relationship was wrong for me, I didn't want to believe it. After a painfully prolonged parting, I met and married Michael. At that point I realized that, sure enough, the breakup of the former relationship was the best thing that had ever happened to me. Had I kept an open mind and trusted my higher self, I could have saved myself some grief.

THEORY OF CRYSTAL CHANNELING

When we channel with crystals, we use the energy information lines that connect everything in the Universe. We all channel information, with and without crystals, unconsciously on a daily basis. But what we commonly refer to as channeling is usually done consciously.

Crystals augment and amplify this natural energy-based data transmission and reception. They are the radios and televisions of the Universe and the Earth Mother's planetary computer. They function as memory chips, capacitors, transducers, amplifiers, transmitters, and receivers. Energy is produced at the Universal power station and transmitted through the lines of force to our minds. The energy is produced by Universal Intelligence, of which we are a part, and transmitted for the creation and re-creation of ourselves and all things in existence. People and crystals function as substations, transformers, and outlets for the growth of an ever-expanding Universe. Channeling is like wiring new outlets that tap into the main power lines. Our minds become outlets for the energy and information that already exists.

It's not, and never has been, necessary for people or crystals to try to transmit power back to the source. The power from the Universal power station is in unlimited supply. It flows, like electricity, from the higher to the lower, ever outward, through people, crystals, and other created forms. Attempts to transmit energy back to the Source are going against the flow. This causes shorts or openings in the power lines, blocking or interrupting the smooth flow of energy. In other words, we get inaccurate information if we try to impose our beliefs or egos on what's being transmitted.

The flow of energy from the Source and through crystals always seeks to balance itself harmoniously. Like the poles of a battery or magnet, both the positive and the negative poles are necessary to complete the circuit. This balance of male and female, or yin and yang, produces a harmonious energy field that radiates as a circle or sphere of energy. Universal Energy creates new forms and remains connected to the new creations. It then continues to power the new forms it has created.

Many human expressions such as song, dance, and art are channeled. They always have been, we just haven't used that term. Many other life experiences—perhaps all of them—also involve the channeling of energy and information. A channel, or medium of expression, has always been required for Universal Energy to manifest the physical reality we see. Our reality is just Universal Energy manifesting as form within an electromagnetic field.

The true nature of the Universe is channeled energy, which manifests through an infinite variety of mediums. The mediums include all physical forms, sentient or not: atoms, rocks, plants, insects, animals, people, planets, stars, etc. Some people like to make channeling mysterious. While it is special, significant, and sacred because it's everywhere and everything, it's not particularly mysterious. An inspirational work like the Bible is channeled, but so is the idea for an electric can opener, a television, disc brakes, and a political doctrine. If you exist, you're channeling energy in one form or another. It's all that exists. It's all that is.

How to Channel with Crystals

Although crystals aren't necessary for channeling, we think that they help us focus and clarify communications. Even when we don't actually pick up and hold a crystal or crystal tool while channeling, the authors always make sure that there are plenty of crystals nearby, which isn't difficult since we wear them, carry them with us, and decorate with them.

What is necessary for a successful channeling is the willingness to set aside disbelief and let the information come through without judgment. That should be easy if you think of it as an experiment. If the material is valuable to you, use it; if it's not, ignore it, much as you would use or ignore what you read or hear in the process of living. You're always in control of the things that affect your life.

Channeling is a lot safer than asking advice from others or having psychic experiences because you can tell yourself to filter out anything negative, or information that you can't handle emotionally. Once you give your mind that direction, it automatically selects what comes through. Also, keep in mind that the higher portion of your consciousness, or your higher self, is as protective of your well-being as you are. After all, it's a part of you. It will tell you what you need to know in the kindest way possible.

Since we outlined how to do a written channeling in an earlier section on recalling past lives, we'll use a tape recorder for this one, although either technique can be used. First, you need to get comfortable and relaxed. Pick up a crystal or crystal tool, then take a few deep breaths or use a short meditation if you like. It's not necessary to put yourself into a trance or hypnotic state. Channeling works best if you think of it as a natural process that doesn't take a lot of ceremony or preparation.

Turn on your tape recorder and get the process started either by asking a question or just saying, "Hello, higher self." After that, all you have to do is repeat whatever thought comes into your head into the recorder. Even if your answer is something like "I feel really stupid doing this," go ahead and record it. If you persist in asking questions and recording whatever answers come into your head, eventually you'll get comfortable enough with the process that the answers will become more relevant.

The worst that can happen is that you'll have a nice conversation with yourself. It's okay if that's what you think you're doing, because in a way that's what's really happening since your higher self is a part of you. Chances are, when you listen to your tape later, you'll find out that you told yourself some things that were relevant and probably of a higher spiritual quality than you knew you possessed.

When Lin first began channeling, she didn't want to go overboard about the phenomena. Although the information she was getting seemed to be of a very high quality, she thought maybe it came from things buried in her subconscious. The following experience convinced her that she was wrong.

A musical friend and I were discussing channeling and, to prove my point, I said that I could never channel something like a song because I just didn't have the technical knowledge to write it down, even if one miraculously came to me.

That night, an original melody started running through my head. That had never happened before and I wondered, "Is the Universe trying to tell me something?" Although I don't play the piano, I borrowed my roommate's and was able to pick out the melody by ear and write the notes down on a scored page. It was so pretty that I decided I should write words for it. That part wasn't difficult, since I often write poetry, but after that I was stumped. I just didn't know enough about chords and note values to go any further with my experiment. But I told myself, "You never thought you'd get this far, why don't you see what you can do? Maybe it is possible to channel something beyond the realm of our knowledge."

It took a long time, but hours later, by using the piano to match the sounds in my head, I'd written eight-part chords and assigned time values to my notes. Unfortunately, I couldn't play the song so I didn't know if it would sound like what I was hearing. My roommate came home about that time and offered to play it for me. I was truly astonished when it sounded just like what I'd heard, and began to revise my opinion of what could and couldn't be channeled. Later, my roommate wrote a piano accompaniment for me, and a friend sang the song at a large Christmas gathering. It got a standing ovation. So much for my original theory.

That story just goes to show that we shouldn't put limits on our ability to channel knowledge. The authors still don't try to do much second-guessing about where channeled knowledge comes from, but we do know that we're all much more than we seem and that a loving force in the Universe wants to help us.

Although we've never known it to happen, a person with a negative outlook could, presumably, get messages that are negative or hostile.

Negative messages would indicate that the channeler's personal computer is interfering with the process, because the nature of the spiritual realm is that it's loving and non-judgmental. If your channeled answers are negative, stop and concentrate on surrounding yourself and your crystal with love and white light. Work on loving yourself first, and then expand that aura of love out into the Universe. When you're ready, start recording your questions and answers again, or just wait until you're in a better mood.

Below, we've reprinted some of Lin's channelings. Your answers to the same questions may be very different. When we've channeled with a group, the answers were compatible but each channeling focused on different aspects of the question.

A CHANNELING

Q: Why am I here on Earth?

A: Why not? It is the journey back to the Source that is the fun part, not the goal. For you have accomplished this goal many times before, and yet you choose to do so again and again, in many different ways. Your spirit is a restless, inquiring one. Why not just accept that fact and enjoy it? You cling so hard to each experience, as if it might be your last. Experience is as infinite as you are. You know this, but your ego doesn't. Let the divine you do the knowing.

Q: What is a master?

A: A master is one whose mind is open to the universe. He then cannot help but share his thoughts with his fellow people. The true master always tries to tell others that they, too, are masters, but it is only rarely that they listen.

Q: What is love?

A: Love is something you find inside yourself, not something that comes from another. Stop worrying about whether you are loved and start loving. If you love unconditionally, it need not be painful. Just love—yourself and others.

Q: What is a mission?

A: A mission is a project undertaken as a focus for a particular life-
     time. It includes some element to further your personal evolu-
     tion, and may or may not include elements to help others in their
     growth.

Q: Does it change during a lifetime?

A: Not in essentials, but it can change in details.

Q: What's the difference between experience and a lesson?

A: Experience is what happens to you. A lesson is what you do with
     or learn from the experience.

*Few of those seeking spiritual knowledge lead serene, untroubled lives,
and sometimes it's necessary to get a view of the larger picture to understand
what's happening in our world and in our lives.*

Q: What is negativity?

A: It is any ego-based consciousness not born of love. There is much
     of this in your world today. It is standard and acceptable for
     beings at your stage of development. When you choose to fall
     away from the Source as physical expressions, it is part of the
     price you must pay. But the joy when one raises oneself inch by
     painful inch into the light of oneness makes it all worthwhile,
     and many choose to do this again and again. It is the striving and
     gaining, the sorrow and then joy, the climbing out of darkness
     into the light that makes this course so attractive to some of you.
     The creative possibilities are endless, each journey a new canvas
     to be painted into perfection.

     There is no shame in this falling away; it is all a part of the per-
     fection of creation. Cycles within cycles, repeating with never a
     single duplication. Others choose different degrees of falling away
     and different roads back to perfection. Some cannot bear to lose
     their knowledge of oneness and so never choose a physical expres-
     sion. But they still feel the need for creation, and send parts of
     themselves out to express as physical beings with free will. They
     then oversee the results of their creation. There are also those who

oversee the overseers. Life includes endless cycles of breaking away from the Source and rejoining that all participate in. The illusion is the separation, but the reality is oneness.

Q: Why do we have egos?

A: Remember, your ego reacts always to keep you on the course you tell it you have chosen to follow. Too often the ego is portrayed as a selfish, grasping thing that keeps you from your goals, but that is not the case. When the ego is programmed to seek those things which are of a higher order, then that is what is found. It is only when it is programmed with base or hurtful needs that negative results are achieved. Remember to program the real needs of your divine self in the ego and it will be your friend. The ego in itself is simply a tool for achieving your ends and should be perceived as such. Like any other tool, use it properly and it will benefit you.

Sometimes, our group channeling assignments would lead to new assignments for all of us.

Q: Why don't people laugh more, since it's so healing?

A: If your perception is that people don't laugh enough, then it is probably because you yourself don't feel that you laugh enough. It is not a question of whether people are laughing or not, but your selective perception of the phenomenon of laughter. You will notice that when you are happy, you look out on a world that is filled with love and joy. The reverse is also true. What you are perceiving in the world is only a reflection of your inner thoughts and feelings. If you want to check your inner mental state, this is an excellent way to do so. Look around you. Are people happy or sad? Are they rich or poor? Is the world full of peace or violence, love or strife? What you answer to these questions is the best indicator of your mental state on any given day. Frequently, this will change from day to day, and this lets you know that what you are seeing is a reflection only of your changing moods.

If, however, you always see a world of poverty or where violence is rampant, then you know that you are dealing with a core belief.

In order to change this belief, if you wish to do so, you must first change your perception. If violence has been your experience, try to notice all the loving acts you see around you. At some point you will notice that the world has miraculously changed from a place of violence to one of love.

To prove my point, I have an assignment for you. In the coming week, pick something that you typically perceive to be true and focus on its opposite. Make a point of really noticing the opposite, and also involve your emotions and feelings in this experience. At the end of seven days, examine how you now feel about both your original perception and its opposite. Has your perception changed? If it hasn't, pick another perception that is less emotionally charged for you and repeat the experiment. You will, perhaps, be surprised at the results. Good luck and happy experimenting. Have fun with this.

Often our questions involved where we come from and why we're here. The following is an interesting explanation of why metaphysical people say all is one and yet we seem to be separate.

Q: Why did we split off from the Source?

A: At the Source, as well as for all aspects of life, it is necessary for growth and change to take place. Without growth and change life would soon die out. Therefore, the Source must continually throw off fragments of itself to develop on their own. These fragments, in turn, throw off fragments so as to form a complete experience of whatever aspects of life have been chosen. When these scattered fragments and aspects eventually rejoin with each other and with the Source, the Source experiences growth. Thus life is an expanding creative process that is never-ending. How could it be otherwise?

Eventually your higher self may develop a distinct personality or way of speaking. For instance, my higher self is called David and often addresses me as "my dear." Just to make sure it was really my higher self that I was communicating with, I asked a few questions.

Q: Who are you?

A: Why, I am you, of course—one of your many aspects. I have chosen to help you and others along the way, on my path to reunion with the Source.

Q: Your expression feels very male to me. Why not female?

A: You always related well to father figures, so I chose a male role. Besides, that's the personality I like to wear when I'm teaching. You humans tend to listen more closely to a man.

Q: Tell me what it's like for you, wherever you are.

A: It is very pleasant. I have many interesting beings that I communicate with. Perhaps it's a little dull compared to the rigors of physical life, but very nice. My work is important to me, not only because it promotes my own spiritual growth, but because I find it stimulating.

Q: Have you had a physical life on Earth?

A: Yes. Many.

Q: Did I ever know you as a human being?

A: No. You are a lower vibrational aspect of mine. We have, however, had some lifetimes when we were the same person.

Q: Did we share a lifetime when you looked like the portrait Lois East drew of you? (Lois East is a friend and artist who channeled the portrait.)

A: As a matter of fact, we did have a rather similar aspect during the time of Biblical history.

Q: New or Old Testament?

A: New. We lived in a little village by the Sea of Galilee at the time. We were a fisherman and had a wife named Martha, as well as a son, a daughter, an ass, a boat, etc.

Q: What was significant about that lifetime?

A: Many things. For instance, we were not the benign person in your picture. We drank excessively and beat Martha and the children, David and Ruth. We were very poor, both spiritually and materially.

One day when we were working on our boat, a man and his disciples came through our town. The man said that he, too, was a fisherman in the seas of life. A brilliant light surrounded him, and our hates and fears disappeared in that light as if they had never been. We were invited to join the man, but declined. Our mission was to remain in that small town.

After that, we gave up drink and tried to spread light to those around us. We died some years later, when our mission was accomplished, in a violent storm at sea. Our growth was rapid in that lifetime.

Q: Could one at your level, which I assume is considerably higher than mine, be born as a human?

A: It is possible, although not likely. Once a spirit has progressed beyond the realm of the physical, it would be of no benefit to go back to that phase.

Q: What do you do at your level?

A: That is a difficult question to answer in terms you can relate to. You might say I oversee and assist.

Q: Do you just oversee and assist humans?

A: Yes. That is my job, as you might call it.

Q: How long do you do that?

A: Until I am ready to move on.

Q: How many humans do you oversee and assist?

A: Eight. That is the number of fragments I have created.

Q: Did you create me?

A: Yes, although in a sense you created yourself, too.

Q: Have you been overseeing and assisting me since my first physical life?

A: And before that.

Q: What was before that?

A: Consciousness.

All in all, you may find that doing crystal channeling will help you clarify your vision of yourself and your world. Use it as you would any other tool, with love and balance, and it will speed your journey into the wisdom of the shaman.

TWENTY

One-Minute
Crystal Healer

*When we use Universal Crystal tools, we're not only
connected or related to all things, we are all things.*

W hat can we do with a crystal or a crystal rod in one minute—
sixty short seconds? Although shamans spend much of their time on spiritual work, an amazing amount can be accomplished throughout the
course of a busy day in the space of a minute or less.

A minute doesn't sound like a long time, but in the world of faster-
than-light thought transmission, it can be an eternity. And visualization
with a crystal, using the Ki or Chi life force energy, is instantaneous, turning sixty seconds into plenty of time to accomplish a healing.

The Universe is a mind visualization where all things and beings are
connected. It provides instantaneous information communication, and
we can use this capacity to reach anywhere in the Universe with our
awareness. Visualizations with a crystal or crystal tool are immediate, with
no time span required for the reception of the mind picture.

Michael likes to use a crystal rod for his one-minute healings. You
may find other crystal tools, or just a plain crystal that you prefer.

My favorite rod is a half-inch in diameter and four and a half inches long. It has a double termination quartz crystal (chipped and cracked, by the way) on one end of a copper-capped tube. The tube is loaded with pieces of magnetic lodestone and wrapped with black leather, while the crystal, in a half-inch copper coupling, is left unwrapped. This small rod is just the right size to grip in either hand while holding my index finger around the crystal and my thumb on one of the larger facets. The grip is easy for me to use while sitting, standing, driving, or walking, and works for receiving energy or radiating a balanced energy field or aura. I also use this grip for self-healing at times when I don't need to project a beam of energy.

When I'm driving or riding in a car, my grip on the rod produces a white-light energy field of balance around myself and the vehicle. Positive thoughts and feelings of connectedness amplify the energy field, while an attitude of receptiveness produces the flow of energy to accomplish my healing.

When I want to project a beam of Universal Energy rather than create an aura or field, I change the grip by pulling back my thumb and index finger to expose the quartz crystal. In a matter of seconds, a beam of white-light energy can be projected to a reckless driver two car lengths away or to a war area halfway around the world.

In the same few seconds, healing energy can be sent to a passenger sitting next to me who is suffering from a headache; or a beam of particle energy can be projected to hold traffic lights on green or yellow, for a faster trip across town.

The one-minute crystal rod healing can also be done at home, in the garden or in the yard, just as quickly and easily. In less than a minute, I can send healing energy to a friend or family member who is suffering from a head cold. Or I can project the energy to an injured pet or a houseplant that seems to be ailing. All this can be done in seconds and is a wonderful way to improve the balance of energy on the planet.

OTHER ONE-MINUTE USES FOR CRYSTALS

Our experiments frequently call for clear quartz crystals. That's just a general guideline. Actually, a one-minute healing can be done using single or double termination crystals, or even clusters. Crystals can be cloudy, smoky, rose quartz, amethyst, or citrine, and need not be clear or perfect in order to work. Use the crystals or crystal tools in either the right or left hand for receiving or transmitting.

PERSONAL, PLANETARY, OR UNIVERSAL USES FOR CRYSTALS

If you use crystals to move Universal Energy for balancing and healing frequently, you are living more and more in oneness with the spirit, and are healing yourself at the same time. The one-minute crystal healer seeks to show how fast and easily you can become one with the creative energy of the Universe. Your inner awareness grows with each instant you spend healing and balancing. This, in turn, affects healing and balance on the planetary Earth Mother, and the spiritual energy also radiates throughout the solar system, the galaxy, and the Universe. One simple act of love and energy toward a plant in the garden enriches the quality of life in the whole Universe.

When you do a healing, you also get to benefit. What you send out as a one-minute crystal healer, returns to you multiplied hundreds of times over. While healing others, you too are healed.

Knowing our oneness with the Universal for even one minute a day makes a difference in the amount of good energy flowing around the Earth. It doesn't matter if we send the energy or receive it ourselves. In fact, we can produce healing energy by just sitting for a minute and holding a crystal or crystal tool. The very act of looking at the beauty of a crystal, or touching one, can form a field of beneficial energy.

We call the one-minute crystal healing the "fast food" of the crystal world. Many times, in our modern world, we can't or won't take the hour, half hour, or fifteen minutes for meditation or affirmation that some spiritual practices ask for. A minute of time can usually be found by even the busiest people during a hectic day. That one minute can be the one that makes a difference.

ONE-MINUTE CRYSTAL HEALING TOOLS

Although any crystal or crystal tool can be used for healing, the most convenient of these are:

1. Crystals or crystal clusters

2. Pocket or purse-sized crystal rods

3. Crystal jewelry, such as pendants, ankle bracelets, necklaces, earrings, rings, bracelets, pins, and tie tacks

4. Crystal wrist bands and headbands made of cloth

5. Ankle wallets with crystals or healing stones

6. Car crystals and healing stones

7. Crystal pendulums

All of these are easy to carry and use. The crystals, clusters, crystal rods, and jewelry are familiar items to most of us. Crystal and healing-stone wristbands, cloth headbands, and ankle wallets make it easy for joggers, hikers, bikers, dancers, and health club enthusiasts to combine spiritual practice with exercise. We've included a diagram for a sports wristband you can make yourself.

Crystals can also be stored or carried in sports accessories that you can buy. Ankle wallets are frequently found in small mail-order gift catalogues. Manufactured wristbands with or without zippered pockets are usually available in sports or sporting goods stores that cater to runners. For those of you who sew, you can make your own head and wristbands.

ONE-MINUTE HEALING PRACTICES

There are many ways you can use a minute to do a healing. We've listed some of them below. Try the ones that appeal to you, and perhaps you can come up with others of your own.

SPORTS WRIST BANDS
WITH QUARTZ CRYSTALS
IN POCKETS

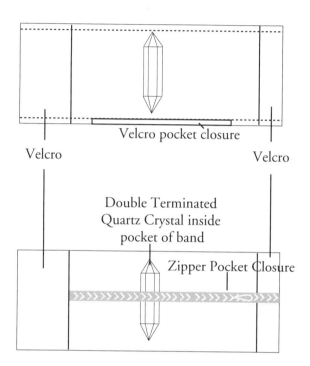

Velcro pocket closure

Velcro   Velcro

Double Terminated
Quartz Crystal inside
pocket of band

Zipper Pocket Closure

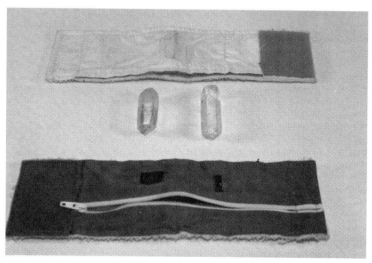

Healing Yourself

1. Sit quietly for a minute, feeling the peaceful energy from your crystal energize your aura while being at one with all.

2. Visualize the energy beam from your crystal pouring healing energy into any area of your body that might need balance.

3. While you're exercising, imagine the Universal Energy flowing through you and surrounding you in an energetic healing aura.

4. Hold your crystal in either hand and receive the energy information you need for guidance or the answer to a question.

Healing Plants

1. Point your crystal or crystal rod at a plant and visualize a beam of blue-white energy flowing down through the soil and roots, then up through the stalk, branches, leaves, and flowers. Imagine yourself as the plant and feel it experiencing the energy.

2. Visualize the beam of energy from your crystal spreading out to form a large sphere of white light surrounding the entire yard or garden for growth and vitality. Experience love, peace, and oneness with the Earth while you're doing the healing.

Healing the Earth

1. Visualize the crystal energy spreading out to form a sphere or aura of good energy surrounding the Earth. Everything within that aura experiences balance and healing.

2. Imagine the beam of energy from the point of your crystal flowing across or through the earth to a specific area that needs help, while projecting love and a sense of oneness.

3. Send the beam of energy to a person who is making an environmental decision—see it helping the Earth.

HEALING AN ANIMAL

1. Visualize the beam of energy surrounding the animal and balancing its energy field. Experience your kinship with the animal's love of life and will to live.

2. Imagine the beam of energy flowing into a specific afflicted area in the animal. Know that the love energy is balancing and removing blockages to restore or promote good health.

HEALING ANOTHER PERSON

1. If the person is troubled or unhappy, experience unconditional love while you visualize energy flowing through the crystal to the person's aura, from near or far away. Concentrate on projecting a healing balance and sensation of well-being.

2. For a person with a specific ailment, visualize the beam of energy pouring into the affected area, clearing blockages to restore balance and good health. In addition, imagine the energy flowing into the person's head and heart area to heal negative thoughts and emotions that might have caused the imbalance.

Something happens for a minute while we're using crystals and crystal tools. It happens for even longer periods when we're building and creating crystal devices. The "something" that happens is within ourselves. That "something" is awareness. Our awareness isn't the result of meditation or philosophical practice. It isn't the result of creative visualization or the mental gymnastics we do with our thoughts. Whatever it is, it happens when we're working with crystals. It's more than just an awareness of what's around us or an awareness of ourselves. It goes deeper than that, to the experience of being one with all other physical and nonphysical forms. Once we have that awareness, there's nothing we can't accomplish or create for the good of ourselves and others.

TWENTY-ONE

Healing Rods

We see and feel the Spirit in our physical world.
Perhaps next, we'll experience Spirit directly.

Healing plays a large part in the path of the shaman. When we think of healing, we often link it to healthy bodies, but healing is actually a catch-all term that includes many different activities. For instance, in order to project healing energy, it's often necessary for the shaman to first heal himself or herself. Then there's the question of exactly what needs to be healed. As we know, healing the body is ineffective if we don't first take care of the underlying problem that causes the dis-ease. Otherwise the person will just find another way to manifest his or her inner discomfort. So we must also deal with mental, spiritual, and emotional problems along with physical symptoms.

Also, there is the fact that some people who ask for help don't really want to be healed. Sometimes, perhaps, the physical ailment is easier to live with than the thought of dealing with its cause. Maybe the person believes that a hatred, resentment, or another negative emotion is all that sustains him or her. That's not true, but there's not much the shaman can do in the face of free will.

However, many people are truly seeking the light and are desperately looking for help in their quest. It's the shaman's job to share what he or she has learned in order to help these people. The healing rods are an excellent tool for doing that, as are plain crystals. In fact, sometimes the shaman can help people heal themselves without doing much at all.

A few years ago, our friend Jerry gave a crystal to his brother, who was a terrible hypochondriac, unhappy, and negative. His hypochondria was aggravated by the fact that he had some real health problems. Jerry would have liked to use a healing rod on his brother, but knew he wouldn't respond well to the idea.

At various intervals over the space of five years, Jerry gave his brother a few more crystals, rocks, and a healing rod, along with snippets of spiritual information when they seemed appropriate. During that time his brother became noticeably more positive, but still held on to his hypochondriac tendencies.

Recently, at a family gathering, Jerry was amazed to hear his brother proclaim that he'd been doing some reading and had decided to heal himself. For the first time in his life, his brother appeared to be happy, in charge of his life, and focused on something other than the state of his health. It wasn't until later that Jerry began to wonder if the crystals, rocks, and wand he'd given his brother over the years had started the process that culminated in his metamorphosis. At that same gathering, Jerry also realized that his other relatives, who had been receiving crystals or crystal rods from him over the years, had changed for the better, too. He said he believed the changes in his family had started when he gave them the crystals or crystal rods and their own evolving spirituality had accomplished the rest. It proved to him that people really were capable of changing and inspired him to continue his healing work.

Another friend, Sara, told us she'd given a healing rod to her sister, Peg, on an impulse about a year ago. Peg never mentioned the rod, and Sara, knowing that her sister's lifestyle didn't include crystals, imagined the rod was gathering dust in a closet somewhere. Recently, she was astonished when Peg called and told her that ever since Sara had given her the rod, her job, relationships, and zest for life had been improving. In fact, she said that her whole life had turned around since that time. Sara told us that she was pleased that the rod had worked so well, but what really threw her for a loop was that her sister realized and admitted that the rod had been responsible.

As shamans, we have to do the best we can to help people, and we don't necessarily know if we've been effective. Sometimes it's amazing to find out how truly effective our efforts are.

Many new crystal rods and other devices for healing are being built around the world. Despite numerous modifications, they all seem to work. As we've seen from the stories above, they often work in unexpected ways. Stories like these demonstrate that we shouldn't be rigid in our perception of crystal tools. Our intuition will not only guide us to build the right tool, but it will tell us the right way to construct it and how to use it. In wrapping the rods, leather, yarn, cloth, plastic tape, shrink tubing, etc., have been used successfully.

The length and diameter of the rods has varied from pencil size to seven-foot models. They've been made with tiny crystals as well as very large ones. All types of quartz crystals have been used—clear, cloudy, smoky, amethyst, citrine—in all shapes, sizes, and conditions. All of the rods worked for the people who built them. The key has always been our consciousness of ourselves as light beings and co-creators. Spiritual expression is working wonders in our world each and every day, and given some general information and the help of crystals, we have the ability to work our own wonders.

HOW HEALING RODS WORK
AND HOW TO USE THEM

Healing rods can be large, medium, or small, but they all work the same way. A beam of energy—subatomic particles, usually outside the range of the human eye's spectrum, but sometimes seen as a blue-white beam—is projected from the point of the crystal at the outer end of the rod.

This beam of energy is visualized and thought of first by the operator-healer. Energy follows thought, causing the subatomic particles of Universal Energy to instantly move in place of the visualized beam. At the same time, the crystal at the inner end of the healing rod, pointing toward the operator-healer, is emitting a field of energy that merges with the healer's aura or bioelectromagnetic field.

PERFORMING A HEALING

Before you start your healing, you can focus and increase your own energy by creating a baseball-sized sun or sphere of energy in front of you. Cup your hands to form and shape the ball of energy, while feeling it grow stronger in pressure. This method of starting the energy flow through the hands will augment the flow through the energy rod and crystal.

After the energy flow is started, pick up the rod in the hand that feels most comfortable. You may want to outline a circle of energy around the subject with the crystal that points outward. This can be done from one to twelve times, starting at the top of the subject's head and moving in a clockwise circle.

At the same time, begin to feel unconditional love for and oneness with the subject. The healer's emotion determines the degree, force, or amplification of the energy flowing from the crystal healing rod.

Starting at the top of the subject's head, slowly bring the rod downward about six inches away from the body. Use your free hand to feel the energy by following the motion of the rod at about six inches from both the rod and the subject's body.

Continue moving the rod and hand downward to the neck and shoulders, along the arms and hands, back up to the neck, down the length of the body and legs, then back up the body. All this time, usually five to fifteen minutes, your open hand is feeling the flow of energy. You may feel warm or hot spots in certain areas. The heat usually indicates a blockage of energy. You can then direct the beam of energy from the rod to the hot spot. After a few minutes, the hot spot usually turns cool, indicating that enough energy has been channeled into the area. If the area is a serious injury in the process of healing itself, it may not change from hot to cool.

After energy blockages in the body have been dealt with and balanced, return with rod and open hand to the subject's head. If there were warm areas of the body, there will usually be warm areas of the head. The subject's mind, thoughts, and feelings reflect or express themselves in the body so that re-energizing and balancing the head area is necessary for an effective and permanent cure. Areas of discomfort, denoted by hot spots or energy blockages, are usually the symptoms, but the cause can usually be traced back to the head area: mind, thoughts, and spirit.

Another area that frequently causes physical symptoms is the heart area. The heart carries negative emotions and the inability to express love for others, which also means an inability to accept and love one's self. Work on that area for as long as you think it's necessary before ending your healing by an upward swoop of the rod and hand to leave the energy flowing in an upward direction.

After the energy balancing of the subject is completed, it's a good idea to return the flow of energy from your hands to a normal flow or balance. There are two commonly used techniques for doing this. One is to clench the fists tightly and release them simultaneously in a sharp movement. The other is to relax the hands and wrists while shaking them rapidly a few times to release the excess energy.

Use the practices and techniques described here as suggestions and guidelines. As you work you can develop and modify these procedures through your own personal experience.

Constructing a Healing Rod

We've included some basic construction techniques below that will help you build any of the healing rod variations offered in this chapter and elsewhere in the book.

1. Before gluing anything, assemble most of the rod first to make sure the pieces line up correctly and fit together easily. Then use instant bonding glue to hold the pieces together.

2. When you're gluing parts together, run a line of glue around the inside of the larger piece. Slide the smaller piece inside to neatly spread the glue to the interior.

3. *Mounting a crystal in a copper coupling:* Chances are the crystal isn't going to fit perfectly into the coupling without some kind of shim material. To ensure a snug fit, neatly wrap the base of the crystal with leather, cloth, copper tape, or copper mesh. The shim material will be visible when the crystal is mounted. Next, insert the wrapped crystal into the coupling and squeeze drops of instant bonding glue onto the shim material. It will soak down to hold the crystal in place. As a final step, use a knife with

a flat blade to push the shim material down so it's even with the edge of the coupling. Let the mounted crystal sit for a few minutes to dry.

4. *Mounting crystals directly into copper pipe:* Some of the rods in this chapter are made in what we call the traditional style featured in Michael's book, *Crystal Power,* where crystal rods were first introduced. These rods use crystals mounted directly into copper pipes and work well when you have a crystal with a larger diameter than the size of the pipe you've chosen. They require a little more fitting, but fewer parts, and leather covers everything but the crystals. To prepare the pipe, use tinsnips or aircraft shears to cut four slots in the end at equally spaced intervals. The depth of the slots will depend on the size of the crystal to be fitted. Bend the cut portions outward with pliers until the crystal fits snugly into the pipe. Insert the crystal and squeeze instant bonding glue down around the places where the crystal touches the pipe. It will drip down to form a bond. If the fit doesn't seem to be secure enough, cut small pieces of leather and poke them down around the base of the crystal for extra support, then squeeze glue over the leather.

5. *Cutting copper tubing:* We use a vise to hold the pipe, then cut it with a simple hand-held tube cutting device. You can also use a hacksaw or get the pipe cut when you buy it.

6. *Buying copper fittings:* Copper fittings can be found at most hardware stores where plumbing supplies are sold.

7. *Wrapping the rods:* Although all the rods offered here are wrapped with leather, any suitable material can be used, or the rods can be left bare. For most wrappings, you'll need to cut the material in strips. We usually use strips ½" wide when we use ½" fittings, and ¾" wide for ¾" fittings. Cut the end of the strip at an angle to get started. Wrap carefully in a spiral pattern, overlapping the material a bit as you go and gluing the underside. If the strip isn't long enough to wrap the whole rod, cut the end off at an angle. Cut a matching angle for the new piece so the two pieces fit exactly together, and continue wrapping. When you

reach the end of the piece to be wrapped, cut the strip off at an angle and glue it down.

8. *To glue or shine the copper fittings:* If the fittings are extremely dull, you can put them in a tumbler with jeweler's rouge to shine them up. They can also be shined with a wire brush polisher, but it sometimes leave brush marks. New fittings can be coated with a fixative or varnish so they won't tarnish, but a bit of tarnish isn't all that unattractive, so we don't bother. However, if you want to shine up the fittings after the rods have been assembled, you can use Brasso, copper cleaner, or a jeweler's rouge cloth. Unfortunately, if drops of glue have spilled onto the fittings, they leave shiny spots that won't polish to the same color and there's not much you can do.

Below, we offer fourteen variations on the basic healing rod. Let your intuition guide you to the one that feels right for you. If innovations occur to you, welcome them and come up with a rod that's uniquely yours. Any of the rods can be modified by using larger or smaller diameter copper fittings and crystals, or adjusting their lengths. Use the general instructions provided above, along with the diagrams, to assemble the rods.

Note: Although the copper fittings in the diagrams are all shown as being the same diameter, copper tubing (or copper pipe) has actually a slightly smaller diameter, allowing couplings, reducers, and end caps to slide over it.

MINIATURE HEALING ROD

One of the most popular healing rods is the miniature version, which can be carried in a pocket or purse. The total length of this rod is approximately six inches and only the central pipe is wrapped, leaving the couplings at either end bare. These rods can also be shortened to four or five inches, if you want an even smaller one.

MINIATURE HEALING ROD

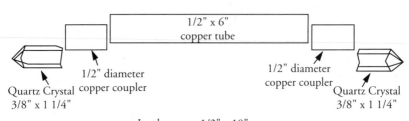

1/2" x 6"
copper tube

1/2" diameter
copper coupler

1/2" diameter
copper coupler

Quartz Crystal
3/8" x 1 1/4"

Quartz Crystal
3/8" x 1 1/4"

Leather wrap 1/2" x 18"

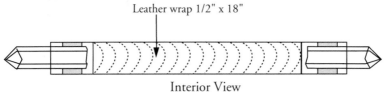

Interior View

MAGNETIC LODESTONE HEALING ROD

Leather wrap 1/2" x 12"

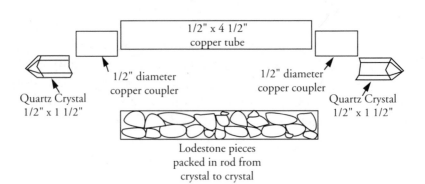

1/2" x 4 1/2"
copper tube

1/2" diameter
copper coupler

1/2" diameter
copper coupler

Quartz Crystal
1/2" x 1 1/2"

Quartz Crystal
1/2" x 1 1/2"

Lodestone pieces
packed in rod from
crystal to crystal

MAGNETIC LODESTONE HEALING ROD

This model, in the pocket or purse size, combines the healing properties of natural magnetism with quartz crystals. Lodestone or magnetite, available from most rock shops, is loaded into the copper pipe before the crystals are mounted. The lodestone needs to be shaken down and sometimes tamped in with a pencil in order to pack it as tightly as possible. Even with packing the rod will probably rattle a bit, but we think the rattle adds to its appeal.

CRYSTAL MAGNET HEALING ROD

Crystals and manufactured magnetic energy complement each other in this hefty rod. The ½" round magnets are available from electronics stores. Since the copper pipe is ¾" in diameter, leather or copper mesh needs to be wrapped around the magnets to hold them stable inside the rod. The 12" pipe takes about sixty magnets, but buy a few extras so you can make sure they touch the crystals at either end. Mount one of the crystals and glue it onto the pipe before adding the magnets. The crystals tend to focus and project the magnetic field with the visualization of the white-light beam amplified by the emotional healing power of love.

TWIN CRYSTAL HEALING ROD

Often two crystals will grow side by side as one. We call these crystals twins, for obvious reasons, and they are excellent for healing work. This rod follows the same pattern as the smaller rods and can run up to 8½" in length, depending on the length of crystals used. The most interesting aspect of this rod is that, due to the two points on each crystal, twin beams of white-light energy projecting from each end of the rod must be visualized for the operation of the rod. These can be visualized as blending into one beam.

CRYSTAL MAGNET HEALING ROD
STANDARD SIZE

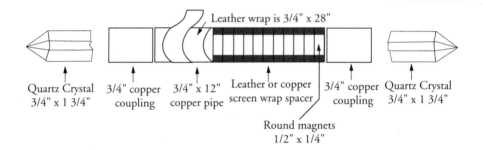

Leather wrap is 3/4" x 28"

Quartz Crystal
3/4" x 1 3/4"

3/4" copper
coupling

3/4" x 12"
copper pipe

Leather or copper
screen wrap spacer

3/4" copper
coupling

Quartz Crystal
3/4" x 1 3/4"

Round magnets
1/2" x 1/4"

TWIN CRYSTAL HEALING ROD

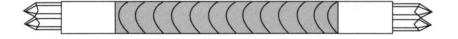

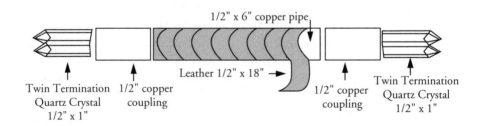

1/2" x 6" copper pipe

Leather 1/2" x 18" →

Twin Termination
Quartz Crystal
1/2" x 1"

1/2" copper
coupling

1/2" copper
coupling

Twin Termination
Quartz Crystal
1/2" x 1"

CRYSTAL PENCIL-POINT HEALING ROD

In our work with quartz crystals, we've found that many of the most beautiful creations are of a smaller size. Some of these are so clear and perfectly formed that they can't be overlooked as a source of Universal Energy. In order to enjoy these crystals, Michael designed a special healing rod to accommodate them. The crystals can be as small as ¼" in diameter and 1"-2" in length. It's possible to mount them in ½" diameter copper pipe by using ⅜"-½" copper reducers. The crystals are mounted in the reducers the same way as they would be in couplings. This is a unique design; the smaller crystals have the same natural subatomic structure that links them to the universal matrix of creative energy, and will operate just as well as the larger sizes.

MODIFIED HEALING ROD

The modified healing rod provides an interesting shape for those of you that want something unusual. To achieve this shape, a piece of ½" diameter copper pipe, 2" long, is inserted through the center of the copper couplings on each end of the rod. The copper reducers on either side of each coupling are then fitted over the protruding ends of the pipe to allow the three pieces to be joined together. Once assembled, the rod works the same way as the others, but its appearance is likely to bring back memories of other times in Atlantis or on other worlds.

AMETHYST HEALING ROD

Many people feel a kinship with amethyst crystals and have asked if they could be used with clear quartz in healing rods. Actually, amethyst and clear quartz crystals are an excellent combination for healing rods. The violet color vibration of amethyst provides a peaceful balance for the high frequency energy of clear quartz. This rod helps us feel our oneness with the creator, while projecting white light for a healthy energy field. It's particularly good for using the power of universal love as a healing energy force.

CRYSTAL PENCIL-POINT HEALING ROD
POCKET OR PURSE SIZE

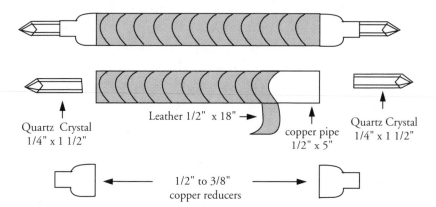

Quartz Crystal
1/4" x 1 1/2"

Leather 1/2" x 18" →

copper pipe
1/2" x 5"

Quartz Crystal
1/4" x 1 1/2"

← 1/2" to 3/8" →
copper reducers

MODIFIED HEALING ROD

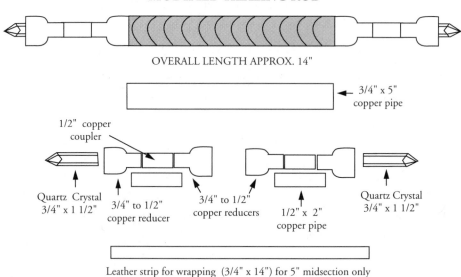

OVERALL LENGTH APPROX. 14"

← 3/4" x 5"
copper pipe

1/2" copper
coupler

Quartz Crystal
3/4" x 1 1/2"

3/4" to 1/2"
copper reducer

3/4" to 1/2"
copper reducers

1/2" x 2"
copper pipe

Quartz Crystal
3/4" x 1 1/2"

Leather strip for wrapping (3/4" x 14") for 5" midsection only

AMETHYST HEALING ROD
LARGE SIZE

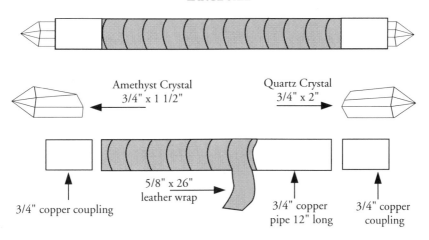

Amethyst Crystal
3/4" x 1 1/2"

Quartz Crystal
3/4" x 2"

3/4" copper coupling

5/8" x 26"
leather wrap

3/4" copper
pipe 12" long

3/4" copper
coupling

TRADITIONAL AMETHYST HEALING ROD
MEDIUM SIZE

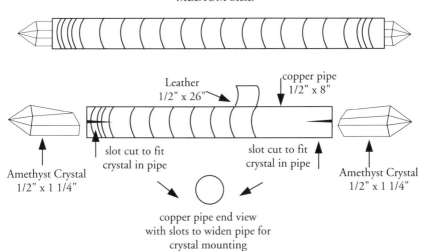

Leather
1/2" x 26"

copper pipe
1/2" x 8"

Amethyst Crystal
1/2" x 1 1/4"

slot cut to fit
crystal in pipe

slot cut to fit
crystal in pipe

Amethyst Crystal
1/2" x 1 1/4"

copper pipe end view
with slots to widen pipe for
crystal mounting

TRADITIONAL AMETHYST HEALING ROD

The full effect of the peaceful balance of amethyst is expressed in this healing rod, and we recommend this choice if the amethyst crystals you buy are too large to fit in copper couplings. The rod is constructed by cutting slots in the copper pipe to accommodate the amethyst crystals, and then wrapping the rod with leather so that only the crystals are exposed. The size is smaller than the standard and larger than the pocket or purse size, with an overall length of about 9½". The color of the amethyst crystals can range from light violet to a deep purple. This rod represents spiritual healing for the light beings that we are. The peaceful emanations of this rod make it a favorite of many healers.

SMOKY AND CLEAR QUARTZ HEALING ROD

At just over 12" long, with the large clear quartz crystal on one end and smoky quartz crystal on the other, this rod provides a striking contrast. It also allows you to use large crystals that won't work for other rods.

This combination provides a powerful balance for healing and eliminating subtle negative emotions and thoughts. Also, the inflowing of positive white light is at a highly refined frequency. The rod is usually used with great care in very special instances. Due to the intensity of smoky quartz, experience with other crystal rods is suggested before building or using this rod. As with all the crystal tools, use the rod in a responsible manner to create good energy for all.

TRADITIONAL DOUBLE TERMINATION HEALING ROD

This rod really is a "double double." Crystals with a point on each end have been favored throughout history as good medicine. These are balanced energy entities in themselves, but when matched in pairs in a rod, they project an intense high energy spiritual healing for all areas of consciousness.

Construct this rod in the traditional style, by slotting the tube to fit the crystals. Its overall length is about 14". Due to the nature of the double termination quartz crystals, it makes a powerful healing rod.

SMOKY & CLEAR QUARTZ HEALING ROD
TRADITIONAL STYLE USING LARGE CRYSTALS

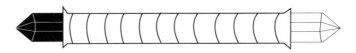

OVERALL LENGTH APPROX. 12 1/2"
(Copper pipe is 3/4" x 10")

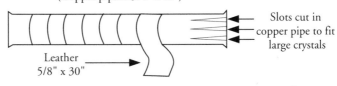

Slots cut in
copper pipe to fit
large crystals

Leather
5/8" x 30"

Smoky Quartz Crystal
1" x 2"

Clear Quartz Crystal
1" x 2"

TRADITIONAL DOUBLE TERMINATION HEALING ROD

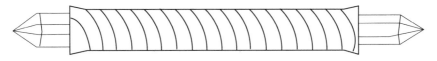

Copper pipe
3/4" x 12"

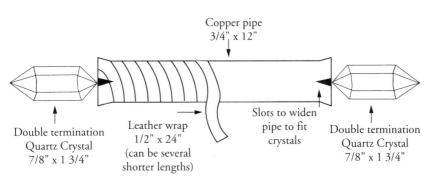

Double termination
Quartz Crystal
7/8" x 1 3/4"

Leather wrap
1/2" x 24"
(can be several
shorter lengths)

Slots to widen
pipe to fit
crystals

Double termination
Quartz Crystal
7/8" x 1 3/4"

AMETHYST DOUBLE TERMINATION HEALING ROD

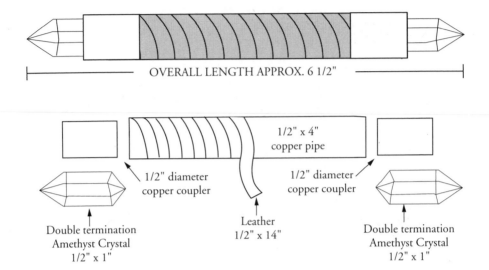

OVERALL LENGTH APPROX. 6 1/2"

1/2" x 4"
copper pipe

1/2" diameter
copper coupler

1/2" diameter
copper coupler

Leather
1/2" x 14"

Double termination
Amethyst Crystal
1/2" x 1"

Double termination
Amethyst Crystal
1/2" x 1"

OPEN END HEALING ROD
(with Double Termination Crystal)

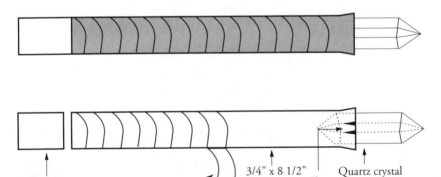

3/4" copper
coupler

3/4" x 24"
leather wrap

3/4" x 8 1/2"
copper pipe

Slots
cut in
pipe

Quartz crystal
3/4" x 2"

Amethyst Double Termination Healing Rod

The intensely peaceful vibration of amethyst is amplified and projected further in this rod. Intensely peaceful seems like a contradiction of terms, but it fits the the feeling this rod provokes. The model shown here is close to pocket- or purse-size to make it easier to have it nearby at all times, but the length can be adjusted to fit your needs. The shade of amethyst can be light or dark, according to what you like the best. This is a very comfortable, personal healing rod that provides a calming effect with a wide energy field around it. It sometimes takes awhile to find double termination amethyst crystals, but it's well worth the wait when you do.

Open-End Healing Rod with Double Termination Crystal

This healing rod uses one double termination quartz crystal rather than the two found in most healing rods. The rod is fairly large and slots are cut in the copper pipe, rather than mounting the crystal in a copper coupler. After mounting a copper end cap on the other end of the rod, leather is wrapped over the copper pipe, leaving the crystal exposed.

With all the energy consciousness focused on one crystal, this rod becomes a very special tool. We don't know its full potential yet, but future experiments will help us understand it and ourselves at the same rate of unfoldment. The difference in this rod lies in the copper chamber. Most are capped or sealed by another crystal to form a closed chamber. In this model, the double termination crystal takes the place of a single termination crystal in each end. The open end of the chamber may make the channeling flow of energy stronger.

Substitute for Double Termination Crystal

In some areas, it's difficult to find double termination quartz crystals, so we designed a device that uses two single termination crystals in place of a double. The small-gauge copper wires used are 2¼" long, but shorter wires can be used if desired. Glue one of the six wires to the center of each

SUBSTITUTION FOR DOUBLE TERMINATION
QUARTZ CRYSTAL

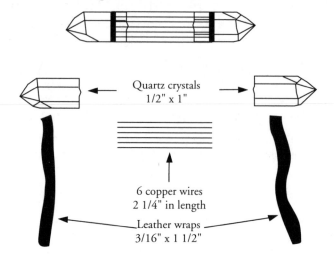

Quartz crystals
1/2" x 1"

6 copper wires
2 1/4" in length

Leather wraps
3/16" x 1 1/2"

PALM-SIZE SELF-HEALING ROD

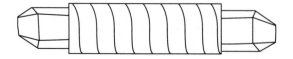

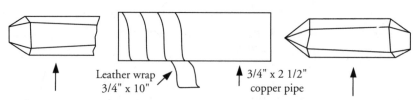

Leather wrap
3/4" x 10"

3/4" x 2 1/2"
copper pipe

Quartz Crystal, Single Termination
(slab/flat sided if possible, but
regular will work) 3/4" x 2"

Quartz Crystal, Double Termination
(slab/flat sided if possible, but
regular will work) 3/4" x 2"

of the six sides of the crystal, keeping them as straight as possible. The wires can then be covered with a thin strip of leather, wrapped and glued around the base of the crystals to cover the wires. While it looks rather fragile, the unit is very stable and can be held in the hand. Use it in place of a double termination crystal for any healing work. The copper wires unify and balance the energy fields of the two quartz crystals into one energy field, tuning them to work together as one.

PALM-SIZE SELF-HEALING ROD

The following rod is provided because self-healing is often our most important job. The rod is slightly less than 5" long and uses one single and one double termination quartz crystal. It's constructed in the traditional style, where the crystals are fitted directly into copper pipe, but without slotting the copper pipe ends. Instead, the crystals are chosen to fit the ¾" pipe. Sometimes, flat-sided quartz crystals, referred to as knowledge crystals, are used. Knowledge is healing, and this is especially true in the case of self-healing.

While any healing rod can be used for self-healing, this rod has been manifested specifically for balancing the light being you call yourself. It's provided for individuals who wish to increase their spiritual expression of light and truth to a much higher degree.

To use the rod, place the thumb of the hand holding the rod on one side of the double termination crystal. Begin with a period of "at-one-ment" with the energy of the creator to the best degree that you know how. Visualize your aura as being very bright, augmented, and amplified by the energy radiating in a field from the rod. With this healing rod, a beam is very seldom used; the energy field is of primary importance for strengthening and balancing. If you're really serious about self-development, this is the rod you want.

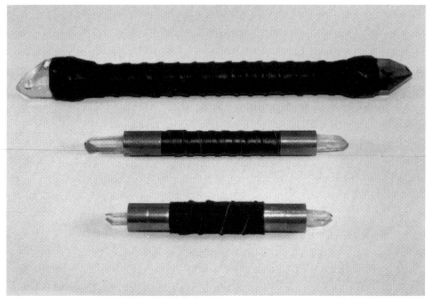

Top: Smoky and Clear Quartz Healing Rod
Center and Bottom: Variations of Miniature Healing Rods

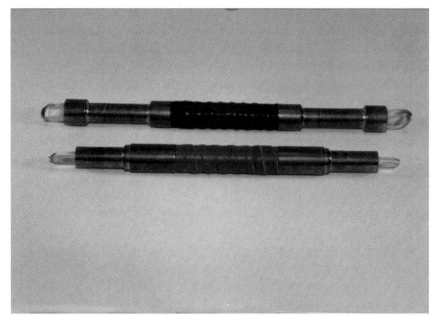

Top: Modified Healing Rod
Bottom: Variation of a Pencil Point Healing Rod

TWENTY-TWO

Pendulums and Dowsing

Could it be that those of us who use copper fittings
to make crystal tools were plumbers in a previous lifetime?

Dowsing is one of those so-called occult practices that has gained respectability because it's so effective. In fact, water-witching, or dowsing for water, is often used even by those who have no interest or belief in the occult. A few years ago, Lin was shocked when her conservative father casually mentioned that the well at his mountain home was inadequate and he'd called in a water-witcher to dowse out the location of a new well. Since drilling a well in the dry Rockies is expensive and risky, she couldn't imagine what brought him to choose that course, but apparently it was a common practice in that area. A few months later, he told her that the well had been dowsed, drilled, and was providing him with plenty of water.

How is it that a person using only a forked twig can divine the presence of water hundreds of feet under the ground? We don't know. All we do know is that it works often enough to have ceased to be classified under the heading of the miraculous.

DOWSING PENDULUMS

The pendulum, which uses a heavy object suspended from a string or chain to answer questions, is another popular tool for dowsing. While any heavy object will work, crystals are particularly effective because of their unique ability to tune into and amplify the energy involved in dowsing.

Michael had been dowsing with various objects for years when his favorite crystal dowsing pendulum literally chose him. It took him awhile to catch on, so the crystal and crystal beings used the direct action approach.

My pendulum was originally a crystal pendant made by a friend at the mineral shop. The pendant had such a unique design that I couldn't put it down. It was beautiful, with a double termination quartz crystal held horizontally by a band of silver, and an amethyst crystal hanging from the center band on the quartz crystal, but its appeal reached beyond beauty.

I bought the pendant and attached it to a silver chain to wear as a necklace. I loved wearing it, but the darn thing refused to hang right; it kept getting knotted up and twisted in the chain. To solve the problem, I switched the pendant to a gold chain instead, but that didn't help. Over a dozen times a day, the chain would come unhooked and the crystals would fall down inside my shirt.

After a couple of weeks, I finally got the message; the pendant wasn't supposed to be a necklace. As I was looking at it one day, the pendant slid down the chain and caught perfectly in the hook on the end, making a pendulum of itself. I've used it that way since then and invariably get a very energetic response from it.

Using Crystal Pendulums

Crystal pendulums are easy and fun to use. Although when you're watching someone else dowsing with a pendulum, it's easy to believe they're making it move by undetectable movements of their hand, when you use one yourself you'll find that it responds even though you're positive you're holding your hand perfectly still. The wonderful thing about dowsing is that, while the movements might be more positive and definite with practice, it works for anyone, even those that are sure they haven't got a smidgen of psychic ability.

To begin to dowse, hold your crystal pendant suspended over a flat surface, such as a table. You can rest your elbow on the table to steady your arm, if you wish. When you ask a question, the pendulum will begin to move of its own volition. There are various ways to interpret the movements. Some people say that a clockwise movement means "yes" and a counterclockwise motion means "no." Others use a vertical swing for "yes," a horizontal swing for "no," and a counterclockwise movement for an "undecided" answer. To choose the method you'll use, you can either arbitrarily decide on one, or you can establish the pattern of the swings by asking a few questions to which you know the answers. Either method works equally well.

To experiment with your crystal pendant, ask questions that have yes or no answers and keep a logbook of your results. Later, you can go back and record the level of accuracy that you've achieved. You may find that the farther the events lie in the future and the more you have invested in the answer, the more uncertain your results. The reason for this is that the pendulum can only tell you what you're currently creating in your future and it often tells you what you want to hear. If you don't like what you're currently creating, change your mind and attract the future you do desire.

In addition to asking questions with yes and no answers, you can use dowsing to find out other information. For instance, if you're moving or planning a vacation, hold the pendulum over areas that you're considering to find the best one. Likewise, if you have any list of possible choices, hold the pendant over each choice. On the first run-through you can eliminate any negative answers. If you have several positive or some undecided answers, go back over the list again until you determine the best choice.

Below, we offer five different crystal pendulums that you can make. Or, if you have a favorite necklace, especially if it includes a gem or mineral, you can use that for your dowsing experiment. It's a good idea when selecting a pendulum to try out several before you decide on one for regular use. For some reason, pendulums work differently for different people, and one that works great for your friend may be sluggish for you. The pendant you end up using most may not be the most visually appealing or expensive. In fact, Lin's favorite is the cheapest and least beautiful of those we offer, a quartz rock on a string.

CRYSTAL DOWSING PENDULUM

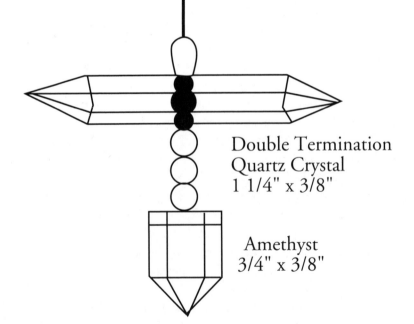

Silver chain

Double Termination
Quartz Crystal
1 1/4" x 3/8"

Amethyst
3/4" x 3/8"

The Crystal Dowsing Pendulum

The crystal dowsing pendulum has two main components. The first is a double termination quartz crystal approximately 1¼" in length by ⅜" in diameter. The second is a small single termination amethyst crystal, approximately ¾" length by ⅜" diameter.

The silver mountings will probably have to be fitted by a jeweler or silversmith, as shown in the diagram, after you choose your crystals. The pendant is then attached to a silver chain. You could also use gold fittings and a quartz crystal on the bottom. The combination of quartz, amethyst, and silver has worked so well for us that we haven't changed it.

Tektite or Meteorite Pendulum

Meteorites or tektites, from outer space, make exotic dowsing pendulums with an unusual energy all their own. These minerals are somewhat rare and can be expensive, but by shopping around, you can probably find one for a reasonable price at a mineral shop or rock show. In fact, Lin even found one by accident while hiking around in the Rocky Mountains. It's also possible that another rock or mineral will thrust itself to your attention when you're searching for a dowsing pendulum. In that case, you can be assured that it's the right one for you.

Once you have your dowsing rock, simply wrap a pliable copper or silver wire around it as shown in the diagram. Make sure you leave a loop in the middle or on one end where the chain attaches. Copper chains are somewhat hard to find, but you can use a silver chain to produce the same results by fastening one end of the clasp around the wire loop.

Crystal Arrowhead Pendulum

The crystal arrowhead is one of the fastest-acting pendulums we've used. It consists of a 12" leather thong tied around a quartz crystal arrowhead, 1" wide by 3" long. The beads shown are for decoration and can be omitted. The most difficult part of making this pendulum is finding a quartz crystal arrowhead. Sometimes old ones can be found or purchased in rock shops. New ones can occasionally be acquired from enthusiasts

DOWSING PENDULUMS

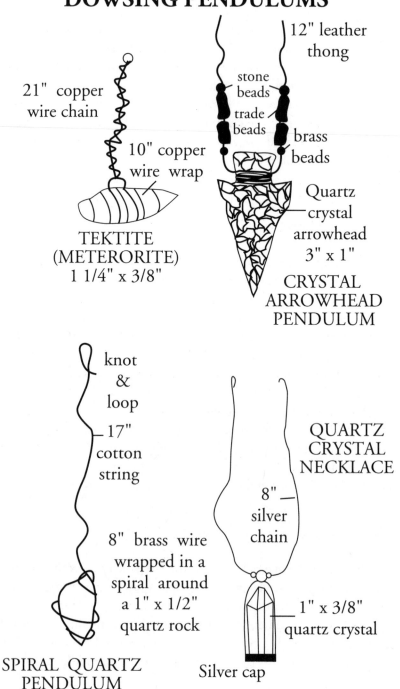

21" copper
wire chain

10" copper
wire wrap

TEKTITE
(METERORITE)
1 1/4" x 3/8"

12" leather
thong

stone
beads

trade
beads

brass
beads

Quartz
crystal
arrowhead
3" x 1"

CRYSTAL
ARROWHEAD
PENDULUM

knot
&
loop

17"
cotton
string

8" brass wire
wrapped in a
spiral around
a 1" x 1/2"
quartz rock

SPIRAL QUARTZ
PENDULUM

QUARTZ
CRYSTAL
NECKLACE

8"
silver
chain

1" x 3/8"
quartz crystal

Silver cap

who practice the art of arrowhead making. If you can't find an arrowhead made of crystal, a rock or flint one can be used.

SPIRAL QUARTZ PENDULUM

One of our favorite and most active pendulums is also the easiest to make. In addition, it's also economical. The weight on the end is any rock with quartz crystals embedded in it, or it could be a small quartz cluster. Most rock shops carry inexpensive rocks like this, and chances are pretty good that you can find one for free if you look around outside. Our rock is about 1¼" long and ¾" in diameter. The string used is a length of cotton. Simply wrap a spiral of copper, silver, gold, or brass wire around the rock. You'll need about 8" of wire, and it should be of a heavy enough gauge to remain fixed in place after it's wrapped around the rock. Use needle-nosed pliers to hold one end of the wire while bending it around the rock. The string is tied to a tight loop in the wire at the top of the spiral.

Another option for your pendulum is to buy a quartz crystal necklace and when you're ready to dowse, simply take it off and begin to dowse.

CRYSTAL DOWSING RODS

For those of you who are hard-core dowsers we've included crystal dowsing rods to add energy and improve the accuracy of your dowsing. To make these crystal dowsers, we added small power rods to the tips of a pair of conventional dowsing rods, which are a high-tech version of the forked twig that dowsers of yore used. Our rods, purchased from a local branch of the American Society of Dowsers, are made of an L-shaped length of stainless steel, with plexiglass pieces on the bottom of the L that function as handles and allow the rods to swivel. These rods are very sensitive and take some practice to use. While Michael can operate the rods the way they should be used, Lin tends to find them going every which way when she tries to use them. If you want to make your own dowsing rods, you can even straighten out two metal clothes hangers and bend down one end to form a handle. However, a heavier metal would be preferable and easier to use, especially if you can find cylinders of plastic to put on the handles to allow them to swivel more easily.

USING THE CRYSTAL DOWSING RODS

To use your dowsing rods, hold one in each hand with the tips out in front of you. When questions are asked, a "yes" answer is indicated by the rods crossing each other to form an "X." If the rods remain straight or swivel outwards, the answer is no.

Constructing a Crystal Dowsing Rod

Materials:

A pair of dowsing rods, either professional quality or homemade

Two quartz crystals, approximately ¼" inch diameter, 1" long

Two lengths of copper tubing, ¼" diameter, cut 1⅝" long

Two strips of thin leather or colored tape, ⅜" wide

Copper, cloth, or electrical tape

Instant bonding glue

Construction:

1. Mount each of the crystals in one of the copper tubes by slitting the end of the tubing. Use glue and/or shims to hold the crystals in place.

2. Wrap the tubes with leather, glued in a spiral pattern, or with colored tape. Don't cover the open end of the copper tube.

3. Mounting your miniature power rods on the ends of the dowsing rods can be a bit tricky as the copper tubing will probably be a larger diameter than the dowsing rods. In order to attach the rods, it may be necessary to use shims of thin pieces of copper, copper mesh, or leather inside the tubing. If this allows them to fit so they don't slide off, they needn't be glued.

CRYSTAL DOWSING ROD

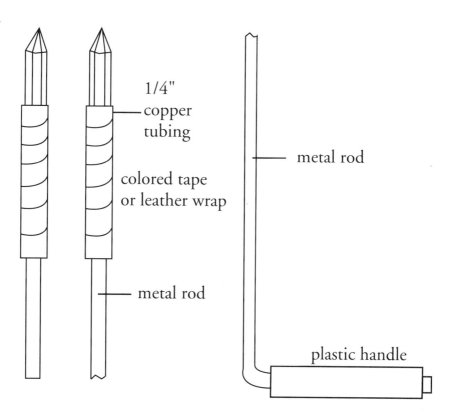

1/4"
copper
tubing

colored tape
or leather wrap

metal rod

metal rod

plastic handle

NOTE: The rod portion is a
continuation of the handle

4. Use copper or electrical tape wound in a spiral pattern to hold the power rods on securely. Start the tape about ⅜" from the base of the power rod and wrap it about an inch down onto the dowsing rods.

Crystal dowsing tools should be economical, easy to use, and convenient to carry. One of our handiest pendulums isn't pictured in this chapter. It's a polished Apache tear with a bell cap glued on one end that holds a 4½" length of chain. It's simple, light, and easy to carry and use.

The most complex dowsing or crystal tool is only going to work as well as the person using it. Buying the most expensive dowsing equipment on the market won't improve a talent developed by experience in the field. Practicing is the best way possible to learn. The more you practice, the more energetic and accurate your answers will be. Before you start, imagine that you and your pendulum are surrounded in an aura of white or golden light. After that, tune into the higher part of your consciousness that has the information you want and simply let it work through you to tell you what you want to know. When we're able to really tune in this way, we almost feel as if we're in a place that exists out of space and time and our answers are amazingly accurate.

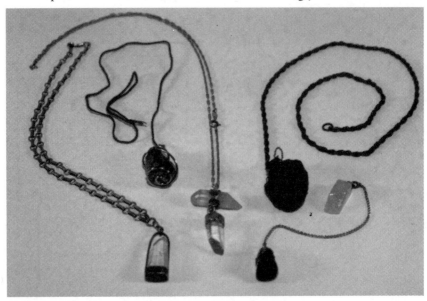

Top: Spiral Quartz Pendulum, Tektite Pendulum
Center: Crystal Dowsing Pendulum
Bottom: Silver and Crystal Necklace, Quartz Crystal/Apache Tear Pendulum

TWENTY-THREE

The Crystal Pipe

Simple existence is not enough.

VISION BECOMES REALITY

The crystal pipe is a shaman's tool that arose out of the current Earth cycle. It merges traditional Native American practices and the science of Universal Energy in the most versatile and powerful crystal tool that we've discovered. The quartz crystal and amethyst pipe, manifested through Michael with the help of crystal beings from the mineral kingdom, is capable of moving spiritual subatomic particle energy in ways that are "awesome." It can be used as an energy-field generator, a power rod, a healing rod, an energy hammer (tomahawk), a chakra/aura balancer, and more. We believe these pipes are destined to become one of the most popular crystal energy tools of the future.

THE PIPE CEREMONY

The most obvious use for the crystal pipe is in performing the traditional Native American pipe ceremony in a healing circle. The ceremony is generally done during the full moon and at the time of the summer or winter solstice. Below we'll outline one version of the ceremony that you can perform for yourself with the crystal pipe. But before we begin, we'll need to explain the Breath of Life used in the ceremony. To perform the Breath of Life with the crystal pipe, purse your lips and place them close to, but not touching, the crystal on the stem of the pipe. Take a deep breath through your mouth until your chest and diaphragm area is expanded as far as it will go. As you draw in the breath, imagine it contains particles of white light or love that light up and fill your entire being. When you exhale, imagine the light surrounding you in an aura that eventually expands until it surrounds your immediate area, the world, and then the entire universe with love and a sense of rightness. With each breath you take during the course of the ceremony, the light expands farther and grows brighter.

The ceremony begins with a group of people standing or sitting in a circle with items of spiritual significance, or items they want to cleanse, in the center of the circle. While a leader is usually chosen to hold the pipe and perform the ceremony for everyone, if all the members know the procedure, there's no reason why you can't pass the pipe clockwise around the circle so that everyone can participate to further blend tradition with a new awareness. Even if one person is facilitating the ceremony, the power of it is magnified if each person in the circle uses the Breath of Life, along with the leader, to add energy to the proceedings.

1. To start the ceremony, the leader says, "We make an offering for the spirit people," and uses a crystal or crystal light rod to circle the amethyst in the pipe's bowl, one to three times in a clockwise direction. Use the same words to make offerings to the mineral people, plant people, sea people, winged people, four-legged brothers and sisters, two-legged brothers and sisters, the Great Spirit, and the Earth Mother/Father. If all are participating in performing the ceremony, the pipe should be passed to a different person for each offering.

2. Raise the pipe silently in both hands skyward to the Great Spirit.

3. The pipe is then offered to each of the four directions. To begin, rotate the stem of the pipe clockwise until the stem crystal points to east, and say, "I call upon the Wind of Wisdom from the east to come into our circle." Then rotate the stem the rest of the way around until the stem crystal points to the person's mouth. Perform the Breath of Life, as explained above. The same clockwise rotations of the pipe, invitation, and Breath of Life are then repeated for the Wind of Growth from the south, the Wind of Regeneration from the west, and the Wind of Purity from the north.

4. Rotate the pipe clockwise until it points upward. Speak the words, "We offer this to the Great Spirit." Rotate the pipe to the mouth and breathe the Breath of Life.

5. Once again, rotate the pipe until it points downward and say, "We offer this to the Earth Mother/Father." Rotate the pipe to the mouth and breathe the Breath of Life.

6. Rotate the pipe for the last time, until it's held at chest level with the stem in the left hand and the bowl in the right. Then lay the pipe carefully on the ground. This completes the pipe ceremony.

At this point, practices vary, according to the purpose of the people involved. The following steps are taken if the circle is for healing.

Members of the circle join hands, with each person who wishes to do so speaking words of healing. Move around the circle in a clockwise direction.

When those who want to have spoken, all join arms and silently send healing energy to friends, family, and anyone else who needs it.

After a few minutes, the leader says, "The visualized heartfelt sphere of good energy in this circle is expanding and growing outward through the Universe." Each person uses the Breath of Life to expand the energy until it fills the Universe.

When sufficient time has passed, the same person closes by saying, "We give thanks for this circle, all the good things experienced, and our brothers and sisters. Thanks are given for our guidance on the path that led us here now, and for guidance on the path to come." Hugs are exchanged.

USING THE CRYSTAL PIPE

Although the pipe was first used to perform full moon and solstice healing ceremonies as described above, it has many other uses. For example, any of the crystals in the pipe can be used as a healing rod or power rod. For healing, try each one until you find one that feels comfortable. In different situations, you may use all of them at different times. Visualize and direct white-light energy from the crystal. At the same time, amplify the energy with a feeling of unconditional love and at-one-ness. Some people prefer the amethyst for healing, while others prefer the double or single termination quartz. Experiment until you feel at home with the three crystal beings of this tool. The same is true when using the pipe as a power rod; usually the amethyst on the bowl is considered best for the single-pointed power rod, but you may find that you get a better energy flow by using one of the other crystals.

The pipe can also be used as an aura/chakra balancer. The amethyst tip is pointed at one of the chakra areas, while the double termination quartz is pointed at another to connect the energies. Visualize healing energy flowing between the two points.

As an energy tomahawk (hammer), this tool is held just the way it sounds. It can be swung in arcs and circles while seeing with the inner eye that it throws a field of Universal Energy from the amethyst and single termination points. If you're familiar with martial arts techniques, you can employ them to help you throw the energy. If you aren't, create your own movements.

The crystal pipe is constantly inspiring new discoveries. One person who held it was reminded of the L-shaped right-angle energy patterns related to UFO propulsion, navigation, and flight paths, using the Universal lines of force and energy. Another used it to recall a past life as a Native American. The pipe will bring out many more discoveries as individuals of different experience and backgrounds build and use them to create a higher consciousness for all of us.

Constructing the Crystal Pipe

Materials:

Quartz crystal, single termination, slightly less than ¾" diameter, approximately 1¾" to 2" long

Quartz crystal, double termination, slightly less than ¾" diameter, 1¾" to 2" long

Amethyst crystal, single termination, slightly less than ¾" diameter, 1¼" to 1½" long

Shim material of leather, copper mesh, or copper tape for mounting crystals

Copper pipe or tubing, ¾" diameter, cut 10½" long

3 copper couplings, ¾" diameter

Copper tee, ¾" diameter

2 pieces of copper pipe, ¾" diameter, cut ¾" long

Leather strip, approximately ½" wide, 30" long

Instant bonding glue

Construction:

1. Mount each of the three crystals in a copper coupler. Wrap the base of the crystal in the shim material you've chosen, then push the wrapped base into the coupler. The shim material will be visible, so make sure you're satisfied with the way it looks before you proceed. Squeeze instant bonding glue onto the shim material, where it will soak down to hold the crystal securely in the coupler. Use a flat knife to flatten the shim material so it's even with the edge of the coupler. Set the mounted crystals aside until the glue dries.

2. Connect the long piece of copper pipe and the copper tee by pushing the pipe into one end of the top of the tee. Wait to glue any of the pieces until you've assembled them all to make sure they fit right, but when you do, run a string of instant bonding

glue around the inside of the tee, and spread the glue by inserting the copper pipe.

3. Fit the coupler with the double terminated quartz crystal onto the other end of the copper pipe. When you're ready to glue it, use the same method you used to glue the pipe to the tee.

4. Connect the single terminated crystal onto the other end of the tee, using the ¾" piece of copper pipe to hold the pieces together. To do this, push the copper pipe into the tee so that half of its length is extending. Fit the coupler over the protruding half of the copper pipe. The copper pipe won't be visible when the pieces are put together. When you're ready to glue the pieces, run the beads of glue around the insides of the tee and the coupler, then use the copper pipe to spread the glue.

5. Connect the copper coupler with the amethyst crystal to the leg of the tee, following the directions in step 4.

6. Use the leather strip to cover the long piece of copper pipe. Cut the end of the strip at an angle and start at the end of the tee, just below it, wrapping and gluing the leather in a spiral. Each spiral should overlap the previous one a bit. If you need to use more than one strip of leather, cut each end off at an angle so they appear to form a continuous piece. When you reach the end of the tubing at the base of the coupler, cut the leather at an angle and fasten it with glue.

7. Like other crystal rods and energy tools, the pipe can be left unwrapped and/or decorated with your favorite gemstones, beads, feathers, gold or silver bands, and more, if you desire.

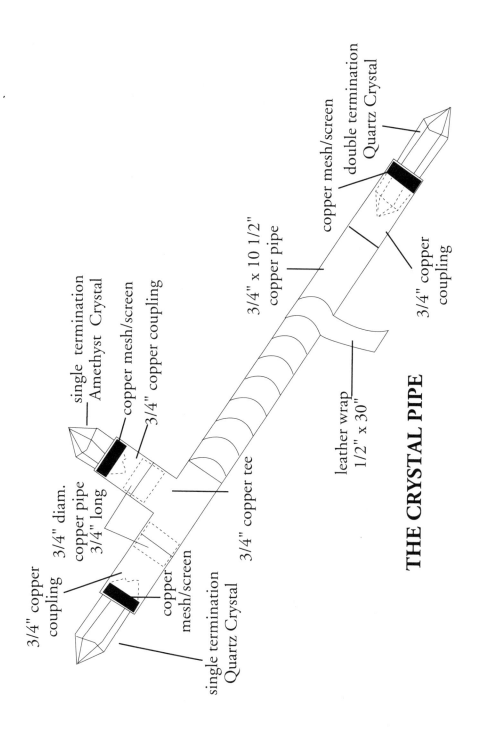

single termination Amethyst Crystal

copper mesh/screen

3/4" copper coupling

3/4" copper coupling

3/4" diam. copper pipe 3/4" long

copper mesh/screen

single termination Quartz Crystal

3/4" copper tee

copper mesh/screen double termination Quartz Crystal

3/4" copper coupling

copper mesh/screen

3/4" x 10 1/2" copper pipe

leather wrap 1/2" x 30"

THE CRYSTAL PIPE

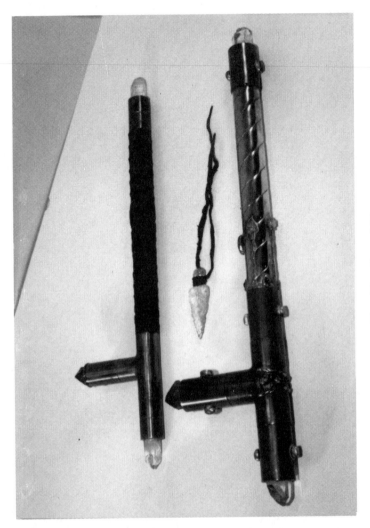

Top: The Crystal Pipe
Center: Crystal Arrowhead Pendulum
Bottom: Crystal Pipe with Silver and Gems

TWENTY-FOUR

Seeking Guidance

*What we call magic, or the miraculous,
is actually the product of laws that we
don't fully understand yet.*

One of the shaman's most important activities is seeking guidance in his or her own life and helping others find their best path. There are many ways this guidance can be sought. Dowsing, channeling, meditation, dreams, and the use of crystal tools and psionics can help us make decisions. For any of these tools to work, all that's really necessary is the faith that the answers are available to us, and the intuition and openness that allows us to recognize the answers when they come.

Although people often go to shamans in their search for answers, the wise ones will teach them how to find their own answers while supplying them with extra energy, rather than giving them the answers outright. The shaman takes this approach because doling out solutions will weaken the person receiving the answer, which isn't the purpose of the truly enlightened shaman. In order for the shaman to evolve into a higher order being, he or she must help others to evolve. With each person that the shaman helps grow spiritually, the greater his or her own power becomes.

It's similar to the difference between giving a destitute person a charity handout or helping him or her find a job. The handout may help the person in the short run, but ultimately it weakens the individual and makes him or her resentful and dependent. Eventually this dependence can drain the donor. On the other hand, with the means to help himself or herself, or find his or her own answers, the person begins to recognize his or her own power and strength. One who might have become a negative drain on the mass consciousness of everyone, including the shaman, becomes instead a source of positive energy, available to all.

Another reason for helping others find their own answers is that none of us, shaman or not, are infallible. We may think that we know another's answer, but that information has to come through our own viewpoint and set of beliefs. It may not be what best suits another's life plan. As shamans, we're here to learn our own lessons, and one of them may involve the proper use of power. We can be pretty sure that when we start thinking we know what's best for everyone, we're heading for trouble. Either we're stifling our own growth by stifling others, or we're going to be disappointed when we discover our own fallibility. There's a fine line between the use and misuse of power that the shaman must always walk. Only intuition and love can allow us to walk that line successfully.

So, now that we've nixed the outright giving of answers, how do we help those in need? We're going to suggest two ways, and both fit nicely into the context of the pipe ceremony described earlier, and the magic circle, which we'll be describing later in this chapter.

The first way to help another is to give the person the energy he or she needs to find his or her own answers. The miraculous thing about energy is that, like love, the more of it you give away, the more you possess. Energy is in unlimited supply in the Universe; the trick is to learn how to amass and control it. Since we can't give away something we don't have, we must first acquire the energy. Once we've tapped into the source of the energy, even after we give it away, the channel remains open, leaving us with more energy and a better means of controlling it than we had before.

BUILDING YOUR ENERGY

Earlier in the book, we described how healers amass energy through their hands by building a sun between their hands. Another good method is to use the whole body as an energy conduit. This method works well when it's used in a magic circle or even when you're alone, and it involves using the Breath of Life described in the last chapter. In order to use this effectively, it's best to practice on your own before using it in other contexts. Pick a time to practice when you're relatively relaxed and untroubled, as it's difficult to achieve the concentration necessary when you're upset.

The first thing you need to do is draw the energy into your body. Pick a comfortable chair to sit in, with your feet flat on the floor and your hands resting on your lap in an open position. It usually helps to close your eyes. When you're relaxed and breathing naturally, visualize a cone of light coming into the top of your head from above. With each breath you draw in, imagine that love-filled light flowing downward, lighting up every nook and cranny in your body.

When the light is too great to be contained, either imagine it coming out of your palms and surrounding you, or let it simply expand out of every pore in your body until the glow has filled the air around you for a distance of three to six inches. Keep in mind that the light is still streaming into your head from above. Soon, even your aura can't contain it.

At this point, depending on your purpose, the light energy can be used in one of two ways. For a general giving of good energy, you can let your aura expand until it fills the room, the city, the entire Universe, if you want. If your purpose is more specific, you can imagine it coming out of your third eye to form a small sun about two feet in front of you. Without letting the size of the sun expand, direct a stream of energy into it, making it glow more brightly with each breath. The glow you see is the energy of love, the driving force of a creative universe.

When you're ready, release that ball of love and energy with the thought that it will go to the person who needs it. You may want to send it with the thought that it will help the person with a specific problem, or just that it will surround any action he or she takes with love and light.

Both of the above techniques should leave you feeling energized rather than depleted, but if you like when you're done, you can take a few seconds to visualize the light filling your aura before you end the process.

This experience can be extremely powerful. To come back to a normal state of consciousness and fully release the energy, we find it helpful to end with a gesture or words to symbolize that we're finished. The words can be something as simple as, "it is done," "so it is," or another phrase that tells you that your purpose has been accomplished. An ending gesture of release might be a flick of the fingers, opening your eyes, or a movement of your hands.

During the course of a magic circle pipe ceremony you may have occasion to use both types of energy sendings at different points. Practicing ahead of time will allow you to do this more quickly and effectively, although sometimes the good energy in a group can help everyone achieve a stronger energy flow than that which they would be capable of alone. We've found that the energy is strongest when love is the motivating force of the group or individual.

You can also use a similar energy-building technique when you're working with crystals and crystal tools. After your aura is glowing brightly, instead of sending the light from your third eye, let the light travel down through your hand to the crystal or crystal tool until it forms an aura or a beam of energy.

The shaman can help others by teaching them how to gather and use their energy. In the following story, we'll see how a very wise shaman, named Gray Seal, helped people he didn't even know by sharing the magic circle pipe ceremony. As a side effect of his efforts, he was able to achieve a long-awaited goal of his own.

GRAY SEAL'S TRIUMPH

Bob and his wife, Liz, met Gray Seal at a party and were invited to attend a magic circle pipe ceremony at his home during the next full moon. When the couple arrived for the ceremony, they were surprised to find, that rather than leading it, Gray Seal encouraged everyone to participate. They were also interested in the crystal pipe that Gray Seal used for the ceremony, rather than the traditional peace pipe. Although Bob and Liz felt a bit uncomfortable at first, worried that they'd ruin the ceremony, Gray Seal told them that it was the spirit, rather than an exact form, that empowered the ritual. After a few sessions where they had to be prompted to perform their parts, Bob and Liz learned the basics and were able to prompt newcomers themselves.

Bob was especially fascinated with Gray Seal's crystal pipe and decided to build one of his own. Although he started out intending to make a duplicate of Gray Seal's, something told him to replace the center section of copper pipe with a rounded piece of African hardwood. When he showed the pipe to Gray Seal, the shaman said gravely, his eyes bright with pride, "You have put your own spirit into this pipe. Now you are a shaman."

That night he asked Bob to start the ceremony using his new pipe.

Shortly after that, Bob found himself in need of guidance in the worst way. Since he and Liz had moved to the small community in the Northwest, Liz had been unable to find a job and they were dependent on his income. That day, Bob had learned that his company was closing. As there were no other jobs in his field in that area, he and his family were going to have to move.

After agonizing thought brought Bob no plan of action, he decided to bring his problem to the next full moon ceremony at Gray Seal's home. Unfortunately, a few days later he found out that Gray Seal would be out of town on that date and there wouldn't be a ceremony. At first Bob was devastated, but then he reminded himself that Gray Seal had called him a shaman. Why not use what he'd learned to help himself?

On the night of the full moon, after their children were asleep, he and Liz formed a magic circle by sitting across from each other on a blanket in their living room. Bob placed a large quartz crystal in the center of the circle, as he'd seen Gray Seal do. Unfortunately, his crystal had a chipped base and kept flopping on its side. He set it upright one more time, and it finally remained upright. Around the large crystal, Liz put smaller crystals of quartz, smoky quartz, amethyst, and citrine, one in each of the four cardinal directions. She also placed some turquoise and silver jewelry around the center crystals so that the rings, bracelet, and necklace would be cleansed and blessed by the ritual. Bob laid his pipe near the center crystal arrangement, and he and Liz held hands across the circle for a time of peace and energy-building before beginning.

Gray Seal had taught him several variations of the pipe ceremony. The one he picked was to sprinkle cornmeal over the crystal in the pipe's bowl while he and Liz alternately made offerings to all the members of the Earth

Kingdom, the Great Spirit, and the Earth Mother. They made an extra offering in thanks and gratitude for guidance.

When the pipe returned to Bob at the end of the ceremony, he performed the last clockwise circle of the pipe, held it out at chest level, and then laid it gently on the blanket near the center of their magic circle.

Holding hands across the circle, he and Liz each asked for a blessing and healing for those they held dear as well as for the Earth Mother and all her children. They asked for guidance for moving and finding new jobs. They each spoke thanks for that guidance with feelings of peace and gratitude. As they sat in silence, holding hands, they were engulfed with a sense of peace and freedom from worry.

Opening their eyes, they stared in silence at the crystal and jewelry arrangement in the center of the circle, enjoying its beauty. Simultaneously, they focused on the fact that the large crystal on its uneven base had flopped over again and was pointing toward the southeast. They looked at one another and both said, "Do you suppose ... ?" then laughed when they realized that they'd both been going to suggest that the center crystal was pointing toward their new home. Bob had sent out resumés in that direction, as well as others, so they decided to wait and see if their interpretation of the circle's answer to their problem had been correct.

Later on that week, Bob still hadn't received any responses to his resumés, but an old friend called to tell Bob about an opening in Bob's field at a company located in Colorado. When he told Liz about the job she said, "Colorado's southeast of here."

"I know. Think you'll like living there?"

"Of course I will, if it's where we're supposed to be."

Bob sent off his resumé, and within a month they'd moved to Denver and his new job, which was better than the one he'd lost. Liz, too, was able to find what she considered her own perfect job, and they marveled at how good the guidance they'd received had been.

It wasn't long before they met people with similar spiritual interests and told them of their success in seeking and finding guidance with the magic circle pipe ceremony. When their friends expressed an interest, Bob and Liz agreed to host a magic circle at their new home. Since none of the people invited were familiar with the ceremony, it was tempting for Bob and Liz to perform it for the others. But then Bob remembered Gray Seal's words, "Now *you are a shaman," that had led to his present success. Instead of leading that first ceremony, Bob handed out a list of the steps to each person and told them that they would all participate in performing it.*

Bob and Liz continued to host the ceremonies for many years, but the thing they looked forward to most was when they could say to one of the participants, "Now you are a shaman." Although they didn't talk about it much, they were disappointed to find how few were able to accept the title and start doing shamanic work on their own. They thought maybe they were doing something wrong.

They consoled themselves with the fact that, while guidance for decisions didn't always come immediately during the magic circle pipe ceremony as it had for them, the ceremony put in motion the energy that usually resulted in a person finding the guidance that he or she needed. At least people were being helped.

Although Bob and Liz continued in Gray Seal's tradition of hosting the ceremonies during the full moon and summer and winter solstices, they also performed the ceremony whenever they felt the need. Liz, who was an early riser, often found herself doing a solitary ceremony in the morning before anyone else was up. Bob was a night person, and got in the habit of doing ceremonies after the others had gone to bed. During their monthly meetings, whenever someone suggested an innovation or addition to the ceremony, they never hesitated to try it, and the purpose of the rituals varied to meet the needs of the group.

They finally knew that their efforts had been a success when a former member of their group wrote to say that he'd formed his own magic circle. Bob felt the sting of joyful tears as he repeated softly, "Now you are a shaman."

A week earlier, Gray Seal had been meditating during the new shaman's first magic circle. He felt a sudden burst of energy that lifted him higher than he'd ever gone before. He smiled and thought, "Another shaman has been born."

TWENTY-FIVE

Fertility and
Harvest Ceremonies

I said, "Go out and populate the earth,
not overpopulate."

Shamanic ceremonies often involve requests for fertility and gratitude for abundance. Although the two ceremonies we've described in this chapter are usually performed in relation to the growing and harvesting of crops, the fertility ceremony can be adapted to produce other sources of abundance and fertility. For instance, the ceremony would be appropriate for any group concerned with cleaning up the environment. Even though the members themselves may not be involved in growing crops, they can help promote a fertile, healthy Earth, and perhaps gain some insight as to how they might help, by communing with the Earth Mother/Father in this fashion. The ceremony could also be performed to promote human fertility by a couple who wants a child. Maybe the fertility you desire is the growth of an idea or product that would benefit humanity, the Earth, or the Earth's creatures. Taken in a larger context, the fertility ceremony can be applied to many situations where growth and abundance are desired.

THE FERTILITY CEREMONY

The fertility ceremony is usually performed during the night of the spring equinox or full moon to establish a productive relationship with the Earth Mother's elemental beings of the mineral and plant kingdoms.

Using the crystal pipe, follow the steps of the pipe ceremony outlined in Chapter 23. In addition, crystal garden rods, crystals, or crystal clusters can be set in each of the four directions at the edges of the garden area or property. A center arrangement can also be added if you desire. The centerpiece can be any arrangement of rocks, quartz, and one or more crystals.

At the conclusion of the pipe ceremony, small amounts of cornmeal or tobacco are dropped in each of the four directions to symbolize the nourishment of the earth.

This pipe ceremony is usually done at night because of another addition to this planting or preplanting ceremony. After the offerings of cornmeal or tobacco, the women walk naked in a clockwise circle around the garden, sometimes dragging a cloak or blanket. Many prefer to chant words or sounds that are meaningful to them at this time. Men are not involved in this part of the ceremony and shouldn't diminish or take power away from it by even watching. Unless your garden is in a secluded area where the naked women won't cause a sensation, the ceremony can be adapted so that the women wear clothing of some type, or it can be performed indoors.

The ceremony was traditionally done to give thanks to the Earth Mother for the good energy and bountiful crops to come during the growing season. If you have a garden, planting of at least some of the crops should be done as soon as possible after this ritual.

GRATITUDE

Native Americans, along with other spiritual groups, have always realized an important Universal rule. The rule is that in order to promote a cycle of abundance, we need to accept and express gratitude for what we already have. Our gratitude is a symbol that we've accepted and claimed the good things that we've been given. Too many of us these days have chosen to focus exclusively on what we want, rather than to appreciate the gifts life has already given us. By constantly dwelling on our dissatisfactions, we create more of them instead of what we really want. On the other hand, by expressing our gratitude for what we have, we start a positive cycle that ensures more good things will come our way.

Perhaps you think you've had a terrible day, week, year, or maybe your whole life is a mess. There's a way to turn that around, by getting in the habit of feeling and expressing gratitude on a regular basis. It takes practice and some self-discipline, but we can testify that the following simple exercise can change your whole life, as it has ours.

BECOMING A WINNER

Do this exercise on paper for at least a full week, or more if you like. After that, you can keep a running tally in your mind. All it involves is writing down every nice thing that happens to you each day for a week. If you have friends or a group you can do this with, compare your results. Call the nice things that happen "wins." It will get you in the habit of thinking of yourself as a winner; we all know that winners magically attract good things. Maybe you don't think nice things ever happen to you, but the truth is that they happen to everyone. The secret of winners is that they recognize and accept these good things.

What are some of the things that could be "wins"? Are you healthy, or even less unhealthy than usual? That's certainly a "win." For winners like George Burns, just waking up in the morning makes it a good day. Maybe someone gives you a compliment. You've got a world-class "win" if you accept it. Other "wins" can be things as simple as seeing a beautiful sunrise, hearing a song you like, eating a food you enjoy, having a bed to sleep in. Instead of focusing on the fact that you didn't get the raise you wanted, write down that you did your best at your job that day, or that you were pleasant to your boss, despite your disappointment. Maybe a friend provided moral support when you needed it. The fact that you're able to attract that kind of friend is a great "win."

If you've been diligent about keeping a list of your "wins," you'll probably be amazed at how many you accumulated in a week. You may notice another benefit. In order to have "wins" to record, you may have gone out of your way to find things that pleased you. Also, you didn't have time to worry about or dwell on disappointments. As a matter of fact, you'll probably find that in order to find "wins" for your list you created the circumstances that provided them. Maybe you went out of your way to be nice to someone, and they returned the favor; or you accepted a compliment that you would have normally brushed off. Also, if you were more cheerful than usual, chances are people responded to you more positively, providing you with lots of "wins."

When Lin first tried the above exercise she was in the middle of a divorce, had no home for herself and her two dogs, very little money, and had just been fired from her job.

I definitely didn't feel like a winner, but I was going to find some wins to write down if it killed me. Amazingly, it wasn't that hard. I found small things to record throughout each day that added up at the end of the week to a changed perspective of just what my life was really about. In the midst of despair, people were nice to me, I had a good job interview, and I had many small, enjoyable moments.

After that, I felt more in control of my life, as if I were the one calling the shots. I saw that the circumstances of my life weren't inherently good or bad, and that I could choose to accept them as positive challenges for growth rather than play the victim. That list of wins made me feel so much better that I continued to keep a running tally of the nice things that happened each day to review and be grateful for when I went to sleep. Instead of waiting for the next disaster, I started expecting to find good things happening— and they did.

Eventually, by looking for the good in every situation, I found a better husband, job, and home than I'd ever had before. All my losses became gains. That simple little exercise has led me from a downward spiral to achievements beyond my wildest dreams. Try it and let it do the same for you.

HARVEST CEREMONY

Like the fertility ceremony, there may be harvests we're grateful for that don't necessarily involve the growing of crops. While the following story describes a harvest ceremony usually performed in thanks for a good harvest during the fall equinox or full moon, there may be reasons and seasons other than fall when you want to thank the earth for nurturing you. Performing the harvest ceremony to express your gratitude for the good things in life, is one way to create more of them.

In her garden, the shaman watched the full moon rise above treetops to the east. Her crystal pipe and three leather pouches lay next to where she sat on the ground. She picked up the first pouch and poured a fine line of cornmeal to start a circle about a foot in diameter on the ground in front of her. She finished the circle with a second handful of cornmeal. With a third handful, she divided the circle with a line down the middle from top to bottom. Her fourth handful was used to make a horizontal line crossing the first, dividing the circle into four sections. She then took four kernels of corn from the second leather bag and placed one in the center of each of the four sections of the circle. Her symbol of Earth and a good life was complete.

Picking up the third leather bag of tobacco, she sprinkled a few grains of the tobacco at regular intervals around the circle to make offerings for the spirit people, mineral people, plant people, sea people, winged people, four-legged brothers and sisters, two-legged brothers and sisters, The Great Spirit, and the Earth Mother.

When her offerings were finished, she picked up her crystal pipe. Dried cornstalks in the garden stood as silent sentinels until a gentle breeze rustled their dry leaves. At the same moment, two of her cats appeared from behind clusters of frostbitten beans and squash.

The animals, one solid black and one pure white, sat at the edge of her circle and watched as she raised the pipe above her head in a silent offering to the Great Spirit. From there, she rotated the pipe in a clockwise direction until the stem crystal pointed toward the east. She called softly for the wind of wisdom to enter into her circle, then rotated the pipe the rest of the way to her mouth and inhaled the Breath of Life. She repeated the ritual for the wind of growth from the south, the wind of regeneration from the west, and the wind of purity from the north, finishing up by offering to the Sky Father and the Earth Mother as she had to the winds. Laying the pipe on the ground on top of her cornmeal circle, she voiced her gratitude to the Earth Mother for an abundant harvest.

The two cats, sensing the ceremony was complete, rose and walked through the circle, sniffing at the cornmeal. Knowing that her gratitude had created abundance and good energy for the future, the shaman picked up her things and walked slowly away, the cats trailing in her wake.

While it's interesting to find out exactly how traditional rituals and ceremonies were performed, and we've provided actual examples of the ceremonies (with the exception of using a crystal pipe and assigning fatherhood as well as motherhood to the Earth), it's important to mention that the real value of these ceremonies lies in the spirit in which they are performed rather than doing them exactly right. Native American and other religious leaders recognize that we have a need for the stability and comfort traditions provide, but that it's our spirit and belief rather than the ceremony's particulars that accomplishes miracles.

If you've ever been present at a traditional Native American ceremony, you may have been shocked to find children and animals running wild through the circle and peace pipes going out, or even being dropped on occasion. The exact form the ceremony takes is also usually slightly different, depending on the tribe or group doing it. The common element you will find is the presence of Universal Light Energy, along with the recognition of our connection to all that is. If you choose to perform the pipe ceremony, do it in a way and for a purpose that is meaningful to you and meets your needs. Keep in mind your connection to the rest of the universe, and you can't go wrong.

TWENTY-SIX

Vision Quest

True vision doesn't require eyes.

Commonly, the Vision Quest is undertaken by strongly motivated people seeking a vision for guidance in their goals, or to find their higher purpose on Earth. It's experienced with four days of fasting and making prayers in a wilderness area with only a prayer pipe, a blanket, and a jug of water for sustenance. The rite was originated by Native Americans, but is now used by people of either sex and all races and religions who are seeking direction on their spiritual path.

Although the original rite lasted four days, modern practitioners sometimes shorten the time spent, depending on the state of their health. Only people in good physical condition should undertake a Vision Quest, and they should inform friends and family where they're going and when they're expected back. It's also a good idea to pick a season when mild weather is the norm and no storms are forecast.

A Vision Quest is meant to be a solitary personal experience that focuses the individual on self-responsibility and self-reliance. The guidance for a life-path or goal is usually found through nature's symbols—encounters with animals or birds (real or spirit), and dreams that occur during the quest.

Many cultures use various methods of fasting and isolation in an effort to free the spirit from everyday concerns. This allows them to become aware of the natural rhythms of the Earth and encourages spiritual visions. People who undertake the Vision Quest should be motivated by the feeling that the time is "right" to discover their true purpose.

To give you an idea of what an actual Vision Quest is like, we offer one woman's experiences.

THE VISION

As night fell the first day, the wind whispered gently through the trees surrounding me. I wrapped my sky-blue blanket tightly around my shoulders and gazed upward through the swaying boughs to early stars that appeared in the darkening sky. Already I felt the loneliness of my vigil, and sought comfort by touching the crystal pipe that lay on the earth at my feet. Sometime in the coming solitary days and nights I'd pick it up and begin to make prayers for my vision, but I wasn't ready yet. I was too caught up in my fear of being alone in the wilderness at night.

Like leaves caught in a river's current, my thoughts were chaotic, with no volition. Why did I choose this way to find guidance when I could have meditated for direction within the security of my own home? It was crazy for a person who hates being alone and fears the night to fast in the middle of nowhere for four long days and nights. How do I know that I'm one with nature? Wild animals are out there and I don't even have a weapon to protect myself. Is that why people carry guns and knives when they leave civilization? Are they afraid of the dark and wild animals, or are we all just afraid to be alone with our own thoughts?

I reminded myself that even big animals like bears, wolves, and cougars seldom bother humans unless provoked. Since I had no intention of doing any provoking, it had to be my own thoughts that terrified me. What if there was no purpose to my life? Or what if I found it and wasn't strong enough to follow it?

The night breeze touched me with a ghostly hand and I huddled within my blanket, then straightened my back. "Nothing can harm me but my own fear," I said out loud, breaking the stillness. "I'll let go of the fear without judging myself for feeling it. To survive, I'll have to accept myself. Nature doesn't seem to be threatening me, so why threaten myself?"

Despite my little speech, fear pursued me into the long night until, eventually, I wore myself out and fell into a restless doze. My sleep was punctuated by formless dreams that evaporated with the predawn chirping of birds and a scolding delivered by a squirrel in a tree overhead. Nature certainly was noisy. I stood up, trying to unkink muscles that had stiffened during the long, cold night, just in time to see magical fingers of light creeping through the trees to bathe me in warmth. Never before had I appreciated a sunrise. Its coming was like a benediction, a gift for having survived the night.

During what seemed like an incredibly long day, I sat on my blanket and began to take notice of the sights, sounds, and smells of nature. I thought about how different the reality of the Vision Quest was from what I'd heard. Nothing had really prepared me for the actual experience.

To relieve my boredom, I tried to record and catalogue my surroundings, and made up stories about the lives of the animals and insects I saw. I suffered through the agony of an ant trying to carry an insect carcass much larger than itself, and cheered out loud when another ant came along to help. The squirrels, birds, and insects all became my friends. I was amazed at the kinship I felt with them in their daily activities. By narrowing and focusing my awareness, I was able to see more clearly than I'd ever seen before.

And the smells! Without its cloak of technology, the Earth provided delicate scents of wildflowers, pine, and the pleasant musk of rotting earth. On the other hand, my deodorant had failed miserably by that time, and I was less enchanted with my own scent and the layer of grit blocking my pores. Whoever said that cleanliness is next to godliness was right. I'd have given anything for a bath.

During the afternoon I gave into temptation and removed most of my sweaty clothes. After that, sun and air blended with my odor to form a pleasant scent. The experience ranked right up there with some of my best baths, and I felt more a part of things without my false coverings.

In fact, the patterns and energies of the Earth herself became strong enough that I thought I could see them. Fleeting dots of light punctuated my vision, and I wondered if I were seeing reality or an illusion brought on by fasting. Strangely enough, I wasn't hungry. I just felt a sense of drifting lightness, as if I'd put far too much emphasis on feeding my body in the past. Maybe it was time I concentrated on feeding my spirit for a change.

My daytime boredom, mixed with moments of euphoria, evaporated with the coming of nightfall. Fear returned, but it wasn't as bad as the first night. My fears must have blocked my senses of perception then, because now I found the air filled with sights and sounds I didn't remember. Alone and in the dark (clothed against the night's chill), I heard myriad insect sounds, and at one point I even detected a mouse rustling through the undergrowth.

A bird's call in the distance caught my attention. Black wing-shadows swooped across the starlit backdrop of sky and forest. With a shock of air, the bird descended to sit, almost invisible, in the foliage of a tree. It looked like an owl, but I couldn't tell if it was a real owl or a spirit bird. I squinted into the darkness. "Who, hoo," the low call reached my ears, breaking the silence that had descended when it arrived. What was the difference between a spirit bird or animal, and so-called real ones? Maybe there wasn't any.

Thinking that this could be my vision, I picked up my crystal pipe and gripped it tightly, leaving myself open to any subtle hint of guidance, information, awareness.

As I waited, a bush rustled loudly about fifteen yards away. Paralyzed, I listened intently with all of my being. Out of the corner of my eye, I thought I saw the outline of a head with pointed ears and nose. A coyote, a wolf?

I couldn't move, couldn't stand, and I knew I couldn't run away. Neither fight nor flight instincts would work in this situation. "What can I do?" I asked myself. "Nothing but be aware," came the answer from a small part of my consciousness. I watched and listened. No movement anywhere. Dead silence in the forest around me.

Turning my head ever so slowly, I tried to see the form clearly. Too big to be a coyote, it looked like a wolf. Was this my spirit animal, or was it the owl who sat unmoving in the tree? Maybe it was both. The wolf, the owl, and I all became silent night watchers.

I don't remember falling asleep, but the next thing I was aware of were rays of sunlight streaming through the trees. Did I dream of the owl and wolf in the night? The morning showed no sign of my night visitors and I decided they must have been an illusion.

I passed the second day in a curious state, as if I were in a time warp where everything was still. Yet I was acutely aware of the activities of nature going on around me. When the long afternoon finally descended into night,

I comforted myself with a drink of the water that replaced an evening meal. At that point, the water compared favorably to a banquet.

Huddled in my blanket, hungry and alone, I wondered what the night would bring. Staring into the darkness, I could make out the dark shapes of trees and bushes, but with an added dimension. Each tree and bush was outlined by a shimmering aura of white light. Even the rock outcrop a hundred yards away glowed around the edges with a glistening white halo. I examined the aura and it appeared to be a solid line of light made up of individual dots that flowed around everything I looked at. If I was having an hallucination, it appeared very real. Every shape I saw was alive with the auras, connected by a single light energy field.

Why hadn't I ever seen this before? I was mesmerized by the moving interplay of white light. Maybe I was seeing the essence of creation. I watched the light for hours, until smaller night sounds were stilled by a large dark shape crashing out of the bushes about twenty-five yards away. The shape stopped and stayed perfectly still. Oh God, a bear, I thought. What do I do now? The whole experience was getting far too real; I could even feel the pulsating energy and power of the animal over the distance. I desperately wanted it to be a spirit animal, but it was so real. Then I noticed that an aura of white light surrounded the bear. Was there some meaning to this? Fear and amazement hypnotized me while I held onto my crystal pipe for dear life.

The connection with the big animal was broken as it came a few steps closer, then turned and retreated, disappearing in the darkness. I was still pondering the experience when the first light of the morning sun heralded the third day of my Vision Quest.

Even after a sleepless night, I felt a sense of well-being and happiness to be alive that I'd never experienced before.

What was the meaning of my experience with the bear? I spent the day in silent reflection, alone with my thoughts. What was I learning from my Vision Quest? Did I know who I was, what I was doing, where my life was going? I held my crystal pipe and watched the crystals sparkling in the sunlight. Maybe I was finally ready to make prayers for my quest.

After I made offerings to all the Earth Mother's people, I stood up slowly, a little light-headed, and held the pipe with both hands, skyward to the sun, in an offering to the Sky Father. Then I rotated the pipe and called to the wind of wisdom to come into my circle. Holding the bowl in both hands, I inhaled the Breath of Life, my exhalation bathing the stem crystal in energy that I could actually see. Rotating the pipe again, and again, I called to the other three winds, seeing my breath reach out into the galaxy and into the infinite. I offered thanks to the Sky Father.

With a last rotation of the pipe and several deep breaths, I thanked the Earth Mother, feeling gratitude for all the good things in my life and those coming to me. The formal part of the prayer done, I sank to my blanket and laid the pipe on the Earth in front of me. I brought my hands together and bowed my head. My lips mouthed the silent inner words, "Oh Great Spirit, please guide me on my life's path. Show me my vision."

After that I meditated as I watched the day disappear, listening for the first sounds of night. The call of a nighthawk caught my attention as he fell across the sky and landed in a nearby tree. His eyes shone brightly in the dim light. We watched each other until I was overtaken by a sleep filled with strange dreams.

The fourth morning I remembered my dreams vividly. I thanked my friend and companion, the nighthawk. The bird must, indeed, have been a spirit creature meant especially for me.

It was time to go home. I rose stiffly and stumbled down the twisting animal path to where I'd parked my car. The car seemed like an alien being after my time with nature. Not wanting to forget my dreams, I wrote them down in a notebook before heading home. After a welcome shower, I thought about my dreams and what they meant in terms of the path I should take.

In the first dream, I'd found myself sitting next to a rock on the slope of a mountain. I was bathed in warmth from the sun, the sky a perfect blue punctuated by puffy white clouds. Colorful wildflowers abounded and their heavenly scent, blending with grass and pine, filled the air.

As a bearded man bathed in white light approached me, I realized that I was at school and he was my teacher. We discussed my progress with my lesson, which was to accept myself so that I could grow and be all that I could be. He lovingly told me that only fear could block my expansion. Then he said, "You must love, not just yourself and others, but life and the life force. Don't block the pain of life, but experience it fully. For it's through pain, as well as joy, that you will find greater life." I knew that fear caused by painful experiences in the past had kept me from seeking out new experiences. I needed to go back and experience that pain fully, bless it for what *it had taught me, and release it before going onward. Although I could take as long as I liked to learn my lesson, I couldn't graduate to the next level of life until it was learned. I resolved to work very hard.*

The next dream was an extension of the first one, only my classroom was a cavern filled with crystals and minerals that glowed with an inner light in the dark. An unseen voice explained to me that the crystalline forms were tuning devices. "They have the ability to match their vibrational level to yours at a certain point, and then tune themselves and you to a higher level." I complained to the voice that I sometimes found the tuning process uncomfortable and was told, "The cellular structure of your body is changing rapidly to a higher vibrational frequency. This is physically and emotionally disruptive to normal functioning while it's going on, but it will not be long before the change is complete."

The third dream was very strange because I found myself in a man's body. It was a warm summer day in a small American town. I stopped by a friend's house because I'd agreed to go to a political meeting with him.

We left his home and were passing a graveled playing field with a baseball backdrop. Several men, armed with machine guns, appeared from behind a clump of bushes across the street. My friend, who was well ahead of me, fell to the sidewalk in a hail of bullets. I ran onto the playing field and dropped to the gravel, thinking that I'd be safe since I wasn't a part of my friend's group. A minute later I felt the sting of gravel hitting my body and thought the men were trying to scare me by shooting so close. Then all was silent, and I congratulated myself on surviving the onslaught.

Seconds later, a gush of crimson erupted from my mouth. With a sense of horror, I realized that the gravel stings had been bullets. My body was dead! After a moment of shock, I thought, "Hey, I'm still alive." In fact I felt more alive than I had before I died. I was just about to try separating my spiritual body from my physical one so that I could go exploring when I awoke.

The fourth dream was brief. I was a man again, wearing a white robe. I was standing on a rock, high above a crowd of people, with my arms outstretched. They were looking to me for guidance. A sense of peace and power flowed from my outstretched arms, bathing the crowd in its light.

Before my Vision Quest, I'd been doing healing work with crystals and had been thinking about conducting some classes to teach others about it. But fear had been holding me back. The dreams must mean that I

needed to resolve past issues and then go ahead with the classes. The infor-
mation that we were indeed eternal, and explanations of what crystals actu-
ally do should be shared. I spent the rest of the day doing a painting of my
spirit animal, the nighthawk, who would help me.

The Vision Quest is unique for each individual. The guidance and motivation comes from within, inspired by the Earth Mother with her wild creatures acting as a catalyst. Prayers with the pipe may be done as often as you want. Some practitioners do a prayer to begin and one to end their quest. Others do prayers throughout the process, and some do only one at the end.

One common denominator of the Vision Quest is that most people experience their unity with all life. The knowledge that we are related to each other and all of nature comes out as a deeply understood fact, rather than an intellectual philosophy. A person's personal visions for guidance and understanding are related to the larger vision of all creation as an interdependent whole.

VISION WITHOUT A FORMAL QUEST

Gardeners and farmers, in planting and harvesting crops, often experience much of the same understanding of the unity of all life without a ritual Vision Quest. This is a natural outgrowth of working closely with the Earth Mother herself. Many practitioners of Earth Magic and the old Earth-oriented religions also attain the same awareness by working with the phases of the moon and cycles of the seasons.

Most Earth-oriented ceremonies involve offering something back to the Earth in a ritual prayer of thanks and gratitude for the good things she has given us to enrich our lives. Offerings of ceremonial corn, wheat, cornmeal, and tobacco are frequently used for this purpose. Sometimes part of any crop grown in a garden is left to be tilled back to the Earth as a thankful offering for the crops and recognition of the abundance of nature. Another way of offering thanks is the simple act of putting out seeds or grain in bird and squirrel feeders to share the abundance, acknowledging that all creatures are fellow brothers and sisters living on the Earth Mother. Simple everyday acts of recycling and composting are also direct ways of relating to our sense of oneness and interdependence with the Earth. Our understanding that all ground is Sacred Ground can be expressed in many day-to-day activities with the same sense of spirituality that traditional Native Americans feel.

The sense of oneness with all life is not just for special days, times, and ceremonies or rituals. It's a way of seeing, feeling, and living in recognition of our connection to the whole of life that represents the ultimate vision of the Vision Quest.

STAY IN TOUCH

On the following pages you will find listed, with their current prices, some of the books now available on related subjects. Your book dealer stocks most of these and will stock new titles in the Llewellyn series as they become available. We urge your patronage.

To obtain our full catalog, to keep informed about new titles as they are released and to benefit from informative articles and helpful news, you are invited to write for our bi-monthly news magazine/catalog, *Llewellyn's New Worlds of Mind and Spirit*. A sample copy is free, and it will continue coming to you at no cost as long as you are an active mail customer. Or you may subscribe for just $10.00 in U.S.A. and Canada ($20.00 overseas, first class mail). Many bookstores also have *New Worlds* available to their customers. Ask for it.

Stay in touch! In *New Worlds'* pages you will find news and features about new books, tapes and services, announcements of meetings and seminars, articles helpful to our readers, news of authors, products and services, special money-making opportunities, and much more.

Llewellyn's New Worlds of Mind and Spirit
P.O. Box 64383-728, St. Paul, MN 55164-0383, U.S.A.

* * *

TO ORDER BOOKS AND TAPES

If your book dealer does not have the books described on the following pages readily available, you may order them direct from the publisher by sending full price in U.S. funds, plus $3.00 for postage and handling for orders *under* $10.00; $4.00 for orders *over* $10.00. There are no postage and handling charges for orders over $50.00. Postage and handling rates are subject to change. UPS Delivery: We ship UPS whenever possible. Delivery guaranteed. Provide your street address as UPS does not deliver to P.O. Boxes. UPS to Canada requires a $50.00 minimum order. Allow 4-6 weeks for delivery. Orders outside the U.S.A. and Canada: Airmail—add retail price of book; add $5.00 for each non-book item (tapes, etc.); add $1.00 per item for surface mail.

FOR GROUP STUDY AND PURCHASE

Because there is a great deal of interest in group discussion and study of the subject matter of this book, we feel that we should encourage the adoption and use of this particular book by such groups by offering a special quantity price to group leaders or agents.

Our special quantity price for a minimum order of five copies of *Crystal Vision* is $36.00 cash-with-order. This price includes postage and handling within the United States. Minnesota residents must add 6.5% sales tax. For additional quantities, please order in multiples of five. For Canadian and foreign orders, add postage and handling charges as above. Credit card (VISA, MasterCard, American Express) orders are accepted. Charge card orders only ($15.00 minimum order) may be phoned in free within the U.S.A. or Canada by dialing 1-800-THE-MOON. For customer service, call 1-612-291-1970. Mail orders to:

LLEWELLYN PUBLICATIONS
P.O. Box 64383-728, St. Paul, MN 55164-0383, U.S.A.

CRYSTAL POWER
by Michael G. Smith

This is an amazing book, for what it claims to present—with complete instructions and diagrams so that YOU can work them yourself—is the master technology of ancient Atlantis: psionic (mind-controlled and life-energized machines) devices made from common quartz crystals!

Learn to easily construct an "Atlantean" Power Rod that can be used for healing or a weapon, or a Crystal Headband stimulating psychic powers, or a Time and Space Communications Generator operated purely by your mind.

These crystal devices seem to work only with the disciplined mind power of a human operator, yet their very construction seems to start a process of growth and development, a new evolutionary step in the human psyche that bridges mind and matter.

Does this "re-discovery" mean that we are living, now, in the New Atlantis? Have these Power Tools been re-invented to meet the needs of this prophetic time? Are Psionic Machines the culminating Power To the People to free us from economic dependence on fossil fuels and smokestack industry? This book answers "yes" to all these questions, and asks you to simply build these devices and put them to work to help bring it all about.

0-87542-725-1, 256 pgs., 5¼ x 8, illus., softcover   **$9.95**

CRYSTAL WARRIOR
Shamanic Transformation & Projection of Universal Energy
by Michael G. Smith & Lin Westhorp

Combine the unlimited potential of the human spirit with *psychotronic* power! Venture into the world of the Crystal Warrior, a world of balance that uses "Autoelectromags" with shamanism, the martial arts, magic, and alchemical techniques to aid in THE EVOLUTION OF THE PEACEFUL WARRIOR AND THE EARTH.

Autoelectromags (AEM) are the most powerful of the crystal energy projectors to arise in thousands of years. The AEM isn't a firearm, projectile weapon or laser. It's a psionic beam generator in the form of a handheld projector used for spiritual development—for meeting with and exploring other aspects of the self.

Crystal Warrior contains information that crystal workers around the world have been waiting for! It explores, for the first time, the evolution and workings of AEMs and gives detailed instructions for their construction and use. It also introduces many post AEM inventions from the past decade including Crystal Swords and Daggers, Crystal Self-Defense Sticks, jewelry and other aura amplifiers, and Crystal Container Rods, all which serve to integrate the earth's mineral kingdom into our search for spiritual development and harmony.

0-87542-727-8, 6 x 9, 192 pgs., 20 photos, illus.   **$9.95**

CRYSTAL HEALING
The Next Step
by Phyllis Galde

Discover the further secrets of quartz crystal! Now modern research and use have shown that crystals have even more healing and therapeutic properties than have been realized. Learn why polished, smoothed crystal is better to use to heighten your intuition, improve creativity and for healing.

Learn to use crystals for reprogramming your subconscious to eliminate problems and negative attitudes that prevent success. Here are techniques that people have successfully used, not just theories. This book reveals newly discovered abilities of crystal now accessible to all, and is a sensible approach to crystal use. *Crystal Healing* will be your guide to improve the quality of your life and expand your consciousness.

0-87542-246-2, 224 pgs., mass market, illus.   **$3.95**

CRYSTAL AWARENESS
by Catherine Bowman

For millions of years, crystals have been waiting for people to discover their wonderful powers. Today they are used in watches, computer chips and communication devices. But there is also a spiritual, holistic aspect to crystals.

Crystal Awareness will teach you everything you need to know about crystals to begin working with them. It will also help those who have been working with them to complete their knowledge. Topics include: Crystal Forms, Colored and Colorless Crystals, Single Points, Clusters and Double Terminated Crystals, Crystal and Human Energy Fields, The Etheric and Spiritual Bodies, Crystals as Energy Generators, Crystal Cleansing and Programming, Crystal Meditation, The Value of Polished Crystals, Crystals and Personal Spiritual Growth, Crystals and Chakras, How to Make Crystal Jewelry, The Uses of Crystals in the Future, Color Healing, Programming Crystals with Color, Compatible Crystals and Metals, Several Crystal Healing Techniques, including The Star of David Healing.

Crystal Awareness is destined to be *the* guide of choice for people who are beginning their investigation of crystals.

0-87542-058-3, 224 pgs., mass market, illus.   **$3.95**

LIFE FORCE
The Secret Power Behind Miracle Healing, Martial Arts & Occult Magic
by Leo Ludzia

A secret living energy ... as ancient as the Pyramids, as modern as Star Wars. Since the beginning of time, certain people have known that there is this energy—a power that can be used by people for healing, magick, and spiritual development. It's been called many names: Mana, Orgone, Psionic, Prana, Kundalini, Odic force, Chi and others.

Leo Ludzia puts it all together in *Life Force.* This is the first book which shows the histories and compares the theories and methods of using this marvelous energy. This force is available to us all, if only we know how to tap into it. Ludzia shows you how to make devices which will help you better use and generate this Life Force. This specialized information includes easy-to-follow directions on: how to build and use pyramids, Orgone Generators such as those used by Wilhelm Reich, and how to make and use the "Black Box"designed and used by the genius inventor T. G. Hieronymus.

Scientists, psychics, occultists and mystics of Eastern and Western paths will want to read this book. It will also attract those interested in psionics, radionics, UFOs and Fortean phenomena.

0-87542-437-6, 192 pgs., mass market, illus. **$3.95**

HOW TO UNCOVER YOUR PAST LIVES
by Ted Andrews

Knowledge of your past lives can be extremely rewarding. It can assist you in opening to new depths within your own psychological makeup. It can provide greater insight into present circumstances with loved ones, career and health. It is also a lot of fun.

Now Ted Andrews shares with you nine different techniques that you can use to access your past lives. Between techniques, Andrews discusses issues such as karma and how it is expressed in your present life; the source of past life information; soul mates and twin souls; proving past lives; the mysteries of birth and death; animals and reincarnation; abortion and pre-mature death; and the role of reincarnation in Christianity.

To explore your past lives, you need only use one or more of the techniques offered. Complete instructions are provided for a safe and easy regression. Learn to dowse to pinpoint the years and places of your lives with great accuracy, make your own self-hypnosis tape, attune to the incoming child during pregnancy, use the tarot and the cabala in past life meditations, keep a past life journal and more.

0-87542-022-2, 240 pgs., mass market, illus. **$3.95**

PSYCHIC POWER
Techniques & Inexpensive Devices that Increase Your Psychic Powers
by Charles Cosimano

Although popular in many parts of the world, Radionics machines have had little application in America, UNTIL NOW! *Psychic Power* introduces these machines to America with a new purpose: to increase your psychic powers!

Using the easy, step-by-step instructions, and for less than a $10.00 investment, you can build a machine which will allow you to read other people's minds, influence their thoughts, communicate with their dreams and be more successful when you do divinations such as working with Tarot cards or pendulums.

For thousands of years, people have looked for an easy, simple and sure way to increase their psychic abilities. Now, the science of psionics allows you to do just that! This book is practical, fun and an excellent source for those wishing to achieve results with etheric energies.

If you just want a book to read, you will find this a wonderful title to excitingly fill a few hours. But if you can spare a few minutes to actually build and use these devices, you will be able to astound yourself and your friends. We are not talking about guessing which numbers will come up on a pair of dice at a mark slightly above average. With practice, you will be able to choose which numbers will come up more often than not! But don't take our word for it. Read the book, build the devices and find out for yourself.

0-87542-097-4, 224 pgs., mass market, illus. **$3.95**

CUNNINGHAM'S ENCYCLOPEDIA OF CRYSTAL, GEM & METAL MAGIC
by Scott Cunningham

Here you will find the most complete information anywhere on the magical qualities of more than 100 crystals and gemstones as well as several metals. The information for each crystal, gem or metal includes: its related energy, planetary rulership, magical element, deities, Tarot Card, and the magical powers that each is believed to possess. Also included is a complete description of their uses for magical purposes. The classic on the subject.

0-87542-126-1, 240 pgs., 6 x 9, illus., color plates, softcover **$12.95**

DANCE OF POWER
A Shamanic Journey
by Dr. Susan Gregg
Join Dr. Susan Gregg on her fascinating, real-life journey to find her soul. This is the story of her shamanic apprenticeship with a man named Miguel, a Mexican-Indian Shaman, or "Nagual." As you live the author's personal experiences, you have the opportunity to take a quantum leap along the path toward personal freedom, toward finding your true self, and grasping the ultimate personal freedom—the freedom to choose moment by moment what you want to experience.

Here, in a warm and genuine style, Dr. Gregg details her studies with Miguel, her travel to other realms, and her initiations by fire and water into the life of a "warrior." If you want to understand how you create your own reality—and how you may be wasting energy by resisting change or trying to understand the unknowable—take the enlightening path of the Nagual. Practical exercises at the end of each chapter give you the tools to embark upon your own spiritual quest.

Learn about another way of being … *Dance of Power* can change your life, if you let it.

0-87542-247-0, 5¼ x 8, illus., photos, softbound **$12.00**

IN THE SHADOW OF THE SHAMAN
Connecting with Self, Nature & Spirit
by Amber Wolfe
Presented in what the author calls a "cookbook shamanism" style, this book shares recipes, ingredients, and methods of preparation for experiencing some very ancient wisdoms: wisdoms of Native American and Wiccan traditions, as well as contributions from other philosophies of Nature as they are used in the shamanic way. Wheels, the circle, totems, shields, directions, divinations, spells, care of sacred tools and meditations are all discussed. Wolfe encourages us to feel confident and free to use her methods to cook up something new, completely on our own. This blending of ancient formulas and personal methods represents what Ms. Wolfe calls Aquarian Shamanism.

In the Shadow of the Shaman is designed to communicate in the most practical, direct ways possible, so that the wisdom and the energy may be shared for the benefits of all. Whatever your system or tradition, you will find this to be a valuable book, a resource, a friend, a gentle guide and support on your journey. Dancing in the shadow of the shaman, you will find new dimensions of Spirit.

0-87542-888-6, 384 pgs., 6 x 9, illus., softcover **$12.95**